DELIVERING DEVELOPMENT

Delivering Development

Globalization's Shoreline and the Road to a Sustainable Future

Edward R. Carr

palgrave
macmillan

DELIVERING DEVELOPMENT
Copyright © Edward R. Carr, 2011.

First published in 2011 by
PALGRAVE MACMILLAN®
in the United States—a division of St. Martin's Press LLC,
175 Fifth Avenue, New York, NY 10010.

Where this book is distributed in the UK, Europe and the rest of the world,
this is by Palgrave Macmillan, a division of Macmillan Publishers Limited,
registered in England, company number 785998, of Houndmills,
Basingstoke, Hampshire RG21 6XS.

Palgrave Macmillan is the global academic imprint of the above companies
and has companies and representatives throughout the world.

Palgrave® and Macmillan® are registered trademarks in the United States,
the United Kingdom, Europe and other countries.

ISBN: 978–0–230–11076–2

Library of Congress Cataloging-in-Publication Data

Carr, Edward R.
    Delivering development : globalization's shoreline and the road to a
sustainable future / Edward R. Carr.
        p. cm.
    Includes bibliographical references.
    ISBN 978–0–230–11076–2
        1. Developing countries—Economic conditions. 2. Developing
countries—Social conditions. 3. Developing countries—Economic policy.
4. Poverty—Developing countries. 5. Globalization—Economic aspects.
6. Globalization—Environmental aspects. I. Title.

HC59.7.C31427 2010
338.9009172′4—dc22   2010024200

A catalogue record of the book is available from the British Library.

Design by Newgen Imaging Systems (P) Ltd., Chennai, India.

First edition: February 2011

10 9 8 7 6 5 4 3 2 1

Printed in the United States of America.

For
Robert E. Carr
and
Cleary Jo, R. J., Evie, Jennifer, and Edward

There are more things in heaven and earth, Horatio,
Than are dreamt of in your philosophy.
                    Shakespeare
                    Hamlet Act 1, scene 5, 159–167

Contents

Figures

Chapter 1

Taking It All Apart

In the early evening of July 8, 1997, I found myself sitting in the courtyard of a house in Dominase, a small rural village in Ghana's Central
Region. I was there to pay a social visit to some of the people who were
kind enough to share the history of Dominase with me. It was pitch dark,
and my 24-year-old Ghanaian research assistant, Francis Quayson, and I
had walked about 500 meters from the slightly larger village of Ponkrum,
where I was staying. We had used a flashlight to navigate the overgrown,
uneven remnants of a dirt road between the two places. As per "official"
local custom, I had brought a bottle of (appalling but cheap) local gin with
me as a gift. This was accepted by Kwame, one of three brothers of the only
family still living in this village. We sat and talked by his wife's cook fire
for a while, drinking the gin and discussing everything from the history of
Dominase to the cost of living in the United States.

It was my first trip to Ghana, and I had been in the country only 28 days.
Like Francis, I was 24 years old. I could not speak Fante, the local dialect
of the Akan language, in any meaningful way and so was nearly completely
dependent on Francis for translation. His translations were halting, at best,
and my struggle to comprehend his limited English was compounded by
the fact that any resident of the village within earshot—roughly a dozen
people—felt free to contribute shouted questions and comments from
across the courtyard. He had great difficulty deciding whose comments
to translate at any given moment or what to do when two or more people
were talking at once.

After spending about an hour there, Francis and I prepared to make our
unsteady way back to Ponkrum. As we stood up, Kwame asked Francis to

translate something for him. Kwame spoke quickly, and Francis tried to keep up, giving me this translation:

"Once, the government had to build a bridge over a river. They hired a Ghanaian contractor to do the work. Before he was halfway done, the bridge fell down. The government hired another contractor. This new contractor began to build the bridge, but it fell down before he could finish. The government went and got a white man. He came and bottled the river gods, and his bridge stood."

Kwame then looked directly at me, and as he spoke, Francis translated: "How did the white man do this?" Completely taken aback by the question, I beat a hasty retreat to Ponkrum without answering.

My discomfort was not the product of an inability to explain what Kwame was describing. Of course, the white contractor had not "bottled the river gods." Instead someone had seen the contractor, or one of his workers, conducting some sort of hydrologic analysis necessary to properly design and plan a bridge. However, with no understanding of hydrology as a science, the person who saw this measurement incorporated this event into his or her worldview to create an explanation that referenced local cosmology.[1]

My visceral reaction was to the implication of his story. Kwame described an infrastructural development project, probably designed to better connect various parts of the Ghanaian economy with the global economy via improved transportation access. It was intended to improve the well-being of the people living around the bridge, likely via the benefits of economic growth. In its implementation, however, this project had produced a local understanding of a technology that identified one group of people (generalized as whites) as having control over at least the minor gods of another group of people (generalized as black Africans). Something had leaked out of this project, this engagement with the global economy, that was neither intended nor understood by those who designed and implemented it. This leakage could not be measured through conventional means, such as Gross Domestic Product (GDP), but it mattered greatly. It called into question most tenets of development, as I understood it. How could people who translated the construction of a bridge into a clear statement of their own inadequacies feel comfortable offering their advice and opinions with regard to the design of future development projects? How can someone benefit from participation in the global economy if one considers oneself as somehow subordinate to the other actors in that economy? If development projects create or reinforce a sense of inferiority among "the developing," how much material improvement is a person's self-esteem worth? The trade-offs between the benefits and problems associated with this bridge, as articulated in Kwame's story, were jarring, disorienting, and upsetting.

I have returned to this story many times in my career. I did so a few days after I first heard it, engaging Kwame and one of his brothers in a conversation about technology, hydrology, and development, trying to call into question the problematic relationships I saw emerging from this story. More recently I have come to see it as a tool for thinking about why development and globalization often do not seem to work the way they are intended. The prevalent, though not ubiquitous, view of these closely linked ideas is that by bringing development to deprived areas, we can improve people's quality of life and enable them to sustain those improvements through engagement with global markets of unprecedented wealth and opportunity. Indeed, such engagement is generally seen as inevitable, its benefits obvious, and therefore the achievement of well-being for all is a goal that is just around the corner.

Chasing this dream, hundreds of thousands of highly trained, well-meaning professionals devise plans, policies, and projects that will maximize the impact of more than $100 billion in aid funding[2] each year. These individuals build policies that create ever-freer trade regimes that allow goods to flow from one end of the planet to the other. These projects and policies have reshaped the world. According to the United Nations Department of Economic and Social Affairs, global life expectancy, which stood at 46.6 years in the period 1950–55, rose to 66.4 years for the period 2000–05. The International Monetary Fund reports that global economic production rose, in 2009 dollars, from $12.47 trillion in 1980 to $68.99 trillion in 2009. The production of wealth on planet Earth today is unprecedented in human history.

After centuries of growing global trade and more than six decades of formal development (overlaid on many more decades of colonial efforts), however, the improvement of the human condition has been uneven at best. This fact is visible in the development agencies' own statistics. According to the World Bank, $40 trillion of global economic production is today concentrated in "high income economies" (those with per capita Gross National Incomes of $11,906 or more) that contain roughly one billion people.[3] As a result, in 2010 nearly 58 percent of global wealth was produced and controlled by about 16 percent of the world's population. In addition, while things have gotten much better at the top of the income scale, in many places things have actually become worse. According to the Food and Agriculture Organization of the United Nations (FAO), there is *less* food per person in sub-Saharan Africa than there was 30 years ago. The Human Development Index of the United Nations suggests that average life expectancy in sub-Saharan Africa, which stands at an astonishingly low 46 years, is actually lower than it was two decades ago. Further, recent assessments of the global environment make it clear that whatever benefits we reap from ever-freer global trade and development are coming at a considerable environmental cost that will compromise the well-being of future generations. If free markets, global trade, and development were supposed to move us toward a world without poverty and with greater opportunity for all, then clearly something has gone terribly wrong.

Of course, many have made these same observations. For example, since the late 1960s proponents of Dependency Theory and World Systems Theory have, broadly speaking, argued that the structure of the global economy requires—and therefore produces—inequality as a part of its very workings. Therefore, development is a project at odds with the very economic system that funds projects and shapes policy. Awareness of these problems is not enough, however, as new initiatives framed around reversing this extended failure continue to fall short. Take, for example, the Millennium Development Goals (MDGs), eight broad but noble objectives for development announced by the United Nations in 2000 to be achieved by 2015. In 2010, only six years from the 2015 deadline, it is clear these goals will not be achieved. The 2008 Millennium Development Goals Progress Chart[4] paints a disastrous picture. Sub-Saharan Africa and Oceania are behind target for every single goal, on every single metric. West Asia will not achieve the goals specified in 14 of the 18 total metrics. Latin America and the Caribbean, Southeast Asia, and Southern Asia are all behind on roughly half the goals. By the MDGs' own statistics, we are making satisfactory progress toward these basic goals in only 39.5 percent of the places and problems under consideration. When even the most broad, basic development goals cannot be achieved, it suggests there is something fundamentally wrong with what we are doing to improve the quality of life for people everywhere.

This failure haunts me. I am principally an academic, a geography professor who has spent the last 13 years studying the intersection of development, globalization, and environmental change. I did not start out intending to become a professor who studied these things. Thirteen years ago I was a PhD student in archaeology who headed to Ghana to assist on a

---

THE MILLENNIUM DEVELOPMENT GOALS (AND THEIR SPECIFIC METRICS FOR EVALUATION OF PROGRESS)

1. Eradicate extreme poverty and hunger
   a. Reduce both by 1/2
   b. Provide productive and decent employment

2. Achieve universal primary education

3. Promote gender equality and empower women
   a. Secure equal girls' and boys' enrollments in primary school
   b. Increase women's share of paid enployment
   c. Increase the percentage of women as parliamentarians

4. Reduce child mortality
   a. Reduce by 2/3 for children under age five
   b. Raise rate of immunization against measles

5. Improve maternal health
   a. Reduce maternal mortality by 3/4
   b. Improve access to reproductive health

6. Combat HIV/AIDS, malaria, and other diseases
   a. Halt and reverse the spread of HIV/AIDS
   b. Halt and reverse the spread of tuberculosis

7. Ensure environmental sustainability
   a. Reverse the loss of forests
   b. Halve the proportion without drinking water
   c. Halve the proportion without sanitation
   d. Improve the lives of slum-dwellers

8. Develop a global partnership for development
   a. Amount of internet usage

Figure 1.1   The Millennium Development Goals

dig led by my dissertation adviser and to identify a site for my own dissertation work. As it turned out, one summer of living and working in Ponkrum and Dominase, the two villages discussed at length in this book, changed my life. My understanding of poverty was first thrown into crisis and eventually dismantled by the contradictions around me. People in these villages lived on less than two dollars a day but never seemed to go hungry. They lived in houses that were made of earth and roofed with sheets of tin but managed to maintain a high standard of hygiene; chronic illnesses, such as malaria, were exceedingly rare.[5] Infant mortality had touched nearly every household in these villages, but even so, many people lived well into their 70s and beyond. Few people in the villages had completed elementary school, but they were able to adjust their farms and livelihoods to address the challenges of an unpredictable climate and economy. Despite all the challenges that marked the residents' everyday lives, people were more often than not joyful and full of life. This was not a community of downtrodden individuals. I was overwhelmed with respect for this group of people, who had withstood tremendous challenges and remained living in a place that had given them every reason to leave.

Understanding how they stayed alive and in place with so few resources, and so little outside information or help, became a central part of my research. I am convinced the people living in these villages, and in other places like them around the world, are repositories of information about how to improve the human condition cheaply and with minimal environmental impact. This book is, in part, an effort to convey some of this information to a wider audience that rarely gets to see the global poor as anything but helpless victims of circumstances beyond their control.

At the same time, this book is more than the story of the residents of two Ghanaian villages. It is also an effort to create for the reader an experience like the one I have had in the course of my fieldwork in Africa and as author of two global environmental assessments. When we connect the story of how these residents have managed severe economic and environmental shocks for more than 40 years to issues of global economic and environmental change, the result calls into question more than the idea of poverty. It also calls into question how we understand globalization, how development works, and the environmental implications of these processes.

Getting It Wrong: Development and Globalization

Implicitly, conversations about development long ago turned into conversations about globalization. While particular discussions of development might be focused on specific problems, such as the eradication of various diseases (for example, malaria, cholera, HIV/AIDS) and parasites (such as former president Jimmy Carter's work on eradicating guinea worm), these specific discussions are couched within larger conversations of how to convert these small victories into long-term improvements in people's lives. In the policy world, and in much popular literature, these discussions are rather rigidly tied to the goal of incorporating people into ever-freer global markets. Development has become a means by which people around the world might engage with these global markets to maximize their incomes and their well-being. This basic assumption is at the heart of many discussions of globalization and development, to the extent that even many critiques of globalization fail to challenge it, instead arguing that globalization is not working correctly because the markets are somehow distorted or perverted.

This linking of development and globalization is decades old. While the era of global free trade has resulted in the greatest generation of wealth the world has ever seen, it has not yielded expected improvements in well-being for those in the developing world. The vast majority of wealth generated by this belief in globalization, and the use of development to globalize ever-larger numbers of people in the world, has accumulated in the already-wealthy classes of already-wealthy countries. We may be living in the era of the greatest wealth in history, but we are also living through the most unequal global distribution of that wealth in history. Not all boats are rising on the tide of global economic growth.

There are many who look at outcomes, such as the falling life expectancies and declining access to food seen in Africa over the past two decades, and see an intentional effort to keep the poor "in their place" both poor and located far from the wealthiest countries in the world.[6] I disagree with this view strongly. While there are significant political challenges to the successful design and implementation of any development project or program, the vast majority of people working for development organizations are intelligent and good-hearted. They care deeply about the plight of the global poor and labor each day on projects and policies that might, finally, reverse the trends of inequality and unsustainability that mark life in much of the world.

What we are left with, then, is a much more interesting question. If these agencies and individuals are, by and large, trying their hardest to do good and have billions of dollars to work with, why are they failing? The answer lies in the character of development. As writers such as the anthropologist James Ferguson have demonstrated, contemporary development is not the product of a single organizational mission, a single theory, or a particular set of practices. It is the congealed outcome of more than six decades of often-uncoordinated administrative decisions, monitoring reports, economic theories, academic studies, and local responses. These ideas, such as the value of free trade and global markets for the global poor, are repeated so often and in so many venues that they seem to lack a single author or source. For the contemporary development practitioner, they seem to come from nowhere and everywhere at the same time. The same assumption is repeated over and over in development documents until, for example, it is impossible to talk about development in the absence of markets. The results are practices and ideas that seem both universal and eternal.

This, in turn, is the problem with the most visible, influential books that purport to explain the failure of development to live up to its most noble aspirations, such as the eradication of poverty. None of these books fundamentally questions the assumptions at the heart of the prevailing understandings of development or globalization. Instead they tweak the edges of these assumptions, leaving the core beliefs untouched. For example, the Columbia economist Jeffrey Sachs (*The End of Poverty: Economic Possibilities for Our Time*; *Common Wealth: Economics for a Crowded Planet*) and *New York Times* columnist Thomas Friedman (*The Lexus and the Olive Tree*; *The Earth Is Flat*; *Hot, Flat and Crowded*) make basically the same argument for development and globalization, respectively: if we want to improve the quality of life for people around the world, we need to foster policies that will enable the engagement of the global poor with global markets, and leverage these policies with the infusion of relatively large amounts of aid in strategic areas, such as health and education. Such a "boost" will push individuals, communities, and entire countries out of the "poverty traps" in which they find themselves and set them on the road to productive futures. This approach never examines whether or not globalization, the engagement with global markets, is in fact such a good idea for the poorest on Earth.

On the other hand, when economists such as William Easterly (*The Elusive Quest for Growth: Economists' Adventures and Misadventures in the Tropics*; *The White Man's Burden: Why the West's Efforts to Aid the Rest Have Done So Much Ill and So Little Good*); Raymond Fisman and Edward Miguel (*Economic Gangsters: Corruption, Violence, and the Poverty of Nations*); and former development consultant John Perkins (*Confessions of an Economic Hit Man*) argue that the central problem inhibiting the improvement of people's well-being in the developing world is not financial commitment but corruption, with various individuals and institutions acting in their own self-interests, either stealing donor funds or hijacking otherwise useful projects, they are not questioning the fundamental value of markets or the idea that globalization will work. These books, and others like them, are attractive at least in part because they do not challenge our understanding of how the world works. They tell us that what we are doing is fundamentally correct, if only we make a few small adjustments to get things right.

This implicit optimism about the relationship between globalization, development, and human well-being comes apart in the face of events taking place along what I call "globalization's shoreline." This shoreline is not a boundary between land and sea but the point of connection between people living in communities at the edges of global trade and politics, and the economic, political, and environmental decisions of those living in other places. Because this connection is often tangential and indirect—such as when the decision to drive a car in the United States contributes to climate change that disrupts precipitation in Southern Africa—those living along this shoreline have relatively little information about decisions that shape their everyday lives and little, if any, voice in them. I call this extended, complex world region "globalization's shoreline" because this connection is often intermittent, strong for one season, a year, or even a decade, while weakening at other times. Thus these communities exist on something analogous to a shoreline, with the waves and tides of global markets and politics ebbing and flowing through their lives, except that on this shore, neither the waves nor the tides are regular and predictable.

The experiences of most residents of globalization's shoreline are not to be found in the optimistic stories set in lobbies of expensive hotels in major cities of the developing world or in Internet cafés and shops near those hotels. While these are often the experiences and stories that support the belief that we are already on the path to well-being for all, they represent a small minority of those living along this shoreline. The experiences of most residents of this world region take shape in peri-urban and rural settings hours from these hotels, even by the best, most comfortable transportation. It should be of real concern to anyone interested in the world that so few of those who purport to explain globalization and development to us have actually lived on this part of globalization's shoreline.

Perhaps this part of globalization's shoreline is overlooked because, at first glance, a few villages and a few hundred residents in a West African village—or in rural India, or in rural China, or in rural Brazil, and so on—do not appear to be as important, in the global scheme of things, as the new millionaires and politics most commonly discussed in the context of globalization. In their analyses and stories, people tend to focus on these big players and movers. Certainly when Bill Gates, Warren Buffett, and George Soros decide to shift their considerable wealth, global markets notice. In comparison, the actions of a few hundred farmers living on two dollars per day are hardly about to cause significant ripples in the national economy, let alone the global economy. This sort of thinking, however, overlooks a critical fact: Villages are not islands, and the ebb and flow of global markets and politics on one part of globalization's shoreline is often mirrored in many other places.

Connecting the Dots: Globalization's Shoreline and Environmental Change

In the first phase of my career I was narrowly focused on issues of development and globalization and how they played out in rural communities in West Africa. Like many who work in development, I became frustrated with the pervasive misunderstandings of life on globalization's shoreline— misunderstandings that marked policy discussions and also inevitably spawned failures in policy and projects. I felt tired and helpless in the face of conversations with friends in Ghana, such as the colleague who, referring to Ghana's then-new development plan, barked, "Ghana 2020? What good will it do me? I am 50 years old!" In a country where the life expectancy for men is 57 years, telling a 50-year-old to wait 20 years for a better world is, indeed, absurd. I began to wonder if there was any point at all to development, and to question my engagement in the field.

Then, in 2003, I was asked to join the Millennium Ecosystem Assessment as a Young Fellow and a Lead Author of the Scenarios Working Group. For the first time I was asked to think about how my work in West Africa might inform broader understandings of current and future environmental changes. In the course of this assessment, I had two revelations. First, I realized that what I was seeing with regard to economic, social, and environmental change in Ghana's Central Region might have global implications. I had never before considered the global impact of the actions and decisions of those I worked with in the course of my research. After all, the decisions of a few dozen villagers about how to use their land and resources have a minuscule impact on massive global biogeochemical processes, such as hydrologic cycles and carbon cycles. As I worked on the Millennium Assessment, however, this myopia fell away. I realized events in these villages were in many ways representative of the situation emerging in many places. Taken in aggregate, lots of small environmental and economic changes can become large and powerful forces. Development did matter, and more than just to those living along globalization's shoreline. Without significant efforts to work with those living along this shoreline, the economic and environmental choices made by a huge percentage of the global population would seriously impact even the wealthiest, most insulated communities in the high-income economies.

When, however, I tried to express this in an early authors' meeting of my working group, I had my second revelation: Those concerned with global environmental change were operating from the same deeply rooted assumptions about development and globalization that marked policy in the development community. My efforts to suggest alternative framings of the relationship between development, globalization, and the environment were too far outside the expectations of those in charge of the assessment and were completely shut down, without discussion or consideration.

Lest I seem to be picking on particular individuals in a particular global assessment, let me make it clear that these assumptions, and this attitude toward the reconsideration of these attitudes, are pervasive in the global environmental policy community. When I joined the United Nations Environment Programme's (UNEP) Fourth Global Environment Outlook (GEO-4) as a lead author in 2005, I ran into the same problem. During a plenary session for all of the authors at UNEP's headquarters in Nairobi, I tried to argue that the document's very framing of environmental problems suggested the ultimate causes of environmental and economic change are processes that can be managed only by national governments, international organizations, or individuals with comparable resources. Local populations and their responses were treated as having significant impacts on the local context, but there was no mechanism for thinking about the aggregate effects of many local decisions on the global environment and economy. Reading this document, one could be forgiven for assuming that the rural parts of globalization's shoreline are not all that important in the grand scheme of things. The team in charge of GEO-4 brusquely responded to my comment with, "Thank you for that comment, we will take it under consideration." A German friend and colleague who had picked up on the tone of the response leaned over to me and whispered, with a chuckle, "Thank you, we will consider how to best ignore your comments." He was right. There was no further discussion of the conceptual framework of the assessment.

Let me be clear here: I am not dismissing the scientific basis of either the Millennium Assessment or GEO-4. Both assessments were written by some of the best people in the world on their subjects, and I was consistently humbled by the knowledge and passion of my colleagues on both reports. Yet, in both assessments the dismissal of alternative framings of the connections among development, globalization, and environmental change does a deep disservice to this expertise and information. As both economic and environmental policy are increasingly dominated by the goal of environmentally sustainable economic growth, globalization, development, and the environment are being linked into policies predicated on shared but often incorrect assumptions about how the world works. I have become concerned about a mounting misunderstanding of what is happening along much of globalization's shoreline. If we do not understand what is happening with more than four billion people on this planet, we will have significant problems understanding future global changes and their impacts on human beings.

This is not to say that I think claims about global environmental change are overstated. Indeed, I fear that much of what is accepted as "mainstream" understandings of climate change greatly underestimate the scope of the challenge before us. I worry, however, that we are misattributing future changes. For example, many economists interested in the issue of climate change—including Lord Nicholas Stern, the lead author of the highly influential *Stern Review on the Economics of Climate Change*—argue that high rates of economic growth along globalization's shoreline will be an important factor governing future amounts of greenhouse gas in the atmosphere, as such growth will eventually generate high rates of emission unless something is done to enable "clean" (read: low-carbon) growth. I am all for the transfer of low-carbon technologies to low-income economies, but my experience along globalization's shoreline leads me to believe these projected high rates of growth are not possible, nor sustainable several decades into the future. Much of the growth we will see along this shoreline will be on paper, like the recent tech and real-estate bubbles in the United States, and much of this (or any other) growth will be concentrated in the hands of a small percentage of the population. Neither of these scenarios (fictive growth or growth highly concentrated in the hands of the very few) will result in massive increases in greenhouse gas emissions over the long term.

Unless economic policy and development-project design are changed, the continued failure of economic growth and development to improve the quality of life for most people living along globalization's shoreline will place enormous pressure on natural resources, such as forests and farmlands, as people struggle to earn a living. In these places the resultant degradation of these resources (such as through deforestation) will be a much more significant future contributor to global climate change than emissions related to economic growth. Therefore, while I come to roughly the same conclusions as these economists with regard to the likely levels of future concentrations of greenhouse gas in the atmosphere, and while I agree with the general findings of the physical scientists who translate these emissions projections into future environmental scenarios, I see a different source for these emissions and therefore for these impacts. The difference between my view and their view lies not in the likely future impact of these changes, but in where those changes will come from and, therefore, how to address them. This is no small quibble. This is fundamental to understanding how to build a sustainable future for us all.

Four Claims to Frame the Argument

I am fundamentally concerned with taking apart the prevailing assumptions about development and globalization that make it so difficult to understand why development is going so badly, why a globalized world appears to be creating more poverty than it solves, and why all of this seems to be driving us toward a bad environmental end. Let us start our examination of this situation with four claims about development and globalization that run contrary to the tone and content of assertions by those who purport to tell us how the world works and why it works that way.

1. **Places we characterize as lacking, or needing, development are often better understood as the outcomes of development and globalization.**[7] The single greatest misconception shaping contemporary views of development and globalization is the idea that the problems of poverty in the developing world are the result of an absence of development. When we see malnourished children, disease, conflict, and environmental problems along globalization's shoreline, we tend to see these as the outcomes of lives, economies, and politics that lack development. The solution to these problems then seems self-evident: We need to bring development to these people. This argument is extended in policy circles to mean that development should be a tool by which people are integrated into global markets to leverage and consolidate gains brought on by development.

Think for a moment about this set of purported explanations and justifications. There is nothing explanatory there. Blaming things such as malnutrition or disease on a lack of development does not tell us how malnutrition came about or why disease has become an issue in a particular place. It merely asserts a condition and then immediately proposes a set of solutions. If we ask how environmental challenges, malnutrition, and other challenges came to be in particular places, however, we find these problems all have histories. These histories, in turn, are usually connected to long-standing efforts to link particular places to global markets, first through colonialism and, more recently, through development. Emerging networks of global trade, new crops, and new commodities have reshaped the lives of even the most remote and marginal people living in Africa, Asia, and Latin America for centuries. When commentators, authors and policy-makers argue that this era of globalization is somehow different from anything that has come before, they are allowing themselves the right to ignore this long history of connection and its impacts. This, in turn, allows them to talk about current efforts to integrate particular places into larger economies and political processes as new experiments in progress, experiments whose outcomes remain uncertain.

These are not new experiments, however, nor are their outcomes all that uncertain. History shows that development and globalization have been central to the production of adverse conditions, such as poverty and malnutrition, along many parts of globalization's shoreline. This means that our treatment of poverty, malnutrition, and other problems has, in many cases, been a greater application of the underlying cause. This is similar to treating the victim of poisoning with larger and larger doses of the same poison in the hope that its effects will suddenly be reversed. This otherwise senseless program of treatment is facilitated by the fact that the doctor is not reading the patient's chart and is therefore unaware of, or able to ignore, the poison that created the initial problem and the previous doses of poison given by other doctors in an effort to deal with that initial problem. Instead, the doctor gets to apply a remedy as if nothing else had been tried up to this point, and to act surprised when it not only fails to cure the patient but makes the patient worse. In the field of medicine, we call this malpractice. In development, it has become business as usual.

2. At globalization's shoreline the experience of "development" is often negative. The integration of local economies, politics, and society into global networks is not the unmitigated boon to human well-being presented by many authors. Those living along the shores of globalization deal with significant challenges in their lives, such as degrading environments, social inequality that limits opportunity for significant portions of society, and inadequate medical care. The integration of these places into a global economy does not necessarily solve these problems. In the best cases such integration provides new sources of income that might be used to address some of these challenges. In nearly all cases, however, such integration also brings new challenges and uncertainties that come at a cost to people's incomes and well-being.

For example, the members of a subsistence-farming household have limited income potential. Even so, they may have a fairly stable food supply and worry only about managing environmental shocks—for example, drought or pest infestation—for which they have means of management drawn from long experience. These shocks might be significant, and in bad years lead to situations of malnutrition or outright shortage. Now, assume this same household has decided to grow cash crops on a significant proportion of the farm to earn income to address these environmental challenges. To raise these crops, they have to cut back on their subsistence cultivation, and therefore they no longer grow enough food to feed themselves. Instead, they rely on the income from their cash crops to buy the food they no longer produce. If the global market for this crop remains stable or expands, the household will likely do quite well under this strategy. Its members will likely have plenty of income to buy the food they need and have money to spare for investment in businesses, children's education, or other productive activities. Commodity markets are notoriously unstable, however, and fluctuations in agricultural prices are typically passed on to the producer. If the price of this household's chosen cash crop crashes, even for a single year, they might not be able to raise enough money through the sale of this crop to buy the food they need, let alone finance other activities, such as education, needed to improve the long-term status of the household. The globalization of this household, while creating new opportunities for its members, has also introduced new uncertainties and challenges over which they have no control.

On globalization's shoreline this sort of trade-off takes place far more often than anyone seems to admit. Further, households and individuals in the developing world often have little in the way of resources for addressing these sorts of uncertainties. Two dollars a day does not provide anyone much capacity for managing uncertainty or addressing economic and environmental shocks. While I am tremendously impressed by the ability of those living on globalization's shoreline to deal with these sorts of issues, piling ever-more uncertainty onto already-stressed people with limited resources is a recipe for disaster. As a result, these trade-offs end badly far more often than anyone wants to discuss.

3. Globalization is not a one-way process. Globalization, understood as the integration of peoples and places into global networks of trade and politics, is not a conquering, absolute way of participating in the world. At most points on globalization's shoreline, the everyday lives of people, and the situation of places, are not so bound up in global markets and politics as are lives and homes in the developed world. For example, in sub-Saharan Africa a household might own a Chinese-made radio powered by Chinese batteries as well as used clothes imported from the United States, locally manufactured ceramics, food raised on the household farm, a kerosene lamp made from a tin can (formerly used to hold imported canned food) and a wick, and a stool made by a local carver. An economic or political shift resulting in the loss of these batteries, radio or even the tin-can kerosene lamp might inconvenience this household, but it will not compromise the overall well-being of its members. The loss of imported used clothing might force the household to turn to local tailors and seamstresses, but they will remain clothed. People like having access to global goods, but they do not *need* these goods to survive on a day-to-day basis. The difference between the situation at the shores of globalization and that in the "globalized" world is that those in the former *like* to have global goods and those in the latter *need* to have global goods. This is why it is so difficult for those living in Europe and the United States, for example, to imagine a deglobalized world. The loss of global goods would have a pervasive impact on residents' lives and would change everything from their economic productivity to their diets.

Because people living on globalization's shoreline are not as dependent on global goods as are those of us living in more thoroughly globalized economies, their connection to these markets and processes is far less direct than ours. On the shores of globalization the choice to deglobalize can be as simple as changing a single crop on the family farm. The impact of this change on the day-to-day lives of those in that family might be tiny, but in the absence of that crop and its connection to global markets, their linkage to the global economy becomes distant and tangential. On one hand, this can present limitations to this family's opportunities because sales of commodities on global markets can be quite lucrative. On the other hand, this distance from global networks provides a level of insulation from economic shocks that might otherwise be crushing. Those living on the shores of globalization strategically globalize and deglobalize all the time in order to take advantage of opportunities or to manage challenges.

4. Globalization and development do not directly create positive or negative outcomes for those in the developing world.[8] A fundamental misunderstanding of development and globalization is that they improve people's lives (or destroy people's lives). Neither development nor globalization does anything to people in a direct way. These activities (development) and processes (globalization) generally lack the coercive force of arms or the threat of imminent death by flooding or volcanic eruption. Instead, development and globalization are catalysts for change in particular places. When we build a road through a rural village, we do not create higher incomes or a greater connection to global markets. Rather, we create a set of opportunities and challenges for those living in that village. How they leverage opportunities and manage challenges are generally the result of a set of decisions made with regard to local needs and conditions, not to universal expectations of human behavior. Some people might see the road as an opportunity to market more of their crops and increase their incomes. Others might see the road as a threat—such as men who are preoccupied with their wives' rising incomes due to greater petty trading opportunities. These different views will result in varying behaviors and outcomes, even within small villages.

The same could be said for globalization. A connection to larger networks of economy and politics might be seen as a huge opportunity for some farmers, who restructure their farms to include more cash crops. For others, however, this connection might undermine their authority, which is grounded in local social and political processes, such as control over farmland. How individuals in these two particular groups respond to globalization, then, will be different. There is no universal response to either development or globalization. The constant quest for such responses are a waste of energy and time, as are efforts to explain away our continuing failure to identify such universals.

In the first half of this book, I will illustrate each of these points through an intense focus on the experiences of those living in two villages in Ghana's Central Region. I am not going to make universal claims about development, globalization, or environmental change through these villages. Instead, the experiences of those living there allow me to call into question the assumptions about globalization, development, and environmental change that undergird much of development and economic policy.

My desire to foster serious discussion about globalization's shoreline by throwing into question (and crisis) some of the central tenets by which we understand this part of the world is not an end unto itself. After more than a decade in the classroom, I have learned that the best way to enable new learning is first to strip away the familiar. This book, then, is a means to the end of creating a space for a new form of development that might just get us to a sustainable, more just future. The second half of the book opens up this space by examining how our assumptions about globalization and development have become durable as a result of the very data we gather to measure these activities and processes and the ways we think about "global" events—such as the financial crisis and the coming end of oil—and it presents one particular vision of global participation and cooperation that can achieve this goal.

Chapter 2

Getting to the "Beach"

The villages of Dominase and Ponkrum are located in Ghana's Central Region, about 90 miles west of Accra, the capital. This description does little to illustrate what it means to live on globalization's shoreline. To explain what this means, we must first leave the comfortable hotels and restaurants of Accra and make the journey to these villages, starting with a trip to the town of Elmina. The only way to do this is to drive along the two-lane highway between Accra and points west. Until recently, describing the condition of the road as poor and potholed did not do it justice. My friend and colleague, Ben Kankpeyeng, came much closer when he referred to these ruts as "potwells," as they were usually deep and full of water. Traffic on this road routinely slowed to a crawl as it passed through busy towns, such as Kasoa and Mankessim, or as cars and buses bogged down behind giant old trucks with top speeds of 40 miles per hour. People and animals from the villages that line this highway dart across the road constantly. On my first trip between Accra and Elmina, the bus in which I was riding hit two goats and a dog. I stopped paying attention after that. Even in the best of conditions, the trip between Accra and Elmina routinely took more than four hours.

The road is now greatly improved. After several years of rebuilding, much of it is a newly surfaced dual carriageway with wide shoulders. As a result, travel times between Accra and Elmina are down to less than two hours. At night, however, the road remains extremely dangerous. For most of its length it is poorly lit, putting the people and animals crossing in the low visibility even more at risk. Further, after dark an astounding percentage of the drivers on the road are intoxicated. The risks of nighttime driving

Figure 2.1 Locator map of Dominase and Ponkrum reprinted from *World Development*, 36(5), Edward R. Carr, "Men's Crops and Women's Crops: The Importance of Gender to the Understanding of Agricultural and Development Outcomes in Ghana's Central Region" 900–915. Copyright 2008, with permission from Elsevier

along this highway came home to me in 1999 when the minivan (*tro-tro*, in local parlance) in which I was riding collided with another vehicle parked on the side of the road, an accident at least partially attributable to the fact that the *tro-tro* driver had been drinking.

The journey from Accra to Elmina, however inconvenient or dangerous, is really only half the trip to Dominase and Ponkrum, located about five miles northwest of Elmina. There are two routes and several options for those seeking to get from Elmina to these villages. The first route passes through the town of Eguafo, the most important in the traditional area to which Dominase and Ponkrum belong. If you are wealthy, you can hire a cab in Elmina to drop you off in Eguafo. The cost of such a ride can be as high as three dollars, more than a day's earnings for most people. For those who cannot afford to hire a cab themselves, there are shared cabs. These run fixed routes from Elmina up to, and often beyond, Eguafo for fixed prices (usually around 25 cents for the trip from Elmina to Eguafo) per passenger. To catch one of these shared cabs, passengers go to the taxi station in the center of Elmina and wait for a cab to Eguafo to fill up. Typically this involves cramming at least five adults (and their attendant baggage and animals) into the compact cars that pass for cabs in this area. I have been in a cab from Elmina to Eguafo that carried seven people (a

Figure 2.2 Elmina town, taken from Elmina Castle

driver plus three adult and three child passengers). The wait for passengers can range from minutes to more than an hour. The operating margins on these cabs are tiny, and a driver will not move a car until it is as full as possible. This also makes it difficult to catch a shared cab from anyplace outside the Elmina station, unless you happen to be standing where someone chooses to disembark on the way to Eguafo. I have waited for more than two hours for such an opportunity at the junction between the east-west highway and the road to Eguafo, watching completely full cabs pass by until I finally got lucky. *Tro-tros* are even cheaper than cabs but far less numerous on the relatively poorly traveled road to Eguafo. These are also found at the station in Elmina, and there are often empty seats for travelers attempting to join a *tro-tro* outside the station.

However one chooses to go, the journey does not end at Eguafo. From there it is a two-mile trip to Ponkrum via a hilly route along a newly graded road that was, until 2004, an impassable combination of dirt road and footpath. Cab drivers will take passengers to Ponkrum via this road but will charge an exorbitant amount (in excess of five dollars, more than several days' pay for area residents). Despite recent improvements to the road, which includes grading and new culverts, parts of the route still become lightly flooded in the rainy season, and cabs can bog down easily under such conditions. No shared cabs or *tro-tros* pass along this route into Ponkrum.

Figure 2.3 The footpath from Eguafo to Ponkrum, facing Ponkrum, in 1999

Therefore, if you cannot afford a hired cab, your only option is to walk the road. The path is lined with farms, and bemused residents working there will warmly greet passersby in Fante, the local language. The trip from Elmina to Ponkrum along this route takes anywhere from an hour and a half to three hours, depending on transportation availability.

The other route to Dominase and Ponkrum is less traveled by visitors but very familiar to residents of these villages. Rather than passing though Eguafo, a traveler can go from Elmina to the east-west highway and then head west to the village of Bronyibima before turning north along a newly graded road that passes through Dominase and Ponkrum on the way to Berase, a large village five kilometers to the north. Today, it is possible to catch a cab or *tro-tro* following this route from Elmina to Berase and get off in Dominase or Ponkrum along the way. However, these modes of transportation move far less frequently than those that go to Eguafo. A traveler might wait two or three hours for the vehicle to fill with passengers before setting out. These shared cabs and *tro-tros* are also more expensive than those going to Eguafo. Therefore, most people who use this alternate route walk.

Until 2004 it was not possible to get a cab to travel this route for less than ten dollars, or more than a week's pay for most residents of Dominase and Ponkrum. This was also a steep price for a graduate student on a thin budget, and as a result I became quite familiar with this walk. From Elmina you walk about a mile along the northern road and then turn west along the east-west highway. After a mile along this road, you come to the village of Bronyibima. Just on the other side of Bronyibima is a relatively wealthy, small community of new houses called Bronyibima Estate, or Estate for short. Turning onto the dirt road that tracks north and gently west through Estate, you pass through this settlement and, after less than one-quarter of a mile, under the high-tension power lines that skirt its northern edge. These wires carry electricity from Akosombo Dam on the Volta River, the principal source of electricity in Ghana, to the western parts of the country. This is the last electrical infrastructure you will see on your walk.

Here on the coastal plain the vegetation is low and scrubby, and the land relatively flat. With the exception of the odd stand of coconut trees planted by local farmers, there is little shade. The northernmost reach of the Benya River burbles gently a few feet to the east of the road, audible but invisible behind heavy brush. It is a hot walk at any time of the year but not a lonely route. After a mile and a half the village of Sanka appears. Sanka has a large elementary school, and many residents make the short trip to Bronyibima and Elmina several times a week, creating a constant light flow of foot traffic on the road.

About a mile north of Sanka, the landscape turns hilly and the vegetation gets taller and more lush. This used to be where the coastal plain transitioned to forest. Today, after centuries of human occupation and decades of development-driven deforestation, only a few tall trees remain. The road turns to the west and winds along between farm-covered hills. At first glance, much of the landscape appears to be untamed brush and overgrowth. There is, however, nothing natural about this scene. Every inch of this land is either under cultivation or lies fallow between cultivation cycles. Even the few remaining tall trees are cultural artifacts that mark the boundaries between different landholdings.

While birds fly overhead, very little moves on the ground. There are many snakes in the area, but they have long learned to flee before footsteps, as farmers will kill any snake they find. I witnessed this during my first few months in the village. While walking back from a farm toward Ponkrum, I nearly stepped directly on the back of a six-foot-long cobra that was sunning itself on the footpath after what appeared to have been a large meal. Everyone agreed the snake had to be killed, but among a group of at least six farmers, not one was carrying a machete or knife of any sort. This is odd for two reasons. First, the machete is the principal farming implement in these villages, and every single man, woman, or child above the age of six or seven owns at least one. Second, we were returning from a farm and were accompanied by several farmers. The likelihood that nobody would have a machete in this particular moment was infinitesimal. When the farmers realized that this was the case, the ensuing argument ("I thought you had a machete. You mean nobody has a machete?") was pretty funny and reinforced my feeling that the situation was somewhat absurd. The snake, slowed by a recent meal, barely moved during this entire exchange. Eventually, in frustration, two of the farmers grabbed some shoots of cut bamboo from a nearby farm and beat the snake mercilessly until it was dead.

Snakes are not the only wildlife living on this land. Anyone paying careful attention while walking along the road north of Sanka can hear the occasional rustle of an animal moving through the bush on the sides of the road. Such sounds could come from grasscutters (a sort of giant vegetarian rodent that is considered a local delicacy), rats, mice, or perhaps one of the few small antelope that remain in the area. Any of these mammals unfortunate enough to raise their heads, however, are quickly trapped, killed, and, in the case of antelope and grasscutters, sold at market in Elmina. Rats and mice are eaten in the village. Local fauna is both exceedingly rare and very valuable. In my eighteen months of living in and around these villages, I saw only two antelope and perhaps three grasscutters. The antelope were both trapped and sold at market for 10–15 dollars, more than a week's earnings for most of these farmers. A grasscutter could fetch eight to ten dollars. In 2000, while walking from Dominase back to Ponkrum after a hot, exhausting day of archaeological excavation, my field crew and I saw a grasscutter cross the road about 50 yards ahead of us. Without hesitation the three-person crew put—well, threw—the archaeological equipment and artifacts down and took off after the grasscutter. For more than ten minutes they tried to corner and catch it, only to have it escape through a hole in some farmer's fence. Frustrated, the men returned to the archaeological equipment and artifacts, carried them back to Ponkrum, and then went in search of the owner of the farm to complain about the grasscutter they had lost because of his poorly maintained fence. The shouting went on for more than half an hour and could be heard throughout the village.

There is a new pressure that all but ensures the complete destruction of edible fauna around these villages in the near future. The fishery in the Gulf of Guinea is collapsing as trawlers from the European Union harvest tremendous numbers of fish for consumption far from West Africa. Those living in Elmina and its hinterland have largely relied on fish caught by local fishermen for much of the protein in their diets. The decline of this fishery has resulted in reduced hauls by local fishermen, driving up the price of fish when they can be had at all. In response to this pressure, coastal communities throughout West Africa are now hunting down local wildlife to make up for the declining availability of fish.[1] I saw clear evidence of this trend in the summer of 2006 as hunting parties of younger men and dogs drove grasscutters, mice, and rats across fields in an effort to catch them. These activities were taking place in the middle of the day, when in previous years these men would have been farming. When I first traveled to Dominase and Ponkrum in the late 1990s, hunting was a passive side effort. Farmers set snares on their farms, hoping for opportunistic catches that would both protect their crops and provide a little variety in their diets. However, since 2004 dog ownership has been on the rise in these villages. In Dominase and Ponkrum dogs have only one publicly stated use: hunting. Privately it is well-known that if they are no good at hunting, they become food. The rise in dog ownership, then, is a clear marker of increased pressure on the animal resources of this area. All these pressures mean the trip from Estate is not much of a nature walk, at least in terms of animals.

The use of either route to reach these villages, of course, assumes the roads are passable. In the primary rainy season, which runs from mid-May to mid-August, heavy downpours sometimes fill seasonal channels that cross the roads to these villages, making them unwalkable for hours and unmotorable for days. In July 2000 I was running an archaeological field school in Ponkrum when unusually heavy rains started. Our tents were inadequate to keep the excavation area dry, so I closed the site for the day and loaded the students into the car of Ben Kankpeyeng, a colleague and friend in the Department of Archaeology at the University of Ghana. Before we left, we heard that the road to the north of Ponkrum was washed out. At that time the path between Ponkrum and Eguafo was impassable by car even in the best of conditions, so we set out to the south, following the road/path back through Sanka to Bronyibima. Just north of Sanka we came upon a flow of water more than four feet deep washing across the road. After we had waited for several hours for the waters to recede, a member of my field crew came from Ponkrum to tell us that the road to Eguafo was passable on foot. We drove back to Ponkrum, and I sent the students to Eguafo with a member of the crew as an escort. In Eguafo they caught a taxi and eventually made it back to our project base in Cape Coast. Ben and I prepared to spend the night in Ponkrum, which was not a problem since I own a house in the village.

Just as night started to fall, however, we heard that the road to the north of the village was now passable. By passable, I should note, the villagers meant that a good driver and a team of people to help push might get the car up the dirt road to the paved surface roughly two miles to the north. The team of people was necessary, as the road was cut by gullies and full of bogs that a four-door Nissan sedan could not negotiate. As Ben drove, my field crew and I ran alongside/behind, catching up whenever he bogged down and pushing him out. After about 30 minutes of running and pushing, we reached Berase and the paved road, seven hours after we set out. I have since referred to that day as the inaugural "Ponkrum Invitational," as four of us effectively raced against a car for two miles along a muddy trail in the rain, conditions that any cross-country runner would have been proud to endure.

While unusual, rain events such as the one that trapped us in and around Ponkrum for seven hours on that day occur several times in a typical year.

They are unpredictable, so while every villager can tell you the road will be cut a few times each year, they cannot tell you exactly when or for how long. Since 2004 the installation of cement culverts at key points in the roads around Ponkrum and Dominase has helped reduce the impact of flooding on these routes, but has not completely resolved the issue. As a result, the persistence of long and often uncertain travel times to get to employment opportunities or markets for their crops cost residents time and money and make living in these villages and reaching these opportunities, if not mutually exclusive, quite difficult to rhyme.

For the purposes of understanding the trip being described, though, assume the road from Bronyibima is passable. After three and a quarter miles of walking from Estate, the road turns to the north again, and we reach Dominase. Walking this route from Elmina to Dominase takes at least two hours and usually longer. Ponkrum is an additional third of a mile, or ten minutes, up the road. For the residents of these villages, the trip to Elmina and back takes at least two hours each way regardless of the route or the means of conveyance. Those who choose motorized transport for the journey will pay at least 50 cents, or a quarter of a day's earnings in these communities. After two hours on the bus and another two hours of walking, we have arrived at our spot on the beach.

Chapter 3

A Day at the Beach

Dominase sits on the eastern edge of roughly 11 acres of flat land surrounded by hills to the east, south, and northwest. It is comprised of a
tight cluster of a half-dozen earth-walled structures with tin roofs and a
single open well with a concrete shaft. The ground around and between
these structures is packed earth. There is no vegetation at all within the
boundaries of the village. Though it is only three miles from the highway
and the high-tension lines, Dominase has no electricity, no running water,
and no formal toilets or sanitation facilities.

Arriving in the daytime, we are unlikely to see anyone around, as most
of the residents are at their farms on the surrounding land. Yet, no local
guide is needed to see this settlement was once much larger. A few yards to
the south of the village there is a circular berm that forms an earthen cistern about the size and depth of a large above-ground swimming pool. The
capacity of this cistern, now in disrepair and overgrown with bamboo, was
well beyond the needs of the dozen or so current residents. Surrounding
the standing structures of the village are overgrown mounds of earth, the
remains of structures that were abandoned and eventually collapsed. These
mounds cover much of the flat area between the hills and spread up the
hillside on the eastern side of the road. Clearly, Dominase is much diminished from what it once was.

Continuing to the north for another third of a mile, we arrive in
Ponkrum. The junction between the road to Eguafo and the one from
Bronyibima is near the northern end of the settlement. Ponkrum is a
collection of 171 houses on about 12 acres that gently slope upward to
the west and south. The village is completely ringed by low hills. As in

Figure 3.1   Dominase from the east, 2006

Dominase, the ground around and between the houses is packed earth, though in some places the soil has eroded down to subsurface stone. Also as in Dominase, there is no electricity or running water in Ponkrum. Toward the northern edge of the village, at the intersection of the roads to Eguafo and Bronyibima, lie the remains of an earthen cistern much like that in Dominase. This cistern, which was supplied by rainwater when it was in use, was intentionally destroyed in 2004 when the roads were being improved. Before its destruction, children and a few adults bathed in the water, while nearly everyone used it for washing, drinking, and/or cooking. It is therefore of little surprise that the residents of Ponkrum were plagued by guinea worm and other waterborne illnesses until 1997, when a French nongovernmental organization (NGO) installed a borehole and foot pump that draws clean groundwater up for drinking.

Since 1997 residents have paid a small amount (the equivalent of less than a cent) to collect a bucket of water from this borehole. The money is saved by the villagers and used to pay for new parts or repairs if the pump fails. Most residents of Ponkrum are willing to pay for this water, at least for drinking purposes. The supply of water from the borehole provided an alternative source for the villagers and made feasible the destruction of the

Figure 3.2 Ponkrum from the south, 2006

cistern and the draining of its polluted waters. Today, there is no guinea worm and very little waterborne illness in this or nearby villages.

When I first arrived in Ponkrum in 1997, there were no improved sanitation facilities in the village. Those who needed to defecate did so in specific areas around the edge of the settlement. Today, while there is a public pit latrine on the north side of the soccer field in the northwest corner of the village, and Francis Quayson has constructed a pit latrine behind his family's houses, many people still relieve themselves in unimproved areas around the village.

When we arrive in Ponkrum, as in Dominase there are few people around—just a small number of children and some women who are cooking. Both villages remain largely uninhabited until around 3:30 or 4 in the afternoon, when residents begin to return from their farms.[1] These farms ring both Dominase and Ponkrum, and members of some households will walk as far as a mile and a half back to their villages carrying harvested crops and farm tools. The villages fill quickly as women, and often children, return from the fields together to begin preparing dinner. The children who attend school—either in Breman, a village nearly three miles to the northwest, or at a mission school near Amoana, a village nearly three miles to the southeast—also arrive after making the walk back to Ponkrum. Men tend to return to the village about a half hour after the rest of their families, having done some extra work while their wives cooked.

Most residents of Ponkrum and Dominase bathe before dinner. As there is no running water here, people take bucket baths, typically using a five-gallon bucket of water to wet themselves and rinse off the soap. Some use borehole water for bathing, but this is unusual due to the cost of that water. More commonly people use stored rainwater, while a few might try to use what little water collects in the remains of the cistern. To preserve their modesty while bathing, households construct small enclosures with fence-like walls made of long slivers of bamboo. Paradoxically, these enclosures are often rather publically situated. I discovered this firsthand during my first field season, when I found my designated enclosure to be located along the road through town from Bronyibima. While there was no motorized traffic along the road, it was still a busy part of the village. Further, these

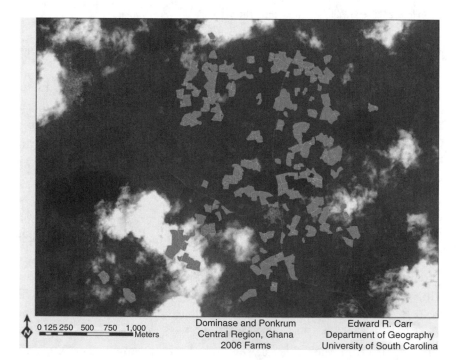

0 125 250   500   750   1,000   Dominase and Ponkrum   Edward R. Carr
                          Meters   Central Region, Ghana   Department of Geography
                                            2006 Farms   University of South Carolina

Figure 3.3 Satellite image highlighting the location of Dominase's and Ponkrum's farm plots in 2006

enclosures are simple walls meant to reach to the neck of the occupant. I, however, am 6 ft. 2 in. tall, roughly eight inches taller than the average man in these villages, and so my enclosure barely reached above my navel. I was a source of amusement for many residents on a nightly basis. In subsequent fieldwork I arranged for a more secluded bathing enclosure.

Most people eat between five and six o'clock in the evening. Because Ponkrum and Dominase are located just a few degrees north of the equator, the sun sets just after 5 p.m. all year long, forcing most households to eat by the light of kerosene lamps. They do this in front of their houses, either near the outdoor hearth on which the food was cooked or at the opposite end of the yard. Those households that own a kitchen structure may eat inside the kitchen. During the rainy seasons, rains rarely fall in the early evening, allowing residents to continue eating outdoors. If it does rain, people have their meals in their rooms or in their kitchen structures.

The dinner meal in Dominase and Ponkrum tends to be spartan. The Fante diet, like that of other Akan groups, is based around starches, the most common of which in these villages is *fufu*, a thick, pastelike concoction made by pounding boiled cassava, yams, or plantains with a large mortar and pestle. *Fufu* can be made of these starches separately or in any

Figure 3.4 Kitchen structure in Dominase

number of combinations and ratios, depending on individual tastes and the availability of ingredients. *Fufu* is filling but also bland. This is especially true if made only from cassava, which is quite common in these villages.

Fufu is shaped into a ball, placed into a bowl, and topped with a stew that adds flavor to this starchy staple. You then use a small piece of the *fufu* as a combination of edible spoon and sponge, soaking up and shoveling the stew and *fufu* into your mouth. There are several common stews in Akan food-ways, but in Ponkrum and Dominase the ingredients for most are inaccessible due to their cost or the distance to markets in which they are sold. Most of my meals were *fufu* topped with a brutally spicy version of palm nut stew. The Ponkrum version of this stew is largely comprised of palm oil, ground hot pepper, a tiny amount of tomato, and a few chunks of bony smoked fish (called "stinking fish" in local parlance) purchased from fishermen in Elmina. Occasionally I would get some form of meat, depending on my cook's luck with traps. Even more rarely I would get *banku*, a vaguely tangy fermented corn dough paste formed into balls and served in the same manner as *fufu*. Though the meals are simple, they provide more than enough calories to fuel the population. They do not, however, always provide all the nutrients needed to ensure healthy growth in children. When I first arrived here in 1997, I noticed a large number of children with reddish hair. This struck me as odd, especially because only one adult had reddish hair. It was not until some time later that I found out that the reddish tint to their hair was a marker of *kwashiorkor*, a form of childhood malnutrition linked to deficiencies in protein and other micronutrients. People with diets heavy in starches, such as cassava, are particularly prone to this form of malnutrition, as these starches can lead to dietary imbalances in protein relative to caloric intake. The long-term impacts of *kwashiorkor* include stunted growth, hair- and tooth-loss, and even an inability to form antibodies following vaccination for serious diseases. *Kwashiorkor* is far less common in Ponkrum and Dominase today, at least in part because after 2004 representatives of Ghana's Ministry of Health began monthly visits to evaluate the health of infants and toddlers in the village.

After meals the residents of the villages socialize or conduct business with neighbors. Some visit friends in other households. For the foreign visitor, the experience of this socializing can be quite disconcerting, as these villagers have a very different sense of personal space from that of a typical American or European. Several evenings during my first field season, I found myself entertaining 6 or more villagers in my 12-ft. by 15-ft. room. Roughly a third of the room was taken up by my bedroll and mosquito net. I had one chair, which as many as four people would share—even when I was sitting in it. The closeness of these visits was compounded by the near-total absence of small talk among these villagers. In the United States we abhor silence in social situations and tend to fill it with innocuous comments meant to move conversation along. Members of other cultures often misinterpret our fear of social silences as an unhealthy obsession with the weather. In Dominase and Ponkrum there is no such fear. If nobody has anything to say, nobody says anything. At the same time, nobody gets up to leave when conversation dies down. Everyone just sits in silence for a few minutes, until someone remembers something else worth discussing. For me, an American who is well known by friends and colleagues as something of a motormouth, these moments of silence were at first excruciating. Over time I have come to appreciate this mode of interaction, though I am still a motormouth.

Few people leave the villages after dark. The vast majority of nighttime travel in the area involves people on the way home, not on the way to another village to visit. The only real exceptions to this are residents of Dominase who routinely come up to Ponkrum after dark to hit the bars (both of them). To the visitor, the bars in Ponkrum look exactly like other houses in the village. Indeed, each bar *is* part of the owner's house and typically consists of a roof supported by four posts, free-standing or leaning against the side of the owner's house. There is usually a bench or two for the patrons. Tables are less common. All furniture is transitory—one day there might be two benches, the next, only one. As anywhere else in the world, you can place drink orders with the man or woman manning the bar (usually a window in the owner's house). You can have any drink you like, as long as it is *akpeteshi*, a liquor made by fermenting the sap of oil palm trees (often called palm wine) and then distilling it. While it is impossible to be sure of the exact proof of *akpeteshi*, it burns with a sustained blue flame, which suggests it is well over 100-proof. I have used it as a disinfectant for cuts and seen it take the tarnish off silver. A 12-ounce soda bottle of *akpeteshi* costs between 25 and 50 cents and contains more alcohol than anyone should consume in a single sitting. *Akpeteshi* is consumed in shots, usually using a communal shot glass. While there is no explicit prohibition on women's consumption of alcohol, and rarely have I heard anyone in these villages complain about women drinking, the consumption of *akpeteshi* in bars is almost entirely by men.

There are few late nights in Dominase and Ponkrum. Most of the residents go to bed before 9 p.m. Until midnight one can hear battery-powered radios throughout the village playing music, Akan-language news, or Akan talk radio. The din of the radios is significant and can be hard to adjust to initially. After midnight the villages go silent, and the only sound is the rustling of leaves and the footsteps of the occasional insomniac goat or sheep. The temperature rarely drops below 80° F, even at night. During the dry season entire households sleep in front of their houses in an effort to stay cool. During the rainy seasons this is not an option, as downpours can come during the night.

There are exceptions to these early bedtimes. If you happen to visit these villages on the day of a major football match, you will see what I mean. I watched the final of the 1998 World Cup and, in 2006, the Ghana-Italy group-stage match, in Ponkrum on a television powered by a car battery. A few residents of these villages own televisions, stereos, or other electronics that work only if plugged in. While plugging in is, of course, impossible, there are well-known ways to rig nearly any of these devices so that a car battery can power them. On the day of a major match, someone is sent with the car battery to one of the service stations along the highway three miles to the south to charge the battery. The fully charged battery can power a small television for several hours, if the charge and television-use are carefully managed. In 1998 the failure of the television's owner to fully charge the battery led to the fluttering in and out of the TV during the final five minutes of the match. A riot was narrowly averted, and the owner's health preserved, when he managed to keep the TV working long enough to reach the end of the match. Nearly the entire population of these villages came to watch the game in 2006, creating a somewhat unusual all-village gathering, where even children were up well past 10 p.m.

The villagers wake with the sun, which rises around 5 a.m. each day. Some residents who choose to bathe twice a day take a bath when they wake up. Women begin to prepare food for the breakfast meal, some cooking for their households, while some sell the cooked food to others in the village. Common breakfast foods include a spicy porridge made from cornmeal and hot pepper and sweetened with sugar, or beans and rice. Men follow up on business with neighbors and sometimes run out to nearby farm plots to collect needed ingredients for breakfast. Households eat breakfast together, in more or less the same places where they ate dinner the night before.

The villages begin to empty out by 7:30 a.m. Men leave for the fields first. Schoolchildren leave around this time as well, heading out for the long walk, either to Breman or Amoana. Wives clean up the kitchens and any cooking and eating utensils, while older girls who are no longer in school sweep the yards in front of the houses until they are clear of all debris. On Wednesdays, women gather up the crops to be sold at market and carry them to Elmina via Bronyibima. Nearly all crops grown for market sale in Dominase and Ponkrum are sold in Elmina. The only crop sold in the villages is palm nuts, which are processed into palm oil. Buyers for charcoal will also come out to the settlements. In both cases these are large operations with heavy dump trucks that can negotiate the road under nearly any conditions. They pass through the villages every week to collect these items from farmers.

In Dominase and Ponkrum, taking crops to market is considered women's work. It is also extraordinarily labor-intensive. Before 2004 it was impossible to catch a ride all the way from Ponkrum to Elmina. Today it is possible but often not practical, as traffic on the road is irregular, which can lead to long waits. It makes little sense to wait two hours for a car when one can make the walk in that amount of time. As a result, most women do not bother with motorized transport and walk the entire five miles to Elmina with up to 50 pounds of crops from their households on their heads. They return from market by the same path, carrying fish and other items purchased with the profits of their trading.

Nonmarket days are not times of rest for the women of these households. On these days, when they have finished their domestic tasks, they join their husbands in the fields. By 9 a.m. families have made the walk to their farms. While not quite as arduous as walking five miles carrying 50 pounds on one's head, getting to the farms is a task unto itself. Some people farm plots more than a mile and a half from where they live and must walk out to these plots carrying all the tools and food they will need for the day. This is not an easy walk. The terrain is hilly, and during the rainy seasons dirt paths turn to slippery mud. The paths can be difficult to see, and navigating between farms is impossible without a local guide. Further, men farm an average of three different plots at the same time. These are often separate, reached by a mile or more of walking. Francis and I mapped many of these farms in 2004 and 2005, and there were days when we had to walk three or more miles just to measure all the plots associated with a single man's farm.

The average man's farm consists of roughly 7.5 acres spread across three distinct plots. Women, by and large, farm a single plot of about an acre near one of their husbands' plots. Women in female-headed households farm a single plot, about three-quarters of an acre, near a plot of the person who gave them the land (usually a father or uncle). Husbands and wives may work separately on their own plots or work together on one or the other's plot, depending on the task at hand. Children who are not in school help on the farms or play near their parents. Infants are often strapped to their mothers' backs and are along for the ride as she works. Husbands, wives, and children eat lunch, prepared by the wife, together on their farms. These meals are exceedingly simple, such as a few pieces of boiled cassava with some palm oil and pepper. Away from their kitchens and in the middle of an arduous workday, women do not have time to prepare more elaborate meals.

The residents of Dominase and Ponkrum pass their days on their farms from March to December of each year. While the sorts of activities you might see vary depending on when you visit, conditions are usually difficult. From March through mid-May the sun can be harsh, and temperatures reach nearly 100° F every day. Men, using only machetes, clear away the dense brush that overgrows fallow fields. This work is done either alone, with the assistance of hired labor (the daily rate for agricultural labor is about $2.50 plus meals), or collectively with other members of their family or friends. Any brush with large enough branches or trunks is burned into charcoal and sold at market. The remaining loose brush is burned on the fields. Agricultural extension officers debate the value of this burning and in the past have discouraged this practice. Farmers in these villages argue that it serves to drive out insects and other pests from the farms. I suspect the principal reason for burning the brush is that doing anything else with it takes time and energy away from farming. As one farmer told me, "I know I am not supposed to burn, but I do it anyway." Once the plot is cleared, men and women begin to plant their crops, using machetes and hands to dig holes or build mounds for seeds.

Starting in mid-May, as the major rainy season begins, rain falls every day, often for long stretches. Large storms pass through frequently. I have been forced to ride out more than one large thunderstorm in a small temporary shelter on someone's farm; the sense of exposure is stressful, to say the least. During the rainy period the fields must be constantly weeded with machetes and hands, and rain-sensitive crops, such as tomatoes and peppers, are added to the crops already growing on the farm. Work is wet, and despite daytime temperatures that often reach into the low nineties, hours in soaking clothes leave farmers cold.

In August the rains taper off, and farmers harvest the crops planted during the first rainy season. The exception is cassava, which is left to mature for another seven to nine months. The weather is hot, sunny, and humid during this lull in the rain, and the crops are harvested by hand and carried from the farm plot back to the villages by everyone—men, women, and children. Once these crops are harvested, most farmers plant a second crop. Generally speaking, farmers simply replant many of the same crops on the same plot they used in the major rainy season. Those few who do open up new plots for the minor rainy season tend to keep them small.

Between late September and the end of October, the minor rainy season is in force, with conditions similar to that of the major rainy season. The rainfalls are often a bit less intense and not as frequent in the minor season

Figure 3.5 A farm plot near Ponkrum. Visible in the picture is maize and a few oil palm trees. Harder to see in this picture are cassava, pepper, tomato and other crops, all planted among the corn stalks and in various stages of development

and shorter in duration. The farmers are engaged in the same sorts of manual labor in their fields that occupied them during the major rainy season. They harvest the crops watered by the minor rainy season in November and December. January, February, and March are too hot and dry to farm productively. Individuals may try to burn charcoal or engage in short-term wage labor outside the village to earn money during this lull in the agricultural cycle.

The relative isolation of Dominase and Ponkrum, and the near-universal engagement of the population with farming, can make it easy for the casual visitor to overlook the importance of wage and commercial income to the livelihoods of the residents. In married households, the ratio of agricultural income to wage and commercial income (often referred to as non-farm employment, or NFE) was roughly 60–40 from the mid-1990s until 2004. For female-headed households, this ratio was 75–25 across the same period.

Men's wage and commercial activities are particularly difficult to observe, as they mostly take place outside the villages. While there is a limited need for agricultural labor here, the prevailing rate for that labor is now so high that it consumes all profits from a day's income, making it impractical as a long-term practice for all but the most prosperous farmers raising the most lucrative crops. Paid farm labor is more commonly employed strategically—for example, to clear the new farm plot or to help with a particularly critical point in the harvest. People who live outside of these villages supply this temporary labor. Therefore, men's principal employment opportunities lie in the short lull in agricultural activity from late December to April, when people are not tied to their farms on a daily basis. Some men go to nearby towns looking for temporary labor jobs. Others travel much farther. One resident of Ponkrum routinely went to Abidjan in Côte d'Ivoire (Ivory Coast) to work as a baker for part of the year. Another worked as a fisherman in Liberia and Guinea. Both sent a portion of their wages back to their families in the villages. Thus, men's wage income is not visible in local industries or businesses. Instead, it is best "seen" in the absence of husbands from their households at noncritical parts of the agricultural calendar. It is, therefore, easy to overlook, unless you know what part of the agricultural calendar you are in and for whom you should be looking.

The only exceptions to this rule are those who make *akpeteshi* and a single carpenter living in Ponkrum. Making *akpeteshi* requires setting up a still near the trees that are to be tapped for their sap, and the final product is usually bottled directly from the still. This is a labor-intensive process that can employ up to five people per still for a month or two each year. There are two or three stills running in these villages each year. The carpenter spends most of his days on his farm but also makes stools and coffins in a spare room in his house, generally working to order.

If men's wage and commercial activities are difficult to see in Dominase and Ponkrum, such work by women is highly visible in the villages and goes on all year long. The most common women's economic activity is petty trading. Women use their limited profits from their farms to purchase goods at market during their trips to sell household members' crops. They then resell those goods out of their homes in the morning and evening, and at a slight profit, to those in the village who cannot or will not make the market trip themselves. As a result, despite the difficulty of moving back and forth between Dominase and Ponkrum and better-connected towns, such as Elmina, a surprising number of goods are available in these villages. You can often purchase a (very warm) Coca-Cola in the bars in Ponkrum. These villages also maintain an active trade in goods such as kerosene, corn meal, bread, and even AA batteries. I bought sugar several times a week from one of the women in Ponkrum. She regularly bought a large sack in Elmina, divided it into individual servings of about one tablespoon contained within ingeniously tied plastic bags, and sold off the individual servings at a slightly higher price than her cost for the sugar and the bags. If a particular trader does not have what you need at the moment, she can get it for you—assuming, of course, that you are willing to pay and willing to wait the better part of a day for someone to go to market and return. Women also make food for sale in the villages. In the 13 years I have been working there, I am aware of only one or two women who have taken up manual labor jobs away from their homes and farms.

From all this hard work, the residents of Dominase and Ponkrum earn a living. They raise enough food to feed themselves and make a small profit. Residents engaged in commercial activities invest part of this profit in their businesses, leveraging their agricultural profits for slightly greater commercial profits. However, any such investment is small. The average villager earns less than two dollars a day beyond subsistence needs from their particular combination of agricultural, wage, and commercial activities. When one distributes the meager income of an average husband and wife across the average household (6.33 people in 2006), it becomes clear that most households work with less than one dollar per day per person beyond subsistence. From this tiny sum of money the residents of Dominase and

Ponkrum must clothe themselves, purchase fish or other meat they cannot catch themselves, purchase medicines, buy batteries for radios, procure books and uniforms for school-age children, and pay school fees for children in the mission school, middle school, and secondary school (there are no fees for children in state-run primary school). Most income in these villages is immediately consumed in an effort to meet these and other household needs. It is telling that during the late 1990s, when the government of Ghana still charged school fees at the elementary level, many children in Dominase and Ponkrum routinely missed days of school because of unpaid fees. The fees for a term were small, around $4.50; therefore, the fact that they went unpaid speaks to the limited amount of money available in these households.

Because of the small margins within the households of these villages, the population owns little in the way of material goods and has little savings. A typical house has one or two rooms. The wealthiest households might have a bed, a table, chairs, a storage chest or two, machetes for farming, several cooking pots and utensils, bowls for eating, and perhaps a radio and/or a bicycle. The poorer households might have only sleeping mats, a single chest in which all of their clothes are stored, a single cooking pot, and a few bowls for eating. What savings these households do have is concentrated in limited livestock holdings, such as sheep, goats, and chickens.

A day among the residents of Dominase and Ponkrum will leave a deep impression on any visitor. Like billions of other people living on the shores of globalization, these people work hard all year long and seek out any opportunity they can find to earn just a little more money. On this stretch of the shore, like many others, the returns on all this hard work and initiative are small. Financially speaking, the residents of Dominase and Ponkrum live largely hand-to-mouth and have few material assets to liquidate if they run into unforeseen health or livelihoods challenges that might compromise even a single agricultural season's income. Unfortunately, the economy and environment of these villages, like so many other places along globalization's shoreline, are full of unpredictable challenges. By looking carefully at the instability and uncertainty that mark this particular place along globalization's shoreline, we can better understand what is happening to those living in this part of the world, why these things are happening, and how remarkable it is that so frequently these people somehow negotiate these challenges while armed with so little.

Chapter 4

Living with Uncertainty

While daily life in Dominase and Ponkrum can be repetitive, it is not predictable. The environment and economy of these villages, as in many other places on globalization's shoreline, are subject to sudden changes (often called "shocks") that create constant uncertainty. In Dominase and Ponkrum this uncertainty is deeply ingrained. Every night when Francis and I parted, I would say, "See you in the morning." Francis would always reply, "In the morning...if God permits." In these villages, even going to sleep for the night requires a caveat.

This deeply felt uncertainty is not a form of paranoia, but rather a response to the realities of life in these villages. First, the environment in which the residents live and farm is changing in unpredictable ways. The backbone of livelihoods here is rain-fed agriculture. This means none of the farmers has access to irrigation to help deal with years of light or ill-timed rainfall. Further, almost nobody uses fertilizers, because they cannot afford them. They are, therefore, completely dependent on natural rainfall for the success of their farms. This is typical of agriculture on globalization's shoreline. According to the World Bank's World Development Indicators, 82 percent of the farmland on Earth is rain-fed. In sub-Saharan Africa this figure rises to 96 percent of all farmland.

Therefore, recent trends in the West African climate are of significant concern. Numerous studies, including the Fourth Assessment of the Intergovernmental Panel on Climate Change (IPCC), have traced a steady decline in rainfall across West Africa, most clearly along the edge of the Sahara Desert, over the past several decades. The IPCC report does not provide an explanation for this trend, and without a causal explanation of why it is taking place, all I can say is that it is a trend. It could end tomorrow or could intensify tomorrow. What I do know is that the farmers of Dominase and Ponkrum recognize there has been a loss of precipitation on their fields over time, and they blame this change for their declining farm yields.

More troubling is the recent identification by the geographers Kwadwo Owusu (now at the University of Ghana) and Peter Waylen (at the University of Florida), of a trend toward the drying out of the second rainy season.[1] Again, the cause is unknown. Therefore, it is difficult to say with any certainty how long the trend will persist, or if it will persist at all. However, the pattern is very worrying. The loss of the second rainy season would greatly compromise the food and income streams of everyone in Dominase and Ponkrum, making current livelihoods strategies untenable for the poorest households and life difficult for everyone else.

While these large-scale, multidecadal trends are certainly having an impact on the agricultural livelihoods of those living in Dominase and Ponkrum, farmers more acutely feel what appears to be a greater variability in year-to-year, and even month-to-month, rainfall. For example, in 1998 the monsoon failed, and these villages went without the major rainy season. There was some rain for a few days, but for the most part the stretch from late May to August was sunny. Fields dried up and, in an effort to salvage what they could, farmers began to harvest ears of maize that were only a few inches long. There were a few days when there was absolutely no food to be purchased at any price—what had been harvested to that point had been eaten, and the remaining crops in the fields were not yet mature enough to reap. While I had access to sums of money that most villagers would consider vast, there was nothing I could buy. Like everyone else, I went hungry. In contrast, in 2005 the rains were unusually heavy, and waterways that had not run in years filled with seasonal streams. Unfortunately, these streams often pass along the bottomlands between hills, flooding farms and drowning crops. This did not create widespread hardship, as did the 1998 drought, but many lost a significant percentage of their farms to flooding, including crops of cassava they had invested up to nine months in tending.

Most years at least one major rain event occurs, when a tremendous storm drops a large amount of water in a short time. This heavy rainfall can wash a newly planted farm down the side of a hill, so the timing of its arrival is crucial to its impact. When these events will take place, however, is not known a month or two in advance, so there is no way to time the planting of crops to avoid having them washed away. Occasionally, a tremendously powerful storm passes east to west, across West Africa and out into the Atlantic Ocean (where sometimes they become hurricanes). These storms pack hurricane-force winds and rain.

In 2000, my field crew and I were surprised by one such storm while digging at Dominase. The sky to the east suddenly turned an extremely dark gray, even though it was late morning. Samuel Mensah, a member of my field crew, looked up, saw the clouds, and began throwing all our tools and artifacts into buckets as quickly as he could. At that point I had known Samuel for three years, and this was our fourth field season working together. I had seen him get hurt in various ways (the most gruesome of which was when he dropped a bucket full of dirt, which scraped down the side of his leg, peeling off a lot of skin), but this was the only time I ever saw him look worried about anything. Following Samuel's lead, the rest of the crew began hurriedly packing everything around them. I had no idea what was going on and could not understand why they seemed so concerned about rain, but in my years of fieldwork I have learned that when the locals start running for cover, it is wise to run with them and save the questions for later. As we finished packing, it became clear there was no way we would get back to Ponkrum before the storm hit, so we took shelter in a kitchen structure in Dominase. As the storm broke over us, I realized why Samuel had moved with such urgency. Torrential rain drove horizontally for more than fifteen minutes, and as we watched, the wind tore the roofs off two nearby houses. Farmers in the fields had no hope of reaching their villages and shelter in their houses, so they were forced to huddle behind trees to avoid being hit by flying debris. It is a miracle nobody was hurt by this storm, as it damaged or destroyed more than 10 percent of the roofs in the two villages, including one house in Ponkrum whose roof was removed intact and deposited thirty or forty feet away.

While access to improved weather forecasting might help farmers avoid being caught in powerful storms, such reporting does not help them time their plantings to mitigate the impact of such events. The information these farmers need about the likely character of the seasonal weather is not available to them. Even if it were, there is no way to predict a thunderstorm two months in advance. Where formerly some degree of security could be derived from generations of experience farming these lands, such historically tried and tested strategies were developed for a different climate regime, when there was more, and more predictable, rainfall. Today, in the face of regional drying trends and increased variability in the weather, these farmers often find themselves flying blind.

Weather and rainfall are not the only environmental challenges facing these farmers. None of the farmers in Dominase and Ponkrum uses pesticides regularly, as these are too expensive to be practical. As a result, their crops are vulnerable to blights and pest infestations, such as the blight that killed more than 80 percent of the coconut trees in and around these villages in 2000. Even today the frondless trunks of coconut trees stand as a reminder of the farmers' impotence in the face of this blight.

While the rain-fed agricultural activities at the heart of life in Dominase and Ponkrum make it particularly easy to see the impact of environmental change and uncertainty on the well-being of those living here, their livelihoods and welfare are not exclusively tied to the environment. They sell their crops at market to buy fish and other goods they cannot catch or make for themselves, or to raise the cash needed to send children to school or pay medical bills. Nearly everyone is engaged with either some form of commercial activity, such as petty trading, or wage labor. Both the availability and cost of trade goods and the availability of and income from nonagricultural economic activities are tied to the larger, unstable Ghanaian economy. A brief discussion of the collapse of the Ghanaian *cedi* (the national currency) between late 1999 and early 2001, an event that probably deserves its own book, illustrates these connections and their impact on those living in Dominase and Ponkrum.

In the fall of 1999 the Ghanaian cedi began to fall precipitously on global currency markets. Those trading in these markets had come to doubt the strength of the Ghanaian economy. These doubts had long been present, for the Ghanaian economy was (and still is) largely predicated on the export of two commodities: cocoa and gold.[2] The price of both commodities can fluctuate significantly on global markets, greatly impacting government revenues year-to-year. This economic structure, common in countries on globalization's shoreline, is not conducive to a stable national economy. While currency markets are complex, the principles behind them are fairly straightforward. Currency traders make money by buying up a particular currency they expect will rise in value against other currencies.[3] For example, as this book was being written, currency traders were buying euros with dollars on the bet that the euro would, over time, gain value against the dollar. A trader buying euros would have paid about $1.35 per euro in May 2009. This would have been a good investment, because by November 2009 one euro was worth $1.45. This means the trader could realize a 7 percent profit by converting his or her euros back to dollars. Put another way, a trader investing $1.35 million in euros in May 2009 could have sold those euros for $1.45 million in November 2009, a profit of $100,000.

While speculation is a tremendously important force in global currency markets, underlying this speculation is the perception of the government and economy behind a particular currency. If investors feel a particular country is pursuing an unwise economic path that, in the future, will make it difficult for the country to support its currency (e.g., by racking up unsustainable debts), they will tend to sell that currency and buy another that appears to be more stable or even growing stronger over time (e.g., the euro). When lots of people holding a particular currency try to buy euros, basic supply-and-demand functions come into play. If many people are trying to buy euros with cedis, the demand for euros will rise and they will become more expensive in cedis. At the same time, if a lot of people who are holding cedis try to get rid of them by buying euros, the market for euros will become flooded with cedis and the value of the cedi will drop against other currencies.

These currency fluctuations are a major problem for governments along globalization's shoreline because their revenues tend to be collected in their national currency, while most of their debts, and therefore their debt payments, are held in major currencies such as the dollar and the euro. If the value of the local currency drops against these major currencies, the government's ability to meet its debt obligations will fall even in situations where its revenues (as measured in local currency) are rising. Imagine a scenario in which the government of Ghana in a given year is able to gather 10 percent more revenue through a more efficient and effective system of taxation, but the cedi falls 12 percent against the dollar and the euro in that same year due to currency speculation. In this scenario the devaluation of the cedi wipes out the added revenues collected by the government and, in dollar terms, actually results in reduced revenues that might have been used to pay off outstanding debts. This, in turn, will raise doubts in the currency markets about the ability of the government to back its currency, which will lead more traders to sell that currency for more-stable major currencies, perpetuating the oversupply that drives down the price of the local currency.

Between 1997 and 1999 the cedi lost value against major currencies such as the U.S. dollar, as those trying to sell cedis outnumbered those trying to buy them. On June 1, 1997, one U.S. dollar was worth roughly 2,040 cedis. A year later one U.S. dollar bought roughly 2,350 cedis, an annual change of about -15.2 percent. On June 1, 1999, one dollar bought 2,500 cedis, an annual change of about 6.4 percent (and a total drop of 22.5 percent across the two years). In other words, across my first three visits to Ghana the cedi steadily lost value against the dollar and other global currencies, a sign of the vague discomfort of global currency markets with Ghana's economic structure. The impacts of this devaluation for the residents of Dominase and Ponkrum included steadily increasing prices for anything manufactured outside the country (as the cedi bought less and less of any product denominated in another currency) and somewhat smaller increases in prices on anything manufactured or transported in the country, as fuel and material costs also gradually rose. As this change was steady, most villagers could manage by gradually raising the market prices of their crops to enable continued purchases of needed goods.

This all changed in October 1999 as the bottom fell out of the cedi (then trading at 2,750 to 1 dollar) because of the convergence of three factors. First, foreign aid was less than expected, creating a revenue shortfall. Second, the price of petroleum rose, straining the government's ability to ensure a stable supply and price for its citizens. Third, and perhaps most important, the global cocoa market's long-term status came into question. The price of one of Ghana's principal exports, cocoa (worth roughly 5 percent of GDP), wavered dramatically amid fears that the European Union was going to change the regulations for what could legally be called "chocolate." Where previously the EU had required anything labeled as chocolate to use only cocoa butter as a vegetable fat, the new regulations required only 95 percent cocoa butter. The potential decline in demand for cocoa created by this shift created tremendous instability on global cocoa markets, for if this rumor became a reality, the world would face an oversupply of cocoa and a likely crash in the price of this commodity. Currency traders saw this instability as a threat to Ghana's economy and, therefore, to its currency. Nobody wanted to buy or hold cedis, and the surplus of sellers began to drive the price of the cedi downward.

One U.S. dollar bought roughly 3,050 cedis by November 1, 1999, and 3,500 cedis a month later. The Ghanaian currency had lost 40 percent of its value against the dollar and other major currencies in just six months. The currency stabilized somewhat in January and February 2000, before the EU moved forward on the new regulations, which precipitated a new run on cocoa and a new currency collapse that drove the price to over 3,800 cedis per dollar by the first of March. At this point a full-out run on the cedi was in progress as global traders tried to unload the currency at any cost. By May 1 the cedi was trading at 5,000 to the dollar. I was forced to revise my field crew's pay schedule on an almost weekly basis to keep up with the staggering rate of inflation. By July 1 the rate was 5,500, and by August 1 it was 6,150.

The cedi did not stabilize until January 2001, at a price of roughly 7,000 to the dollar (after bottoming out at 7,500 to the dollar earlier in the fall). At the time Ghana was servicing more than $6 billion in debt to the International Monetary Fund (IMF) and various multilateral and bilateral donors. The payments on this debt in 2000 alone cost the country 15.6 percent of the value of its total exports of goods, services, and income for the year. The debt was denominated in U.S. dollars, but Ghana gathered revenues in cedis. In part because its revenues from cocoa were badly damaged by market instability, and in part because its currency could buy only one-third the number of dollars it had bought 18 months earlier, the government of Ghana could not meet its debt-repayment obligations and required an emergency loan from the IMF to allow these payments to go forward. This economic failure had, in the end, nothing to do with Ghanaian governmental policy, actions, or even corruption. Ghana could not pay because two global markets over which it had no control (cocoa and currency) had been greatly upset by a set of possible decisions in Europe.

In 2000 the largest banknote in Ghana was the 5,000 cedi note. Between May and August, I made weekly trips to the bank to fund the archaeological field school I was helping to run. Paying for the food, petrol, housing, and local labor force necessary to keep a team of up to 12 people working required weekly million-cedi hauls (the daily max at an ATM). Each week, however, that withdrawal cost less and less in dollars. My bank statements at this time reflect the rapid devaluation of the cedi against the dollar, as the dollar amount withdrawn from my account in the United States with each transaction shrank week by week. Carting off a bag of 200 notes each week added to my feeling that I was robbing the place on a regular basis.

The residents of Dominase and Ponkrum had a very different experience of this crisis. While this collapse had devastating effects on the Ghanaian economy and eventually resulted in the country's qualification for debt relief, little changed in Dominase and Ponkrum as a result of the Ghanaian economy's turmoil. The principal impact on the lives of the residents was a significant loss of access to manufactured goods. The price of everything, even the cheapest plastic bowls and batteries imported from China, rose unpredictably and variably, depending on the seller. Meanwhile the farm gate prices for the crops these farmers were raising did not change fast enough to keep up with the rising cost of these goods. It became more and more economical simply to eat one's crops than to sell the crops at market and try to use that money to buy something else. My experience of this was a sudden, overwhelming flood of available food in the village. Every farmer was happy to sell his or her crops to me, because though I was paying market price for them, I was saving the farmers the time and expense of a trip to market. It took me some time to recognize the cause of what initially seemed to be a remarkable surge in goodwill toward my field school and me.

The situation of those living in Dominase and Ponkrum is emblematic of the issues faced by other residents of globalization's shoreline who live with environmental and economic uncertainty. These villagers cannot, at this time, address the causes of their problems. They are occupied with managing these problems. They do so with almost no material resources, and yet they find ways not only to stay alive but also to improve their quality of life in small ways. That they can do so in the face of so much and with so little is inspiring.

In Dominase and Ponkrum decisions about livelihoods are remarkably high-stakes. A miscalculation can mean insufficient food for the family and outcomes, such as malnutrition, whose impacts might follow a child the rest of his or her life. Every year the members of these households make these livelihoods calculations anew. Every year they take a chance with their lives, and those of their children, as they plan their farms and think about opportunities for wage and commercial income. These villagers live in a remarkably stressful decision-making environment.

For the casual visitor, the ingenuity with which the residents of Dominase and Ponkrum manage these challenges might be hard to grasp. After all, in these villages farm work is done completely by hand; there are no tractors, plows, or harvesters. Individual farmers simply do not earn enough to afford the purchase and maintenance of such equipment. There is enough money, however, to enable particular lineages, or even entire villages, to work together to purchase and maintain a single tractor collectively.

However, collective purchasing power cannot overcome other locally specific barriers to mechanized agriculture in these settlements.

First, the terrain on which many farms are found is hilly. As a result, a tractor cannot be used safely on many of these plots. Further, nearly all farm plots contain several large mounds, which can be as large as a meter and a half tall and five meters in diameter. These mounds are used to raise crops such as pepper, tomato, and garden egg (*solanum aethiopicum,* a small, usually greenish-yellow relative of the eggplant) but are too steep to be managed by a tractor.

Second, the farms of Dominase and Ponkrum are heavily intercropped. Unlike the giant, single-use fields we associate with agriculture in the United States and Europe, the farms around these villages mix as many as a dozen crops onto a single plot. In addition these farms are not segregated by species. For example, maize and cassava are nearly always planted side-by-side. Because they have similar requirements for water, tomatoes, garden eggs, and peppers are planted together on the mounds in the fields and on the upslope areas of farms on the sides of hills. Those who plant orange trees usually do so on active farms, where the saplings are mixed among maize and cassava until they are large enough to yield fruit. The tremendous mixing of crops on farm plots makes the landscape nearly unintelligible to the outsider (see figure 4.1). The average farm around these villages closely intermixes nine different crops on less than 3.5 hectares (8.5 acres). Some farms associated with land-poor households can cram nine or more crops onto an acre. Therefore, to foreign eyes it is difficult to figure out what is growing where, especially in the early part of the major rainy season, when crops are still germinating. This complexity, coupled with locally obvious but otherwise hard-to-see boundary markers, such as specific tree species, creates a situation of unclear demarcations between farms. It is possible for an outsider to wander from one person's farm onto another without noticing any change in the crops or planting scheme.

The complexity of these farms is further complicated by the fact that crops are not planted and harvested at the same time. The typical farming season begins in late March or early April with the clearing of a new plot. Once the plot is ready, farmers prepare it for maize, which generally involves mounding up a little dirt at regular intervals and planting the seed in that mound. The spacing varies depending on the farm, though this variability appears to have more to do with the differing opinions among

Figure 4.1   An example of the slope and complexity of the farms around Dominase and Ponkrum

farmers about the best distance between plants than any consideration for soil quality or other characteristics of the particular plot. Generally speaking, maize is planted two to four feet apart in straight rows. Yams can be planted at the same time, but few farmers raise yams in these villages. Once the maize germinates, the farmers plant a stick of cassava next to each maize plant. Crops such as peppers, tomatoes, and garden eggs cannot be planted until the rains have started and the maize is fairly tall. Some farmers will plant and raise seedlings of pepper under shelters near their houses to protect them from the sun and then transplant them as soon as the rains start. Virtually all other crops are planted as the rains fall, though some—for example coconuts, pineapples, and acacia—can be planted any time of the year.

Harvesting comes in a staggered manner. The first maize, which is an improved variety obtained from Ghana's Ministry of Food and Agriculture, is harvested roughly 40 days after it germinates. Some local varieties come in 60 days after germination, while others may take up to three months to mature. Many farms mix local and "agric" (the government hybrid) versions of maize to obtain a steady stream of food from their farms. Garden eggs, onions, peppers, and tomatoes all come in about three months after they are planted. Sugarcane and yams take about eight months to mature. Bananas, plantains, and pineapples all take a year to mature. The staggered times to maturity of these crops, combined with the ability to plant in two rainy seasons, usually ensures a fairly steady supply of food across the entire year.

While these farms are well designed to maximize the availability of food across the year, even in cases of environmental or economic shock, they are also small, often steep, and complex. Any effort to use a tractor for harvesting one crop would destroy other crops in different stages of growth. Such efforts would also likely result in an overturned tractor. This sort of complexity is common in the agriculture of sub-Saharan Africa. For years, colonial officials, and subsequently development professionals, have attempted to rework what seemed to them to be extremely inefficient agricultural practices. A deep misunderstanding of these complex systems drove these efforts. Officials and professionals alike assumed that complexity was the same thing as disorder and inefficiency.[4] The complexity of farm organization and timing is, however, a strategy borne out of years of experience. For example, in Dominase and Ponkrum maize and cassava are intercropped because the farmers can harvest the maize and use the remaining cornstalks to prop up the more slowly growing cassava stalks until the latter are mature enough to stand on their own.

Even the difficult terrain of these farms reflects efforts by local farmers to manage their often-uncertain environment to minimize the risk of crop failure. The small, steep mounds, while making the use of tractors difficult if not impossible on these fields, allow the often heavy rains to saturate the roots of these plants while providing paths for excess water to drain away without drowning the seedlings. Steep farm plots are not the result of limited land resources forcing farmers onto less-desirable plots. Instead the location of crops on the sides of hills reflects the farmers' efforts to locate plots in varying situations that take advantage of different amounts of rainfall.

A farmer might spread his farm over three plots: one on flat land between two steep hills; one on the side of one of the steep hills; and a third on top of the other steep hill. In years of normal rainfall, the first plot will get plenty of water, enabling healthy farm production. In a dry year, this plot will catch any moisture that comes down the sides of the hills, enabling some production. However, this same plot is vulnerable to flooding in a year when rains are especially heavy, or if there is particularly heavy rainfall on a given day. The plots on the sides of hills are safe bets. They will not fare terribly poorly in a year with heavy rain. Erosion can wash out some seeds or seedlings, but it would take an exceptional rainfall to trigger small mudslides that would wipe out parts of the farm containing mature crops. These plots will perform reasonably well in a dry year as well, though they may be too far up the hill to allow crops access to the amount of moisture needed to produce a large harvest. In a normal year, though, these plots are reasonably productive. Hilltop plots are hedges against the plots at the bottoms of hills, as they work in exactly the opposite manner. In dry years a hilltop plot will be too dry, and crops will fail. In a normal year this plot will get enough rain to allow for some production, but not as much as a plot on the side or at the bottom of the hill. In a year with extremely heavy rains, however, hilltop plots may be the only ones that survive, as excess moisture drains down the hill before it drowns the crops.

Therefore, demanding that these farmers consolidate their farms into a single large plot marked by a single crop, or at least delineated into distinct crop areas, works against local efforts to manage climate risk, minimize labor efforts, and ensure farm production. While all farming is done by hand, and while virtually no farmer uses either fertilizer or pesticides, they produce enough to ensure the food security of their households and a surplus that can be marketed to generate cash for household needs. When the monsoon failed in 1998, what struck me (beyond my rumbling stomach) was the calm of the farmers. They were not panicked about their farms or crops; nor were they terribly concerned about going a day or two without food. They knew their farms would not completely fail and that there would be enough food to survive. They were right. Nobody died of starvation that summer. Their complex farming strategy worked to guard against extreme hardship and death, even in this difficult situation. At the other end of the spectrum, the heavy flooding in 2005 also compromised the livelihoods of some households in Dominase and Ponkrum. Once again there was no panic. While farmers were frustrated by the flooding, most had plots on the sides or tops of hills that fared exceptionally well due to the extra precipitation, which helped balance the loss of plots at the bottoms of hills.

While these time-tested means of managing uncertainty are indeed ingenious, in the end they are technical fixes. For these techniques to work, someone has to decide when and how to use a particular technology, technique, or strategy. These decisions are fraught with issues of social justice that can be hard to see amid the other challenges of everyday life. Though they make decisions about how to earn a living and manage the risk of an uncertain economy and environment each year—and indeed in each planting season—this is not to say that the people of Dominase and Ponkrum start on a regular basis from a blank slate of livelihood options.

Before 2004, when the roads through and around the villages were improved, married households adopted one of two strategies for making a living, strategies principally distinguished by their approach to agriculture (female-headed households are a separate case entirely). The first of these I call the "market" strategy, in which everyone produces crops for market sale. The market strategy is, at its core, an effort to maximize agricultural income within the household to create a set of resources that can meet household needs and provide a surplus that will offset any setbacks from economic or environmental events. When no such events occur, these resources are often used to fund commercial activities, such as petty trading, becoming a sort of investment capital that often results in significant income generation. The households operating under this strategy tend to have the largest amount of farmland under cultivation, an average of nearly 4.0 hectares (9.9 acres). They are also the wealthiest of the households in the community, reporting average earnings of nearly $1,200 per year beyond subsistence.

The second is the "diversified" strategy, by which the male head of household grows crops for market sale and his wife grows crops principally for subsistence production. The diversified strategy is an effort to spread agricultural production across food-generating and cash-generating efforts to cover the risk of either economic or environmental instability. With agricultural production distributed across subsistence and market production, these households limit their exposure to events in one sphere or the other. Environmental shocks such as drought, while compromising both subsistence and market agricultural production, will also have the effect of generating broader regional and national shortages that drive the market price of crops up, providing extra income in times of low rainfall. During economic instability, subsistence production provides a source of food for the household if market crop prices fall behind the curve of inflation, as in 1999–2000. While this strategy is quite robust in practice, it also limits the supply of "investment capital" that might be used during years without significant setbacks, and therefore it constrains the opportunities these households might have to improve their material situations. These villagers farm less total area than the market households do, averaging roughly 3.1 hectares (7.7 acres) per household. Their incomes are substantially lower than those of market households, with an average reported income of $325 beyond subsistence.

This overview of strategies for livelihoods highlights the centrality of agriculture and access to land to the livelihoods of the residents. This, in turn, requires a brief explanation of how people gain access to land in this area. In Dominase and Ponkrum, as in most parts of Ghana occupied by Akan-speaking people, the person farming a plot of land rarely owns it outright. Instead, a husband obtains land for his household each year by going to the local head of the particular lineage (family) in the clan to which he belongs. All Akan people belong to one of eight clans, each of which can, in turn, be divided into families that trace a shared lineage. Each lineage (there are 11 in Dominase and Ponkrum) controls access to some land. The head of a lineage decides how much and which land to allocate to each male member. Under this system women have no direct right to farmland in Dominase and Ponkrum unless they are willing to pay rent for a plot.

This land tenure system is why in these villages the livelihoods strategies associated with female-headed households are distinct from those of married households. Because there are no male heads of household through which to obtain farmland, these women have no formal access to land and usually lack the money needed to rent plots. They are forced to rely on their maternal uncles or their fathers for small grants of "surplus" land from their household allocations. As a result, these women farm an average of about one-third of a hectare (eight-tenths of an acre) per year. They do not plant tree crops, principally because they do not have "legitimate" access to the land and therefore cannot protect that investment in future years when the land is recirculated within the lineage of the uncle or father. With little access to lucrative tree crops, and operating on small plots of land, these households are extraordinarily poor. In 2006, the year for which I have the best data, each reported an average income of about two hundred dollars beyond subsistence each year. This figure represents an astonishingly small amount of money that cannot, by itself, support a family. There is little available for "investment capital," which limits opportunity for activities such as petty trading. This explains why the average female-headed household reports only about 25 percent of total income as coming from activities undertaken away from the farm (versus 40 percent for married households). These women and their households survive because their extended families quietly give them food and money to meet their basic needs.

This land tenure system does not leave women of male-headed households with nothing. Once he receives his allocation of land, each man decides how to distribute it to the other members of his household. Typically, husbands divide the land between themselves and their wives. In unusual cases older children or other relatives living in the household might be given some land. More commonly, they are expected to work on the land of the husband and/or the wife. This division is anything but equitable, as men tend to give themselves four to eight times what they assign to their wives. Yet, once the husband allocates land to his wife (or any other member of the household), he gives up control of that land and its products. Therefore, wives control what they plant, how much they plant, when they harvest, when they sell their crops, and what they do with any profits from those crops. Once the land is handed over for that year, men have no claim over the income from the farms of other members of the household.

The politics of access to land is an important factor shaping how particular farmers employ the agricultural techniques described at the beginning of this chapter. Access to land is not, however, the reason for the different strategies and incomes seen among the married households of these villages. Nor is this difference attributable to different soil qualities or hydrologic conditions on farm plots. Instead, the villagers' smaller landholdings and more limited agricultural incomes are the products of livelihoods decisions that address intrahousehold politics as much as they do the material needs of the household.

Livelihoods in the married households of these villages involve more than making a material living; they also involve social hierarchy and social power. Men rather closely control their families and the incomes in them. While women's incomes should be separate from those of their husbands', in practice men exert considerable influence over the use of their wives' incomes. The clearest evidence for this is in the area of expenditures. Figure 4.2 is a list of responsibilities and activities that, by general agreement across the

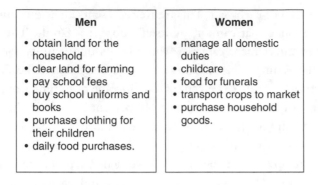

Men	Women
• obtain land for the household • clear land for farming • pay school fees • buy school uniforms and books • purchase clothing for their children • daily food purchases.	• manage all domestic duties • childcare • food for funerals • transport crops to market • purchase household goods.

Figure 4.2   List of roles and responsibilities of men and women from focus groups

residents of these villages, fall to men and women. For example, men are supposed to buy school uniforms, schoolbooks, and clothing for their children. Women are supposed to purchase household goods such as pots and pans. However, when I examined the reported expenditures of women, I found that roughly 45 percent of this income was being spent on purchases that were supposed to be men's responsibilities.

Further investigation into this spending revealed that men in these households often withhold the cash income earned from the sale of their crops and labor from the household. They may use it for their own purposes, such as buying alcohol or batteries for a radio. This is acceptable behavior if the man can demonstrate that his wife did something inappropriate that requires punishment. However, the threshold for actions that justify such punishment seems rather low and includes such things as cooking a bad meal. Women, who farm much smaller plots, have far more limited incomes that, in turn, they might withhold. Most men and women noted that in situations where men withheld their income or otherwise behaved in a manner their wives did not like, the women's principal weapon was withholding sex. They have few other options. If a woman leaves her husband, she is responsible for taking care of the children (under the matrilineal kinship system of the Akan, children in Dominase and Ponkrum are seen as belonging to the mother's family, not the father's) and will lose access to farmland. In addition, there are plenty of female-headed households in these villages to remind disgruntled wives what awaits them if they leave their husbands. As a result, women often find themselves without the capacity to alter the behavior of their husbands. Instead, they pay for the needed expenses themselves—in effect, men control how their wives spend that portion of their incomes.

This situation, however, is not a permanent structure in the society of these villages. It is recreated each year as land is allocated through male heads of households, women plant their farms with subsistence crops, and men withhold their incomes to shape their wives' expenditures. Any number of events could disrupt this process. For example, if incomes in the household dropped to such an extent that food shortage and chronic malnutrition became a significant problem, wives' motivations to stay with their husbands might be greatly reduced. If a woman were to earn larger amounts of money from her farm than her husband did from his, she might start to question the wisdom of remaining with a man who benefited so much from her subsistence and commercial labor. Women with large agricultural incomes might invest heavily in commercial activities, such as petty trading, freeing them from the constraints of the land tenure system and the need to have a husband to access land.

The livelihoods strategies in these households clearly address these possibilities, but from the perspective of the men who shape these strategies through their control over access to land. Men do not want their wives to earn too much money or to become too commercially oriented, as that would reduce men's control over their wives' incomes and well-being. Their principal mechanism for controlling their wives' incomes is through the control of the amount and quality of their wives' farmland. This is because shrinking a woman's farm not only decreases her agricultural production— and, therefore, any agricultural income she might earn—but also limits many commercial opportunities for women, as activities such as petty trading require start-up capital to purchase goods at market for resale in the village.

Access to land is a precise instrument through which men can control their wives' incomes and therefore maintain their own positions as heads of households. Figure 4.3 is a scatter plot of the size of women's farms in relation to their market orientation in diversified households. Recall that these are the households with low overall incomes, which put these men at risk of several of the scenarios described above. Overall, there is a predictable relationship here: As farm size grows, the overall orientation of the farm shifts toward market sales. This is because the larger farms have more surplus that can be marketed after meeting the food needs of the household. Of particular interest, though, are the farms to the far left of the graph. The curve

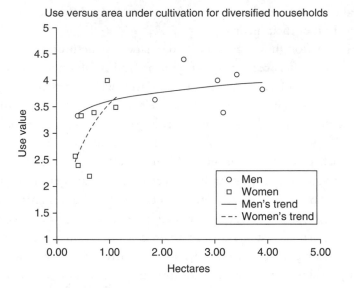

Figure 4.3 Scatterplot illustrating the relationship between the size of a farm and its market orientation reprinted from *Global Environmental Change*, 18(4), Edward R. Carr, "Between Structure and Agency: Livelihoods and Adaptation in Ghana's Central Region," 689–699. Copyright 2008, with permission from Elsevier

is stunningly steep for this group of farms, as even the slightest increase in area produces a huge shift in emphasis toward market production. These data suggest that even small increments of extra farmland allow women in these households to produce surpluses that can be marketed.

It is clear that men, who decide how much land to allocate to their wives, know almost exactly how much land their wives need to meet the subsistence needs of their households *without* allowing for significant market sales that might result in resources for women's interests. This plot shows that even tiny additional amounts of land allow women to raise surpluses and start earning their own cash incomes. These incomes can be leveraged as investments in commercial activities, which result, overall, in even larger cash incomes for women who can achieve agricultural surpluses on their farms. Men in these households are constraining the size of their wives' farms because if a wife farms more land, her additional income might challenge the man's control over the family.

This decision-making becomes even more problematic when we consider the relative agricultural productivity of men and women in Dominase and Ponkrum. My research suggests that women in these villages are between two and three times more productive than their husbands, in terms of income per hectare. While to some extent this is a result of the fact that women farm much less land and therefore can crop it much more intensely than their husbands can their lands, this higher productivity is apparent even when women's farms increase in size. For example, among diversified households, women's farm sizes roughly doubled between 2004 and 2006. In 2004 these women were twice as productive, per hectare, as were their husbands. In 2006, they were 25 percent more productive. Land allocation within a household is zero-sum on an annual basis. If a man chooses to give most of the land to himself, he is limiting the amount of land his wife can farm. In doing this, men are shifting land from the more efficient producers in the household, women, who are likely to make a greater profit on that land. In short, men are choosing to reduce the overall incomes of their households in order to minimize the risk of economic outcomes that favor women and threaten men's control.

This sort of decision-making makes little sense if we assume that efforts to earn a living are principally about ensuring the material well-being of those living in these villages—or, indeed, anywhere along globalization's shoreline. This assumption is flawed. Livelihoods strategies are double-edged: They are means by which individuals, households, and communities meet their material needs, and at the same time are means by which the powerful in society maintain and consolidate that power. In the case of Dominase and Ponkrum, livelihoods are aimed at securing the material well-being of the household, but only in a manner that maintains men's control over their households. In these villages the material goals of a livelihoods strategy are often secondary to the social goal of maintaining the relations of power in the household.

Life in Dominase and Ponkrum is not easy. The villages lack significant comforts—for example, electricity, running water, and reliable sanitation—that those in the United States, Europe, and some other parts of the world have come to see as minimal components of an acceptable lifestyle. Their core livelihood activity, farming, is subject to increasing environmental uncertainty, and the residents lack the financial resources to employ irrigation or fertilizers to manage that uncertainty. Their nonfarm livelihoods are opportunistic and yield low margins. The markets to which they sell their crops and from which they buy their goods are sometimes unpredictable. In short, because they spend so much time and effort managing uncertainty, there is little chance for these villagers to change their position in the world. Women's opportunities are especially limited by local rules of land access and the resultant livelihoods strategies. Most residents acknowledge that they are farmers and will always be farmers. They hope their children will have other options, but they have few means of financing the education or certification needed to make options a reality. This point is not lost on the residents of Dominase and Ponkrum. My friend and field crew member Samuel Mensah left Ponkrum to live in Eguafo in 2004, even though his extensive farm was located around Ponkrum. When I asked him why he would move, given that he now had to walk two extra miles each way to get to his farm each day, he said with a faint smile, "This place will never change." He saw no opportunity or future in a village without a road, electricity, or water.

This is the story we typically associate with places along globalization's shoreline. Even the residents seem fed up by the lack of opportunity and the slow pace of change. Yet, the description of Dominase and Ponkrum cannot simply end by framing them as places in need of development. Life in these villages has not always been like this. The challenges these people address in their everyday lives are not timeless but rather are linked to specific events, efforts, and politics that have played out over the history of these places.

The people of Dominase and Ponkrum had no more influence over the economic events of 1999–2001 than they do over the changing rainfall on their farms now. We cannot, however, view these events as acts of God for which there is no explanation and no blame. Climate change and deforestation are the likely culprits behind the changing rainfall in the area. Interests in the developed world drive both of those processes. Narrow bureaucratic interests in Europe, subject to lobbying by multinational companies, drove the collapse of the cedi, making it difficult for the residents of Dominase and Ponkrum to purchase needed material goods or earn enough money to feed their families. Further, Ghana's economic dependence on the commodity cocoa was, itself, a legacy of colonialism that had long discouraged economic independence of exploited areas such as West Africa—to the point that newly independent countries attempting to start industries from scratch could not compete with well-established, highly efficient advanced economies and corporations. For many of these countries, their only option was to continue exporting raw materials, often to their former colonial masters. In other words, human beings cause the environmental and economic challenges that characterize life in these two villages and in many other parts of globalization's shoreline. Most of the people whose activities create these difficulties do not live along this shoreline and have little idea of their impact on this part of the world.

The situation in Dominase and Ponkrum is not due to a lack of development. It is the *outcome* of nearly two centuries of colonial and development intervention in the global, Ghanaian, and village economies and environments.

Chapter 5

Nothing Has Always Been Like This

When I first started working in these villages, elderly residents of Dominase claimed an early chief of the village had been one of those who greeted Portuguese explorers who reached the coast five miles to the south in 1471. Since my arrival I have conducted fairly extensive archaeological investigations in both Dominase and Ponkrum, but have yet to find any evidence of occupation that dates to the late 1400s, when European contact occurred. The earliest materials I have uncovered that relate to the current settlements date to sometime around 1825.[1] Artifacts from the late 1800s and early 1900s are far more numerous than those from the early 1800s, as might be expected from a settlement that was growing after its founding. The bulk of structures standing here by the mid-twentieth century were constructed in or after the late 1800s.

Dominase and Ponkrum were not settled at random in the coastal hinterland of Elmina. Instead the first residents set up alongside a road that the historian and archaeologist Gerard Chouin has identified as Asante Road #7. This road linked Elmina, the principal trading post in the area, to the powerful Asante kingdom inland. In the early 1800s slaves, gold, and various materials passed down this road from Asante to Elmina and the waiting ships of the Dutch, who controlled the trade around Elmina at that time. A tremendous variety of materials returned to Asante by this same route. By settling along this road, the founders of Dominase and Ponkrum positioned themselves to obtain trade goods in exchange for their crops along a reliable route to the markets at Elmina. These settlements are therefore creations of the interaction of a globalizing economy with this part of the world.

Evidence for the close connection between the residents of these villages and this already-internationalized economy is most clearly found in a nineteenth-century burial I uncovered in the course of archaeological excavation. My archaeological work was focused on the yards associated with structures that had been abandoned in the 1960s and 1970s. These yards contain a great deal of evidence related to the spatial organization of the households and hold important clues to livelihoods, gender roles, power relations, and decision-making regarding land use and livelihoods from this time period. While it may seem odd to conduct archaeological investigations into life in the late 1960s, these were needed because few people still living clearly remember life in these villages at that time. In a setting with relatively short life expectancies (59 years for Ghana as a whole) and virtually no written history or documentation, even the recent past can disappear quickly. Though I found and spoke with a handful of people who had lived in Dominase in the late 1960s, it would be problematic to rely on the memories of this small group to understand what was happening in these villages and households several decades ago.

First, nearly all of these surviving residents were men. While they might clearly remember the crops they were planting or the jobs they held in the 1960s, it is unlikely that they would remember with equal clarity what their wives were doing in the domestic sphere. Any view of the economy or society in the 1960s obtained only from men is therefore likely to be slanted toward men's concerns. Second, in settings where dramatic changes have taken place, the past often becomes a tool for the justification of current practices, situations, and inequities. For those at the top of society, the argument that current livelihoods practices and job opportunities are more or less the same as they were 40 years ago might serve to justify their privileges. Similarly, those who feel marginalized by the current social situation might try to present a past that emphasizes the injustice of their current situation. Often, such biases are not conscious and, therefore, are difficult to control and avoid. Those who base their field research or project plans on quick interviews of a limited portion of a community run a great risk of being caught up in these biases; their research results and project designs could reflect the needs and desires of specific constituencies rather than the larger community.

Archaeology is a useful technique for controlling these biases. The archaeological record is a largely unconscious collection of materials that people threw away, dropped, or otherwise lost in the course of their everyday activities. In most cases there is no effort to build such a record to support a particular understanding of the past. Thus, by archaeologically examining the record of household organization in these villages, I was gathering information that might either corroborate or question the information I had obtained through interviews. In any case, I was not looking for burials during these excavations.

In the course of this work my crew and I often came upon trash pits, which were usually holes dug to gather the earth needed to construct a house and then filled with trash and dirt after construction was finished. Because they were full of modern artifacts with well-known production dates, they were a useful means of dating the construction of particular structures. By June 2000, when we hit what we thought was another trash pit, we had seen so many of these that we did not expect anything terribly interesting. A quick glance at the first artifacts out of the pit confirmed a late 1800s fill date, much like all the other trash pits we found. This sort of find had become so routine that I left Francis to supervise its excavation and went to oversee other crew members in another part of the site.

Things changed rapidly when Francis called a halt to his group's digging and came to me with a long bone he could not identify. We routinely found goat and sheep bones in these trash pits, and even found one cow bone, which was surprising, as beef is expensive and cattle are not raised in or around these villages. However, this bone was different. I was reluctant to identify it as human, because the Fante treat their dead with some reverence and usually bury them at least six feet underground, or as deep as they can go until they hit bedrock. After closing that excavation area for the day, I took the bone to the Cape Coast compound where the larger Syracuse University archaeological team was based, and found our physical anthropologist, Joe Johnson. I showed him the bone and said, "Please tell me this isn't people." Joe looked at the bone for a few seconds and then stated, "Oh, that's people."

The next week of my life was dedicated to clearing the trash pit out to find the rest of the body. As it turned out, at the bottom of the pit there was a nearly complete skeleton lying on its side in a slightly flexed position typical of burials in this area (see figure 5.1). There was no sign of a coffin, suggesting burial in a shroud. The acidic clay soil had taken a serious toll on the bones. The smallest and most spongy bone materials had long since dissolved, but the long bones, ribs, and other significant bones were intact. All that was missing was the head. I believe it was accidentally broken up and removed by the person who dug the pit in the late 1800s, unaware of the burial below.

There is something very intimate about sitting in a grave with a skeleton, gently brushing soil off bones, beads, and other burial goods. The bones told us that this was a young man, probably around 19 or 20 years old at the time of his death. They did not provide any clues to the cause of his death. This man was buried wearing a substantial number of beads. While these are common grave goods in this part of Ghana, most of the beads in this grave were waist beads worn only by women. The only men who wear waist beads are fetish priests, suggesting this young man was a fetish priest at the time of his

Figure 5.1   The burial in Dominase, 2000

death. Among Akan groups, fetish priests serve to facilitate communication between members of the community and one or more of the many major and minor gods worshipped in Akan cosmology. The position is largely hereditary and quite important, as the communications that fetish priests facilitate are critical to the well-being of the community. A fetish priest, therefore, is someone of important social standing in the community.

The grave goods associated with this young man told us a great deal about the connections between the people of this village and the larger world in the earliest days of the settlement. The materials in the grave all date to around 1825—the burial is the earliest evidence of occupation we have for this village. Buried with the man were beads from Venice and Bohemia (today the western part of the Czech Republic), a Dutch clay smoking pipe, and British sheet brass that had been hammered by an Akan craftsman into a vessel called a *forowa*, used to hold personal items. The markers of status and respect accorded this fetish priest in his burial were global goods from various parts of Europe. This burial alone makes it clear just how integrated the people of this village were into the global economy, even in the earliest days of Dominase's settlement. These goods were common enough, and had

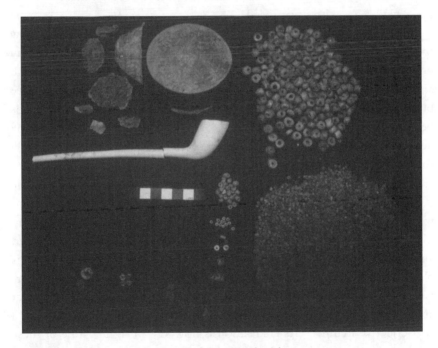

Figure 5.2   The grave goods from the fetish priest burial

been around for long enough, to be incorporated into their lifeways such that they made sense as burial goods. This burial leaves little doubt that those who settled these villages were at least partially motivated by accessing this global trade, as well as integrating into the regional political economy.

Engagement with global trade also radically reshaped agriculture in the area around Elmina. While we have no direct records of the crops farmed in Dominase and Ponkrum at the time of their establishment, we know that engagement with the Portuguese and, later, Dutch owners of Elmina castle contributed greatly to the transformation of agriculture in this area. The Portuguese introduced a large number of crops from South America, including maize, cassava, sweet potatoes, groundnuts (peanuts), hot peppers (capsicums), and tomatoes.[2] Other crops introduced later include bananas, oranges, sugarcane, pineapples, pawpaws, cashews, mangoes, plantains, and many species of beans.[3] These introductions were not, by and large, imposed on the population, but rather were efforts by local farmers to take up some of the crops farmed by the Portuguese for their own needs. Cattle, sheep, pigs, and goats were also introduced to this area in the same manner. Thus, the contact with Europeans resulted in a remarkable transformation of the local agroecology, with farms throughout the region incorporating these new crops with great speed.

Such incorporation is no simple task, as the introduction of a new species to an existing ecology comes with several risks. The species may not survive because the soils, timing of seasons, weather, or pests in the area can present insurmountable barriers. The new plant might survive but cause other crops with which it is intercropped to have lower yields because of the way it uses water and/or soil nutrients or because of the pests it might attract. In some cases new species might become remarkably successful in a new setting and start to take over, choking off existing food crops and other local species. A familiar example of this is kudzu in the southern United States. The planting of kudzu, a Japanese ornamental, was at one point encouraged to create fodder for cattle and to shore up hillsides against erosion. However, in the southern states this crop found an ideal ecological setting and began to take over areas in which it was planted. Today the cost of kudzu control is about two hundred dollars per acre per year, for five years. This figure is so high that forest-product areas (e.g., used for logging) invaded by kudzu cannot be recovered in a cost-effective manner.[4] Its eradication is nowhere in sight. None of these outcomes appears to have occurred with plants introduced in and around

Ponkrum, which speaks to the skill of local farmers in managing this process of incorporation.

Over time the introduction of new crops to the colonial holdings that would later become Ghana, including the area around Dominase and Ponkrum, became a part of official policy. The slave trade, though abolished by the British in 1807, did not wind down for a decade or two, making trade with this area less and less profitable. To earn income for their mercantile efforts, the European powers began to introduce cash crops that might be exported for profit. For example, by 1820 the British were promoting the growth of oil palm in their holdings around Cape Coast, less than ten miles to the east of Dominase and Ponkrum. While Elmina was a Dutch holding at that time, it is likely the oil palm trade reached the newly settled villages of Dominase and Ponkrum. George Mclean, the British governor at Cape Coast, pushed for the expansion of this trade, and by 1850 oil palm products were the principal items of trade in the area.[5]

Without the slave trade, the Dutch owners of Elmina castle found their investment less and less profitable. In 1872 they transferred their West African holdings to the British, who consolidated the territory around Elmina with other territories to the north to form the Gold Coast Colony in 1901. To ensure these holdings were profitable, the British colonial government focused on the export of gold and the introduction of cash crops. Production of oil palm for export peaked in 1884, before going into a long decline due to challenges from other products in virtually every area of its utility.[6] This instability gradually eroded oil palm's popularity as a cash crop. Although palm products accounted for about 50 percent of the total exports of British West Africa in the period up to 1900, by 1930 its export share had declined to 33 percent, and by the 1950s to 15 percent.[7] Therefore, by the late nineteenth century the Gold Coast Colony (it would not be known as Ghana until independence in 1957) was still seeking an alternative export to replace the long-defunct slave trade.[8]

While oil-palm exports began to decline after 1884, the meteoric rise of cocoa production in the forest areas of the Gold Coast Colony furthered this downturn after the turn of the twentieth century.[9] Cocoa production was at virtually zero in 1900, but by 1910 the colony exported nearly 40,000 tons of cocoa, and by 1921 over 130,000 tons.[10] By the end of the 1920s cocoa accounted for 80 percent of all exports from the Gold Coast Colony. By comparison, mining of the gold from which the colony had taken its name, as well as other minerals, made up a mere 5 percent of all its exports by the late 1920s.[11]

The ecological changes created by the introduction of cash cropping in and around Dominase and Ponkrum took a form unlike that seen in other parts of the world. Whereas agricultural efforts in Latin America and Asia were marked by the establishment of large plantations growing crops for export, the palm-nut and cocoa industries were run almost exclusively by peasant farmers who cultivated their own small plantations. This allowed farmers to incorporate small cocoa and palm plantations into the forest areas without destabilizing the long-standing system of shifting cultivation seen in Dominase and Ponkrum.

The discovery of the fetish priest burial helps explain the way these broad trends in trade and agriculture played out in Dominase and Ponkrum. From their settlement until the early 1990s, we have little evidence for the existence of Dominase and Ponkrum or for the lives of their residents. The villages do not appear in any colonial documents until the 1940s. This is perhaps unsurprising for small, relatively remote settlements. There are no writings of the residents to which we can turn, as these villagers were not literate. Indeed, in the early twentieth century it would not have been possible for them to have been literate in Fante, the particular Akan dialect spoken here. Only recently has Fante been transliterated, and even now its orthography is under debate. As a result of all these factors, we know relatively little about life in these settlements before the mid-1990s. In the absence of direct evidence, the archaeological evidence provided by the accidental encounter with burials helps us make at least a circumstantial case for the impact of this trade on these villages and their inhabitants in the late nineteenth and early twentieth centuries.

The position of Dominase and Ponkrum alongside a trade route to a significant center for trade gave them an advantage in the marketing of these new cash crops. We cannot know exactly when the farmers here took up these crops, nor can we know the impact of these crops on the lives of the residents. However, the specific burial mentioned earlier provides us with interesting clues. As noted, the Fante typically bury their dead at least six feet underground. To find this burial less than two feet underground is, therefore, odd. Even odder is the fact that we found another burial about twenty feet to the south of the first. This skeleton, too, was of a man about twenty years old. Like the first, he was buried in a semiflexed position, with the head to the east. The burials were almost perfectly aligned, which suggests their locations were not accidental or random.

Before the British assumed control of this area in the late 1800s, the Fante commonly buried their dead under the floors of their houses.[12] Most commonly the person was buried under the floor of his or her bedroom. These two men were buried too far apart to suggest they were under the same house. However, their shared orientation suggests they were buried under different houses aligned in the same direction, much as we see in the archaeological evidence for later structures in Dominase and the alignment of contemporary houses in Ponkrum. What remains is the odd fact that both burials were less than two feet deep. No Fante family would, if they had a choice, bury someone only two feet under the floor of their house. As neither burial shows any signs of being rushed, the only plausible explanation is that these remains were once much farther below the surface.

In other words, the depth of these two burials suggests that the landscape of this village was dramatically reshaped around the time the trash pit was filled, in the late 1800s. It appears that at least part of the relatively flat area on which Dominase stands was once a bit hillier and was leveled by those living in the village in the late 1800s. This leveling likely removed four or five feet of soil, which perhaps they used to construct the large cistern to the south of the village. After leveling this area, and constructing the cistern, the residents of Dominase began to construct their houses on top of the newly leveled area. In short, something rather dramatic happened in these villages in the late 1800s that led to the construction of the cistern to the south and to some sort of reorganization of the landscape that included leveling a portion of the settlement and the structures that once stood here. Given the coincidence of this reorganization with the introduction first of oil palm and later cocoa to the area, this reorganization speaks to a surge in the size of the village, likely motivated by the relative success the farmers here enjoyed. The landscape of Dominase is therefore anything but timeless. Even its topography has been reshaped by the introduction of cash crops, which derived much of their value from a global market.

Yet, the rise of cash cropping alone is not responsible for the transformation of the livelihoods and landscape of Dominase and Ponkrum at the turn of the twentieth century. Cash crops require markets and means to get them to market. Thus, the development of transportation infrastructure around these villages is a central part of their story. The first significant transportation development in the Gold Coast Colony was the construction of a railway linking the port of Sekondi-Takoradi with Kumasi inland. This line, started in 1898, existed to facilitate the transportation of gold from the mines in the western part of the country. Eventually, a second line connecting Kumasi to Accra was constructed, passing through much of the best cocoa territory in the colony and facilitating its movement to port. Neither of these rail lines passed anywhere near Dominase and Ponkrum. The changing situation in these villages was, instead, tied to the emergence of motorized transport in the colony.

In the 1890s there were only 32 miles of motorable road in all the Gold Coast Colony.[13] Farmers engaged in the growth of cash crops in the earliest part of the twentieth century therefore had to employ people to carry their crops to the nearest market, an expensive proposition that made cocoa production economically infeasible in many parts of the colony. However, by 1919 the colony had 1,200 miles of road, which four years later increased to between 3,200[14] and 3,400 miles.[15] The mid-1920s introduction of tarmac and the growth of private transport in the 1930s eventually lowered the price of motorized transport far beyond that of human carriage, at least for cocoa.[16] Seeing the cost benefits of motorized conveyances, farmers in rural areas constructed their own roads, thus adding to the total mileage.[17]

This form of transport, and the participation of local populations in its expansion, were made possible only through yet another import, the Ford motorcar. The heavy vehicles initially employed in motorized transport along the coast tore up the fragile roads, making successive trips more difficult, shortening the lives of vehicles, and driving the cost of conveyance higher.[18] The lighter Fords, first imported in 1918, were able to make use of even the lightest indigenously constructed roads and soon flooded the market.[19] By the mid-1920s the expansion of motorized transport allowed for the profitable cultivation of cocoa throughout much of the southern Gold Coast Colony.

The extension of roads into the rural Gold Coast Colony had another effect, that of opening the Upper Guinea Forest's valuable hardwoods, including mahogany and teak, to profitable commercial logging. This reserve of resources comprised a significant segment of the colony's economy, accounting for between 5 percent and 6 percent of the total GDP and 11 percent of total commodity export earnings across the colonial period.[20] Most of these earnings were the products of the sale of unprocessed logs. The rapid expansion of roads meant, however, that forests were opened to commercial logging before the colonial government could police them. In many places the forest became a reserve of resources exploited with little governmental control aside from taxation.[21]

As this broad transformation of the economy and environment took place in the Gold Coast Colony generally, and in the area around Dominase and Ponkrum specifically, the voices of those living in these villages at this time can be heard in a letter to the colonial government. The letter, from representatives of those living in the Eguafo Traditional Area—to which Dominase and Ponkrum belong—and the Abrem Agona Traditional Area, requested funds for the improvement of existing feeder roads. This request, submitted by the Eguafo-Abrem Management Committee, was justified in part by referencing the affected villages as "a thick cocoa centre" as well as a center of palm oil production.[22]

This letter illustrates how closely Dominase and Ponkrum were tied to the broader processes of increased cash cropping and transportation development taking place in the larger Gold Coast Colony. It also shows how clearly the residents of these villages understood their position in this world and how to use that position to maximum advantage. They needed a road through the area to improve their connectivity to local markets, which would have enabled more efficient transport and therefore greater profits from their farm products. Yet, they also knew the British colonial government did not care much about a few dozen farmers living in villages that would have likely been deemed within walking distance of regional markets. So, the farmers attempted to play on the economic sensibilities of the British, referencing their growth of key cash crops in an effort to get the attention of relevant officials who might grant their request. This was not the communication of backward, isolated farmers. This was an effort by some savvy people to manipulate the colonial government into giving them a road that, in the colonial scheme of things, their importance probably did not warrant. Clever as it was, this gambit failed. The British never built a road through this area, and the remnants of Asante Road #7 remained a footpath until the 1940s.

The people of Dominase and Ponkrum would get their road eventually, but not through the colonial government. Instead, they benefited from the growth of logging in the colonial economy and what might be seen as an early effort to privatize infrastructural development. In the late 1940s, George Annan, the Ghanaian owner of a private logging company with local connections, began work on a logging concession to the north of Ponkrum, near Berase. Annan had been one of the people behind the earlier letters to the colonial government requesting the construction of a road. Clearly, he was hoping the government would cover some of the costs associated with his logging operation. When the colonial government refused, Annan was compelled to construct his own road to provide access to the concession. The route he graded ran from Berase south through Dominase and Ponkrum and on to Amoana before connecting to the large north-south road a few kilometers north of the east-west highway. This provided easy access from the logging concession to ports from which logs could be exported.

The opening of this logging concession had a number of impacts on the lives of those living in Dominase and Ponkrum. First, it provided opportunities for nonfarm employment in the immediate vicinity of the villages. While few, if any, villagers were employed by the logging operation itself, several were employed to help maintain the graded road. As described in chapter 2, even a well-graded road will be cut by gullies during the rainy season. These are rarely large enough to prevent the passage of the large flatbed trucks commonly used to move harvested logs out of logging areas, but without constant maintenance of the roadbed such gullies can result in damage to trucks that costs both time and money. Second, the newly graded and maintained road opened up transport access to these villages. While most traffic would have been on the way to, or returning from, the logging concession and the larger villages to the north of Ponkrum, the increased traffic created real opportunities to catch rides to towns such as Elmina, where nonfarm employment opportunities were much more numerous.

As a result of these first two impacts, livelihoods in these villages shifted to incorporate much more nonfarm employment. New job opportunities provided a complementary source of income to back up the agricultural incomes of residents. The result was a third important impact on the lives of the villagers: Household agricultural incomes likely rose as increased efficiency in transportation facilitated the movement of greater amounts of crops to market for less cost in time and money. Circumstantial evidence in the form of changes to the landscape of Dominase, starting in the 1950s, suggests the incomes of those living there likely rose as the road was constructed and maintained.

I know about the changing landscape of these villages because in 1997, as part of my research, I hired a team of workers—Francis Quayson and

Samuel Mensah—and surveyed both villages, mapping all structures fallen or standing. In Dominase the vast majority of these structures were long abandoned and collapsed by the time I began my survey. Further, they were often heavily overgrown or even farmed as part of a field. Our efforts to map the 143 structures we could identify took more than a week. Ponkrum had never been completely abandoned, and therefore any fallen structure was located within the boundaries of the village and not overgrown. As a result, the mapping of Ponkrum went much more rapidly.

While this survey mapping was as interesting as it was frustrating, what made it valuable was the connection of individual structures to their dates of construction and abandonment. In Dominase the key resource was the memories of remaining residents. Once we completed the survey mapping, I drew up a map of the village that included the fallen structures. The crew and I then walked over the site with a group of elderly men who had grown up in the village. Remarkably, they were able to identify the owners of nearly every structure and tell when they were abandoned. In some cases they also could remember when structures had been built. They could not provide exact years of construction but distinguished between structures at ten-year intervals; for example, they could separate those that were abandoned in the 1970s from those abandoned in the 1980s. In Ponkrum the absence of abandoned structures simplified our data collection. We simply interviewed the occupants or owners of each to find out its year of construction.

Linking this information to the survey map of the village, I was able to create a series of maps of the landscapes of Dominase and Ponkrum. These maps begin in 1950, the earliest decade for which we have ethnohistorical data, and show paired villages, with Dominase the dominant partner. Dominase grew between 1950 and 1960, likely the result of new opportunities in this village. Ponkrum grew slightly but remained a fairly marginal settlement. This pattern is not surprising. The heads of the principal landholding families in the area all lived in Dominase, and much of the infrastructure of these communities, such as the well and cistern, were located there. Ponkrum had no well and only a simple cistern. Someone moving to this area would likely have chosen to live in the larger village, in close proximity to those on whom they relied for access to farmland.

Reconstructing as best we can from the landscape of these villages, the activities in their wider historical setting, and the memories of the few remaining residents old enough to remember life at this time, Dominase and Ponkrum were prosperous villages in the 1960s. One long-term resident of Dominase told me the land around the village was very fertile and rainfall more than adequate, resulting in years in which "We left crops in the ground because we had more than we could harvest." While this oral historical evidence might be tempered by a rosy view of the past situation of these villages, the 1960s were a period of generally high rainfall in West Africa. Further, many who lived in Dominase and Ponkrum in that decade were highly integrated into the regional economy and, as a result, into the global economy for the commodities that drove the Ghanaian economy. Of the few remaining residents who lived in Dominase or Ponkrum at the time, nearly all reported significant nonfarm employment, ranging from security guards at the University of Cape Coast 12 kilometers (7.5 miles) to the east to laborers on the logging road through the village. All agree that cocoa was a significant crop in the area, an assertion supported by the earlier letters written by residents of these villages to the colonial government.

As the 1960s wore on, those living in these villages had every reason to be optimistic about their futures. Development in the form of transportation infrastructure, cash crops, and nonfarm employment opportunities had allowed them to connect their lives to a globalized market for commodities

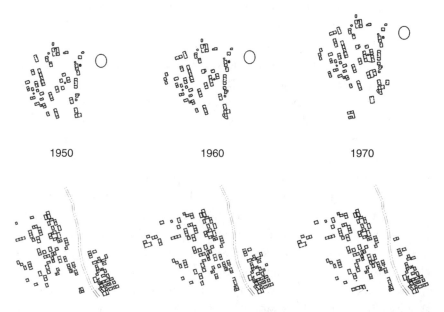

| 1950 | 1960 | 1970 |

Figure 5.3 A map of the rise of Dominase (bottom) and Ponkrum (top), as visible in their changing village landscapes between 1950 and 1970

and created a situation of unprecedented prosperity for the residents. This is how development and globalization are supposed to work along globalization's shoreline. These improvements in local conditions were highly correlated with population growth in the area. This new population needed access to farmland, which they could obtain only through connections to, or renting from, landholding families in these villages. Therefore, these changes worked to consolidate the authority of those who headed these families. Dominase and Ponkrum were the products of a series of development (or at least developmentlike) interventions that began not long after the villages were settled. This was not a place awaiting development but rather something of a development success story.[23]

Chapter 6

The Tide Goes Out

We have clear evidence from the 1940s on that the residents of Dominase and Ponkrum had some understanding of the larger networks in which they were caught up, and they understood how to manipulate those in charge of those networks to get things they wanted. Farmers in these villages were growing cocoa and oil palm as well as various food crops. They buttressed their agricultural incomes with wage and commercial activities facilitated by the road through their villages and the logging operation to the north. Archaeological evidence suggests that by the 1960s livelihoods in these villages were stable and robust.[1] For example, my field crew and I found relatively large numbers of glass shards from bottled beverages littering the yards of houses in Dominase. These bottled drinks were expensive and had to be purchased in town, usually with cash. In 2010 it is rare to get such bottled beverages in the village. The bottles are actually more highly prized than the drinks inside, as the bottles can be reused to hold everything from kerosene (for oil lamps) to *akpeteshi*. As a result, glass bottles are guarded jealously and rarely broken, never discarded. This makes the large amount of glass found in the 1960s-era yards of Dominase surprising. The number of glass fragments suggests a much larger number of these bottles and, likely, the drinks they contained, in these villages in the 1960s than I saw during my fieldwork between 1997 and 2006. This suggests, in turn, that the households living in Dominase in the 1960s were able to make these purchases because they enjoyed greater incomes than do their twenty-first century counterparts.

In the late 1960s, however, a sequence of events in the global economy into which they had been integrated led to dramatic changes in the

situation of those living in Dominase and Ponkrum. As the 1960s pro-
gressed, the favorable global market for timber produced in Ghana fell off.
This weakening market was exacerbated by the post-independence degradation of the national transportation infrastructure, insufficient storage
facilities for harvested timber, high export taxes, and the overvaluation
of the cedi (which made Ghanaian timber artificially expensive and non-
competitive on a rapidly declining global market). After 1970 Ghanaian
timber exports collapsed, bottoming out in 1982.[2] This, in turn, resulted
in a massive reduction in timber-related employment, which fell 25 percent
from 1977 to 1982.[3]

In the late 1960s the by-then-elderly George Annan called an end to
his logging operation. Whether he did so because of declining markets
for timber or because of his advanced age remains unclear. At first glance
it might seem that the end of logging around Dominase and Ponkrum
would, like the decline of cocoa, have only a limited impact on those living in these villages. Relatively few residents were employed by Annan's
operation, and those who did work for it did so to augment their farm
incomes. But Annan still owned the road network that connected these
villages to regional markets for their goods and labor, although why he
still owned it is unclear.

The desire of the inhabitants of Eguafo to improve this network beyond
the work done by Annan had become a matter of public record in the
1950s. First, as mentioned in the previous chapter, the Eguafo-Abrem
Management Committee[4] requested funds to improve the existing feeder
roads in the district. Immediately afterward the committee commissioned
Annan to report on the improvements necessary to bring the roads up to
acceptable quality.[5] In 1957 a group of residents recognized as the Eguafo-
Abrem Local Council again requested funds for feeder road improvement,
this time from the District Development Committee.[6] According to this
letter, earlier requests had been rejected due to questions of road ownership, and the council sought funds to purchase the existing roads from
Annan and obtain the rights to improve them. What is not clear is whether
or not the failure to purchase these roads and improve them with state
funds was stymied by Annan or by colonial authorities. I found no further
reference to this request in the documents of the Central Regional Archive
located in Cape Coast. This is perhaps unsurprising, as independence came
to Ghana on March 6, 1957, and the colonial archive would have had little
reason to continue collecting these documents.

Whatever the reason for Annan's continued ownership of the road, it was a fact of life that became important when the logging operation came to an end and the road fell into disrepair, as Annan had no reason to maintain it. Some residents of Dominase claimed Annan actually closed the road to all traffic, refusing to let cars or trucks pass. Some even claimed that for more than a year he would not let anyone walk the stretch he considered his own. I cannot verify these stories, especially the one related to walking on the road, as I have no idea how Annan might have policed and enforced this edict. The villagers who can remember these events do not believe Annan closed the road because of a particular issue with the people of Dominase and Ponkrum. Instead, most feel he went mad.

Whatever the motivations for Annan's behavior, and regardless of the extent to which he actually "closed" the road, after the end of his logging operation there was no maintenance of the route. The villages affected by this loss of transportation network were small and relatively unimportant, and Ghana was entering a period of economic mismanagement that would arguably make twentieth-century colonial expropriation look benign by comparison. Even if the Ghanaian government had been inclined to do anything about the road network through Dominase and Ponkrum, they lacked the resources to repair and maintain it.

Within a year the road had significantly deteriorated. Those who remember this time agree it was unmotorable within three years. Having seen what rain can do to a dirt path in a single season, I find this completely plausible. By 1970 Dominase and Ponkrum were marginal. The route that had allowed them to diversify their livelihoods through access to regional wage and commercial opportunities was gone. Further, the travel time to market for their agricultural products had increased dramatically, lowering the efficiency of their trade and cutting into their overall incomes. It was much more difficult for any who sought to purchase cocoa or palm nuts from these villages to reach them. The only saving grace for these villagers was the fact that at this time food-crop production was becoming more lucrative than even cocoa production. The Ghanaian government's heavy concentration on industrial development, combined with collapsing producer prices for cocoa, drove food-crop prices up, partially offsetting the increased time and cost of transporting these crops to market.[7]

In the space of a year or two, the globalized political economy receded from the lives of residents of Dominase and Ponkrum. This is not to say they were completely delinked from larger economic and political forces.

Indeed, the decline of the road is intimately tied to global and national processes and policies. The price of their agricultural products was strongly influenced by national agricultural-production policies, which were responses to global markets for commodities such as cocoa. The ability of these residents to link directly into these larger forces was greatly diminished by the loss of the road. To return to our shoreline metaphor, the tide of globalization went out on these villages, ebbing toward towns such as Elmina, leaving Dominase and Ponkrum high and dry.

These shifts were certainly traumatic for the people of these villages, but they need not have been catastrophic. Rising food-crop prices, even in the face of explosive inflation at the time, might have maintained livelihoods at something like previous levels. But the loss of wage and commercial opportunity, and the likely decline in cash-crop incomes as cocoa became less valuable[8] and purchasers for palm nuts found their access to this area constrained, brought a long-standing environmental trend to the fore. Rainfall had slowly been dropping off in Dominase and Ponkrum for years. Whether or not the farmers noticed this as it was happening is hard to say. They had access to other streams of income and cash crops that would have offset declines in food crops, so it is possible they never realized what was happening. However, when thrown back upon their farms and food crops for most of their livelihoods, this trend and the resultant declining income from food crops became very clear.

While local claims about precipitation in this area are difficult to verify, a great deal of circumstantial evidence strongly supports the local population's version of these villages' environmental history. Any farmer old enough to remember the 1960s will argue that rainfall was much greater in the past. However, the nearest continuously monitored weather station to Dominase and Ponkrum is near Cape Coast and therefore cannot reliably record inland precipitation patterns. The nearest inland weather station with measurements that continuously span the past five decades is nearly 40 km (24 miles) east-northeast in Jukwa. This is a vast distance in a part of the world where variations in climate can take place on a very small scale. However, looking at the data from Jukwa, we can see that between 1960 and 2000 the average annual total precipitation fell by roughly 30 cm (12 inches). Further, actual annual rainfall figures vary more and more across the 1990s. While it is difficult to draw strong conclusions about rainfall in Dominase and Ponkrum from data gathered 40 km away, these measurements provide some concrete evidence of a broad regional decline in precipitation, and they support the otherwise anecdotal claims of the farmers.

Also interesting is the decline of cocoa farming in this area. While once the local farmers characterized the area as "a thick cocoa centre,"[9] there is presently virtually no cocoa in the entire Eguafo Traditional Area, let alone Dominase and Ponkrum. When asked about this decline, farmers do not discuss changes in the price of cocoa. Instead they argue that the rainfall in the area is now inadequate for cocoa cultivation. For example, during a conversation in 2000, Samuel Mensah told me, "I would not plant [cocoa], because it would spoil, because of the [lack of] rain." Cocoa requires at least 1,250 mm (49 inches) of rain annually and therefore is susceptible to extended dry seasons that provide less than 100 mm (4 inches) of rain per month.[10] While figures on the exact amount of annual rainfall in the area are not available, it is clear from my own experience that dry seasons last several months, and during such times less than 100 mm of rain falls per month. For an area to go from a "thick center" of cocoa production to nearly no production strongly suggests there has been a decline in precipitation in these villages since the 1960s.

There are also more localized issues that might be contributing to this trend. The negative impact of deforestation on the soil quality and

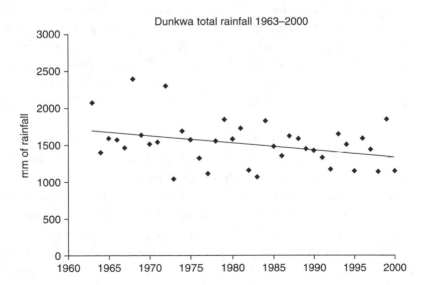

Figure 6.1 Chart of annual rainfall totals at the Dunkwa Weather Station in Ghana, 1960–2000

precipitation of surrounding areas has been documented by many scholars. Changes in local environments created by deforestation are many, from decreasing rainfall and soil fertility to the loss of shade critical for the growth of crops such as cocoa. For example, Gyesi and coauthors[11] describe the leaching of bases from the topsoil of various sites in eastern Ghana's southern forest-savannah zone, which is tied at least in part to the loss of canopy protection from rainfall. Further, they demonstrate that in these study areas deforestation and cultivation reduced organic carbon content in the soil by 37 percent (when compared to virgin forest), and that intensive cultivation had reduced the nitrogen content of cultivated soils by 46 percent.[12] In short, they found that, from the loss of forest cover, farmers in the area will experience significant soil degradation and declining amounts of crops on their farms.

Thus, by 1970 Dominase and Ponkrum were villages beached by globalization, and the residents were forced to deal with the impact of climate variability on their farms and lives. These changes, and their consequences, were brought into sharp relief as the road was closed and residents of the villages were thrust back upon their farms and food-crop cultivation for their livelihoods. Even rising food-crop prices could not obscure declining farm outputs. Coupled with increasing costs associated with the transportation of these crops to market and inflation within the Ghanaian economy more generally, it is likely such environmental changes prevented these farmers from maintaining their previous standard of living. This situation is remarkably common in contemporary Africa and is the focus of much discussion. How the people of Dominase and Ponkrum dealt with these stresses is, therefore, illustrative of the complexity with which we must grapple if we are to plan for these impacts in the near term as well as the longer term.

At first glance, the local response to these changes seems straightforward. Roughly 65 percent of the households in Dominase abandoned the village between 1970 and the early 1990s as residents sought out opportunities elsewhere. A much smaller number of households left Ponkrum in the 1970s and early 1980s. This abandonment does not, however, reflect a singular set of decisions related to livelihoods and migration. Instead, the abandonment throws into sharp relief the real character of life at the shores of globalization. For the residents, these changes created a series of challenges that were principally concentrated on the maintenance of their standard of living. However, the response to these challenges was not uniform. First, the abandonment was complex. Some 33 percent of Dominase households left between 1970 and 1980. Another 16 percent left between 1980 and 1990, and still another 16 percent left in the early 1990s. In other words, roughly half the households that left did so more than a decade after the significant challenges to which they were ostensibly responding took place. Further, 36 percent of the households in Dominase never left. If abandonment was a simple response to the changes in this context, why is it that only a third of the households left immediately? How do we explain the actions of the other 32 percent who left more than a decade later?

When I began my work in these villages, I was obsessed, like many who write about development, with finding *the* answer to why Dominase was abandoned. In an effort to get to the bottom of this issue, I began to ask those who had lived there in the 1960s and 1970s what had happened. When I asked why so many had left, the most common response I received was "because there were no lorries," a clear reference to the collapse of the transportation network and the new costs associated with marketing crops. This might have been the end of my inquiry but for the existence of Ponkrum. While Ponkrum shrank slightly across the 1970s, by the mid-1980s it was growing again. This growth was not a product of people moving there from Dominase; only one household did so. Instead, the new residents came from outside these villages, most commonly from urban areas outside the Eguafo Traditional Area to which these villages belong.

1970   1980   1990   1997

Figure 6.2 A map of the decline of Dominase (bottom) and rise of Ponkrum (top) post-1970, as visible in their changing landscapes

By the late 1990s Ponkrum was larger than Dominase had ever been, and it continues to grow, albeit very slowly. How can events that affected both villages equally lead to such completely different outcomes, especially in communities located only a third of a mile apart on the same road? If people left Dominase because there were no lorries, why didn't they leave Ponkrum as well?

When I presented this follow-up question, I generally received bemused looks and then a series of interesting, if equally unsatisfying, answers. For example, Nana Kofi Akuansanua II, chief of Ponkrum, claimed the reason people did not leave Ponkrum when they left Dominase is simply because he asked them not to leave. When questioned if the last chief of Dominase asked his people not to leave, Nana Akuansanua was unable to answer. The paramount chief of the Eguafo Traditional Area, Nana Kwamena Ansah IV, argued that people left Dominase because "the last chief was no good." This was an uncomfortable explanation for most other informants, who talked around the issue. For example, when I directly confronted a Dominase resident and nephew of the last chief[13] with the suggestion that perhaps the last chief was difficult, he acknowledged, "It is possible," but offered little more information. This discomfort seems to stem from both a loyalty to one's family and to the difficulty in identifying what constitutes a bad chief. However, the emergence of this uncomfortable consensus about the last chief suggests that, after years of successful rule, the new circumstances of Dominase and Ponkrum were more than he could effectively manage.

In short, what happened in Dominase and Ponkrum after 1970 defies explanation through prevailing understandings of globalization. The temptation is, then, to dismiss the various actions taken by residents of these villages as outliers, or as idiosyncratic or irrational behaviors that are particular to this case. However, if in this manner we dismiss these actions and the decisions behind them we lose an opportunity to understand what life is like on the shores of globalization. All that is required is for us to put aside the idea that globalization is inevitable, irreversible, universal, and something new. "Globalization" is simply a word we use to encompass the broad process by which particular places are linked into a global political economy. That linking creates different opportunities and challenges, depending on when, where, and how the linking takes place. In the case of Dominase and Ponkrum, different parts of their populations had different experiences of these changes. They saw different challenges and opportunities and, therefore, responded in different ways. Some residents followed patterns that conform to conventional understandings of globalization. Others made rational decisions that, while responding to events that we might associate with globalization, challenge the idea that the experience of globalization can, or should, be thought of as universal.

By 1970, as the tide of globalization ebbed away from them, the villages of Dominase and Ponkrum were being deglobalized. The loss of their transportation network compromised their ability to engage with markets for their labor and their agricultural products. While they still sold crops at market and certainly still purchased global goods there, their well-being was far less predicated on these markets than it had been just a few years earlier. This apparently negative outcome actually cushioned the residents from the complete collapse of the Ghanaian economy during the 1970s and early 1980s. This collapse had far less impact on the lives of those living in these villages in 1975 than it would have in 1965 because economic collapse generally means: the loss of access to imported goods (either through availability or pricing), hyperinflation, limited access to other manufactured goods, and widespread unemployment. In 1965 any of these outcomes would have immediately and deeply impacted livelihoods and the standard of living in these villages. However, by 1975 the residents of Dominase and Ponkrum were living without much, if any, access to wage-labor opportunities. Their access to imported goods and manufactured goods already had been greatly constrained by issues of transportation access and declining incomes. Much like their experience with the cedi's collapse in 1999–2001, the collapse of the Ghanaian economy in the 1970s had a relatively small impact on the residents' day-to-day lives and little impact on their basic well-being.

Therefore, as frustrating as life became under these circumstances, nobody suffered from food insecurity or outright deprivation during this collapse. Nobody was homeless, and nobody lost farms or crops. People likely cut back a bit on their consumption of kerosene and batteries, which cut into their evening routines to some extent. All in all, however, daily life in these villages continued as it had before the collapse.

Following the logic of many popular framings of globalization, we should expect to see the residents of these villages, now deprived of the benefits of participation in a global economy, attempting to find new ways to connect to those benefits. After all, according to many current authors, once people see the benefits of globalization, there is no going back; they will not accept anything else. To some extent this argument about global-ization is correct, in that it captures the experiences and responses of some members of the population. However, this segment of the population was not chasing globalization or global markets—two abstract concepts that refer to a means of achieving locally defined ends. In other words, if we are to establish a causal link between deglobalization, environmental change, and migration, then we need to understand what were the ends, or goals, for the population of Dominase and Ponkrum.

To better understand how globalization and deglobalization played out in Dominase and Ponkrum, we need to dissect the abandonment of these villages. When we do so, we find at play two different goals that were achieved through three different strategies. First, we need to examine the households who moved almost immediately after the changes came to Dominase and Ponkrum. These were mostly households headed by younger men, usually 30 years of age or under. In the late 1960s, with reliable transportation to and from these villages, people relied on various forms of nonagricultural activity, from petty trading to irregular manual labor, for about 40 percent of their income. Most of this income was concentrated in the hands of male heads of households, but women also earned significant income from commercial activities. The loss of reliable transportation hit all residents hard, as it compromised much of their income. While refocusing on agriculture could replace some of the lost income from nonfarm liveli-hoods activities, the loss of the road through these villages likely resulted in an overall decline in income. It also shifted household power relations, as men's overall income fell relative to their wives', regardless of livelihoods strategy. The material basis of men's control over their households weak-ened but did not disappear, since they still controlled household access to land for farming. However, the stresses from lost income and increasingly contested control of the households were likely significant.

The decision to move, then, was not aimed solely at making more money. Instead increased income was a means to an end—a means to preserving men's control over their households. Confirmation of this is reflected in the fact that a large number of those who left Dominase and Ponkrum had to keep their farms in Dominase because this was the only land to which they had rights. Therefore, leaving Dominase and Ponkrum for new settle-ments such as Yesunkwa, a village two miles due south, along the east-west highway, meant walking extra miles to the farms each day. This is an appar-ently illogical set of decisions about farm, home, and resources if the goal is simply income maximization. However, if the goal is to reinstate wage and commercial income to the household economy in order to strengthen the material basis for men's control over their households, this movement makes more sense.

Why, then, did only the households headed by younger men make this move? Quite simply, young men were the ones most competitive on the local manual labor market. Most residents of these villages had little, if any, education. Therefore, their wage-labor opportunities were limited to various forms of unskilled labor, from construction to security. The Ghanaian labor market of the 1970s, like that of the early twenty-first century, had no effective protections against age discrimination, so younger men were far more likely to be hired for these positions. Older men were unlikely to have much success reestablishing access to wage income by moving. Their employment opportunities were, in most cases, inferior to those of younger, more able-bodied men. However, older men had their own opportunity to maintain their social status and control. By virtue of their seniority, they were the ones in charge of the family lineages that controlled access to land in Dominase and Ponkrum. While these men might not be able to maintain their social status through access to wage income, they could rely on their control over the land around these villages to make even those households that left Dominase and Ponkrum honor their social status.

In short, the older men chose to stay because they had means of maintaining social status, even if staying meant a diminished material quality of life for their households. These men voluntarily deglobalized, in that they chose to pull back from inferior job opportunities in larger labor markets as a means of maintaining their status. Instead, they turned to local markers of status that were not tied in any way to larger markets or political processes. Their opportunity to do so lay in the land tenure system, and they took advantage of it. Women in their households paid the price, for they had to deal with a declining standard of living and with the greatly increased time and expense of transporting crops to and from the market in Elmina.

Any doubt this was happening in these villages is largely laid to rest by the actions of women when they were empowered to make decisions about staying or leaving. Most female-headed households left the village in the first wave of the abandonment in the early 1970s. This makes a great deal of sense. Then, as now, these households were extraordinarily land-poor, as they had no direct rights of access to property in their home villages. Without husbands to procure land, female-headed households found themselves at the mercy of uncles and fathers, who granted them very small plots to farm. These households were not self-sufficient, and so access to land and income was not a significant constraint on their decision to move. Further, with nobody else to move their crops to and from market, these women were acutely aware of the disadvantages of staying in Dominase and Ponkrum. They moved because their situation could hardly get worse and likely would improve at least slightly with better access to transportation.

What of the remaining 32 percent of the village that moved more than a decade after the changes in Dominase and Ponkrum? The answer is surprisingly simple. Almost all were households that moved directly after the male heads died. These families had stayed because the older men heading them fell back on their control of land to maintain their status. When these men died, these households became female-headed, with all the attendant problems of land-access that go along with that status. Further, women finally gained control over household decision-making. They knew the cost of their relative isolation and no longer had land or husbands to hold them back. These women moved soon after the deaths of the male heads. This, by the way, makes intelligible the principal explanation I received during my first field season for the abandonment of these villages. When people reported that Dominase was abandoned "because there were no lorries," they were not offering their own analysis; they were simply reporting the answer given to them by these women as they moved out of the villages. These women were the ones most affected by transportation, and the loss of transportation would have loomed large in their minds as they made the decision to leave. This is the explanation these last few residents would have heard, over and over, for more than two decades.

Therefore, changes in the economy and environment of Dominase and Ponkrum converged in the late 1960s to present significant challenges for the residents. For some, such as those living in female-headed households, these changes wrought such significant negative impacts on their overall well-being that the decision to move must be considered a direct response to the material effects of these changes. However, for the male-headed households that predominated in these villages, the significant challenges were not principally material. As demonstrated above, while these villages became more marginal after the loss of the road, and their farms were less productive than in previous years, these changes did not threaten the survival of these households. Instead, for male-headed households, the concern was over how the loss of wage income presented challenges to men's control of households. The decision to move or remain was made to achieve the end of maintaining the existing social hierarchy, both within the household and, to some extent, within the community.

What is fascinating about this chain of events, and the explanation for them, is the suggestion that some members of these villages behaved as we might expect them to: following the linkages and resources that granted access to globalized markets and their associated income and goods. One group, those living in female-headed households, clearly moved to preserve their connections to a larger economy in an effort to meet their material needs. This is what we expect to hear when we talk about globalization. However, the vast majority of people moving for this reason did so long after the villages had experienced the convergence of economic and environmental changes. In the context of the initial convergence, the majority of decision-makers in these villages were seeking a different end. Approximately one-third of the village may have moved to preserve their connections to a globalized economy, but that decision to move was not predicated on universal motivations, such as maximizing their income and its utility. Instead this movement was an effort to achieve locally specific social goals. The married households remaining in the village chose voluntarily to deglobalize. The male heads of these households turned away from the globalized economy and its income and goods as a source of control over their households and focused, instead, on completely local social resources—their control over land tenure, as a means of maintaining their social position within the households and the community.

Decision-making on the shores of globalization is turbulent and complex. If we want to understand the problems that have already arisen in the context of globalization, and the challenges that remain before us, we must give up on explanations and predictions based on universalizing claims about human nature and motivation. We must, instead, focus on locally specific challenges and opportunities that arise in particular places as the tide of globalization ebbs and flows; we must try to understand how different members of even the smallest communities might address these challenges and opportunities.

Of course, this is not where the story of Dominase and Ponkrum ends. In the mid-1980s, as Dominase was still undergoing abandonment, Ponkrum began to grow. This growth was a result of new residents moving into the village from outside the Eguafo Traditional Area to take advantage of the available farmland left by those who had moved to new villages. Many of these new residents appear to have moved as urban economies in Ghana underwent significant stress in the early days of economic restructuring[14] in the early and mid-1980s. Instability in these economies made employment precarious and, with no social safety net, those who lost their jobs often had to resort to farming, at least temporarily, to make a living. This trend continued through the 1990s. For example, two of the men presently living in Ponkrum were employed as carpenters in the city of Takoradi, located 30 miles (50km) west of Dominase and Ponkrum along the coast. When their carpentry shop burned down due to an accident, the owner was unable to rebuild, and the men had to resort to farming to make a living. They came to Ponkrum because they had family connections that gave them access to land.

Why did others come to Ponkrum when the vast majority of people leaving the area had left Dominase, which had the only well around? The explanation for this restructuring of the relationship between these two villages is closely connected to the explanation of the pattern of their abandonment. The decision of some men in Dominase and Ponkrum (mostly in Dominase) to turn away from the global economy, and toward local resources, made them dependent on that land for their status and as a source of income. With nothing left to fall back on, the male heads of family in Dominase appear to have become surprisingly unreasonable in their dealings with new residents. Rather than deal with these difficulties, new residents moved to Ponkrum and to what appeared to be a more accommodating environment. In 2010 only one extended family, comprised of three or four households and based in Dominase, farmed the land once associated with the village. If those who controlled this land in the 1970s and 1980s made a series of take-it-or-leave-it offers to those seeking land as they moved to the area, it appears that the new residents chose to leave it. The result was the decline of Dominase.

Thus, by the time I arrived in Dominase and Ponkrum in 1997, the conditions of everyday life there, and even the very landscapes, bore the marks of 170 years of economic and environmental changes linked to colonial/ development efforts to connect these people and their livelihoods to the larger global economy. For nearly two centuries residents of these villages tried to manage the challenges and leverage the opportunities that emerged from these changes. Each of these efforts, from the incorporation of cash crops in the late nineteenth century to the decision either to move or to pull back from larger economic engagement, played a role in shaping life in these villages. Therefore, the residents' living conditions as described in the first part of the book are not markers of an absence of development. Rather, these conditions are the *outcomes* of development and globalization.

The situation of those living in Dominase and Ponkrum from 1970 until 2004 might be described as deglobalized—not completely delinked from global markets, but attached only tangentially, and only to the extent that residents were willing to risk their agricultural livelihoods in favor of scarce, unstable wage and commercial opportunities. However, just as tides go out, so too they flow back. In 2004, 35 years after the tide of globalization went out, it returned in the wake of heavy equipment that graded and improved the roads in and around these villages.

Chapter 7

The Tide Comes Back In

The story of my involvement with Dominase and Ponkrum nearly ended with the gradual reoccupation of two marginal villages in Ghana's Central Region. In 2003 I accepted a position in the Department of Geography at the University of South Carolina. I began to write up my data and conclusions through my 2000 field season, with an eye toward closing up the project and moving on to something new. But I was missing some data that was useful for my interpretations of events in these villages. So, in the summer of 2004 I went back to tie up these loose ends. As part of this last field season, I ordered some satellite imagery of the villages and the farms around them in order to map and inventory farms, which would provide data to fill in missing information about agricultural practice in the area. My work in Dominase and Ponkrum seemed to be coming together in a nice, neat bundle. However, as I have lectured many students on the unpredictability of fieldwork, I should have known better.

My first problem was obtaining satellite imagery of the area. Cloud cover is a constant in this part of West Africa. In the course of this project, I ordered imagery of these villages and the surrounding land four times. Not once was I able to obtain an image that was 80 percent or more cloud-free. While many early mornings open to clear blue skies, even in the rainy seasons, by 9 a.m. puffy, low-hanging clouds accumulate as vegetation heats up and releases moisture that rises and condenses into clouds. These clouds obscure the ground, making whole portions of the area invisible to satellites. By midday much larger clouds roll in, completely blanketing the area.

In 2004, though, I was new to the satellite imagery game and did not realize the difficulties I was about to encounter. Despite my ordering the imagery two months in advance, the weather conspired to render several efforts useless. I did not receive an image that was even partially workable until the day before I was to depart on my return to Ghana. In the whirl-wind of packing and planning, I opened it up on my computer to make sure the file was not corrupted and to print out a few versions to show the people of Dominase and Ponkrum as I conducted my fieldwork.

As I pointed out the villages and the road to Dave Vaughn, then a PhD student in the department, he noticed the road did not look like the worn-out, unmotorable footpath I was describing. As we zoomed in, we realized the road was now graded. I had not heard of any plans for this improve-ment, and in my most recent call to Francis Quayson, some two weeks earlier, he had not mentioned any change in the road. Nevertheless, there it was, a newly graded road all the way from Bronyibima through Dominase and Ponkrum and on up to Berase. A quick check showed the road from Ponkrum to Eguafo had also been graded. I stared at the image and real-ized that my entire research plan, both for the summer and for closing up my work in these villages, had come to an end. The tide of globalization and development had come back in to Dominase and Ponkrum.

I was incredibly lucky this road improvement happened when it did. The road was graded in late April, after the farmers had cleared their plots and begun planting crops. The residents had no warning this grading was coming. As a result, they planted just as they had in previous years without the road. In other words, 2004 became the baseline against which the vil-lagers' reactions to the road could be measured and interpreted. With this baseline data in hand, it was possible to track, in great detail, the changes in the lives of villagers after the return of the road. In 2004, 2005, and 2006 I conducted new fieldwork in Dominase and Ponkrum to study the changes taking place in the wake of the road improvements. The resultant data present a vivid picture of the complex return of the tide of globaliza-tion, ushered in by transportation development.

After arriving in Ponkrum in 2004, I began to ask around about the roads. Everyone seemed bemused but pleased by their relatively sudden appearance. Nobody I spoke to in either Dominase or Ponkrum knew the roads were being improved until the heavy machinery appeared north of Sanka one day in April. Until that moment it seemed the residents of Dominase and Ponkrum assumed this opportunity, like so many other things, would pass them by. However, once the roads arrived, people started making plans. As I spoke to more than half of the adults in these

Figure 7.1 The Bronyibima road right after grading

villages, men and women, young and old, (relatively) wealthy and poor, everyone was talking about wage and commercial opportunities outside of Dominase and Ponkrum. At the time it appeared this road was going to result in the diversification of local livelihoods and, therefore, increased local incomes.

I expected to see a suite of related effects cascade from these diversified livelihoods. Despite my scepticism toward much of development's "conventional wisdom," it is sometimes difficult to step outside conventional expectations for development projects. Further, it can be difficult to see past one's own views of the opportunities and challenges presented by a development project to understand the perspective of those living in the affected communities. To make this point, it is worth mentioning my expectations, and the ways in which reality deviated from them. First, I felt that if a significant percentage of these farmers were to find wage labor or commercial opportunities outside the village, even the most efficient transportation system in the world could not enable continued farming through the existing techniques required to achieve a successful harvest. For example, maize requires weeding for weeks after it is planted and, ideally, throughout its maturation. Maize will grow poorly if neglected for days on end. With the cost of farm labor more than two dollars per day, it was not financially feasible for someone holding a job in Elmina or elsewhere to hire someone to work the farm in their absence. Yet most of those seeking employment opportunities outside these villages planned to keep their farms. I assumed that to deal with the impossibility of intensively cultivating a farm while pursuing wage or commercial activities outside these villages, job-seeking farmers would have to adjust their farms to grow lower-maintenance crops that could bear some neglect. For example, I expected to see an explosion in tree crops, such as orange, palm, and coconut, as these are relatively low-maintenance once they are established. I did not have any idea what the local environmental impact of a transition from food crops, such as maize and cassava, to tree crops might be, but there were sure to be consequences from such a change.

Second, I expected to see significant upheaval in the local social order. A shift to tree crops could trigger a crisis in the land-tenure system and the practice of agriculture in these villages. Tree crops are a long-term investment, taking years to mature and then producing marketable fruits for decades afterward. Those who plant these crops are not likely to allow this land to be rotated back into the family's pool of common land. As more and

Figure 7.2 Francis Quayson and the author mapping a farm

more land was planted with tree crops, challenges to the practice of rotating land in and out of production to maintain its fertility seemed likely. Further, I expected to see a change in the way authority was identified and exercised in these villages. If land were assigned to people for long periods of time, the power of those in charge of particular families—which power largely rested in the ability to allocate farmland to other family members— would be greatly diminished. Perhaps we would see a minicapitalist revolution and the overthrow of the semifeudal local land-tenure system, as the anthropologist Polly Hill described in cocoa-growing areas in the 1950s and 1960s.[1]

As it turned out, I was wrong about nearly everything. By 2006 the people of Dominase and Ponkrum had shifted the composition of their livelihoods, changed some of their agricultural practices, and altered the compositions of their farms, but not in ways I had expected. For example, while farms became somewhat larger over the two years after the construction of the road, planting did not shift heavily to tree crops. Stunningly, the place of nonfarm activities (such as wage employment or petty trading) in the household incomes of most people in Dominase and Ponkrum had *diminished* two years after the construction of the road. Further, the social order of these villages emerged unscathed. Intracommunity hierarchies based on the land-tenure system and intrahousehold hierarchies that enabled men to control the incomes and activities of those living in their households remained largely intact. There was no sweeping transformation of village society as a result of the road, or increased engagement with regional, national, and global markets.

I was wrong because, like many others before me, I had based my projections of future outcomes in these villages on universal assumptions about how the world works. Rather than see the return of the road as an event that created opportunities and challenges, I saw the road as having certain inexorable impacts, such as increased wage employment and commercial activity and increased farm incomes (all due to higher transportation efficiency). I assumed that, when presented with these sorts of opportunities, residents of these villages would do everything they could to leverage them to raise their incomes. These "universal" outcomes drove all my other expectations for these villages and their residents. My initial assumptions were wrong, however, as were all my other analyses that were contingent on these assumptions. Only by returning to the locally specific opportunities and challenges presented by this road can we understand what happened in these villages and what it really means to talk about the tide of globalization coming back in.

Though only slightly more than 100 adults live in Dominase and Ponkrum, the responses to the road improvements were quite complex and varied because these improvements created different opportunities and challenges for different households, and even for different people in these households. Therefore, it makes little sense to discuss the impact of these new roads on the villages as a whole. Such an effort runs the risk of smoothing over important differences between and within households, differences that are keys to understanding the causes of the changes in these villages.

Let us begin with the market households, which in 2004 were the wealthiest in these villages. In the two years after the construction of the road, local market households maintained their overall strategy of maximizing income to address the ever-present economic and environmental uncertainties in these villages. Their income trends and the composition of those incomes ran contrary to my expectations. The average reported household income hovered around $1,200 in 2004 and 2005 before falling to $1,050 in 2006. At the same time, wage and commercial income, as a portion of the household income, fell from 40 percent to 30 percent. These households increased their average landholdings from 3.8 hectares in 2004 to 4.6 hectares in 2005. In 2006, however, the average farm size fell back to 2004 levels. Across all three years, farm productivity per hectare held steady around a reported $185 per hectare. In summary, two years after the road improvements these households were earning less, were less engaged in nonfarm employment, and were farming more or less the same size farms at the same level of efficiency.

These outcomes run directly contrary to every expectation in the academic and professional literature on the impacts of road construction on local livelihoods. Increased access to transportation did not raise incomes, increase engagement with local labor markets, or improve the efficiency of agricultural production. Not only do these outcomes call into question the assumptions linking transportation development and human well-being, but they also point to a serious problem in Dominase and Ponkrum. Under this livelihoods strategy, the maximization of income is the principal safeguard against the impact of shocks to the environment or economy. Since 2004 these households have seen a decline of more than 12 percent in their incomes, suggesting they are now more vulnerable to these shocks than

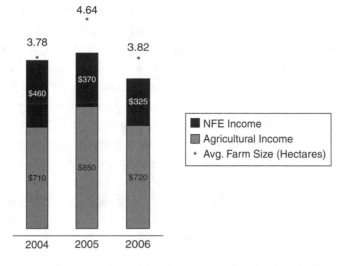

Figure 7.3 Chart illustrating the livelihoods outcomes of market households

they were before the road was constructed. Further, the turn away from wage and commercial income means these households are more dependent on their farms than ever before. As a result, they are now more susceptible to environmental shocks than before the road was constructed.

Because these outcomes run contrary to expectations, some might feel a strong temptation to dismiss these households, and even these villages, as outliers, exceptions that somehow prove the rule of rising incomes and employment in the wake of infrastructural development. Such an attitude, however, would be a serious mistake. Because they jar us out of the rut of expected outcomes and assumed causes, these outcomes are an opportunity to think differently and carefully about the connections among development, globalization, and human well-being. If, instead of dismissing these surprising outcomes, we take the opportunity to explore them carefully, we can understand how they came about and can better comprehend how globalization and development work on the shoreline.

To understand what caused these surprising outcomes, we must first realize they were actually the products of different trends *within* these households. Four key trends tell us a great deal about the decisions these villagers made in the wake of the road improvements: overall income, agricultural income, farm size and the number of plots farmed, and the percentage of income dedicated to wage and commercial activities. Men's reported average income fell from $950 per year to $650 per year. Their average farm income was fairly steady at $570 in 2004 and 2005 but fell to $475 in 2006. This is linked, at least in part, to a decline in the size of their farms, from 3.5 hectares in 2004 to 3 hectares in 2005 and 2006. In 2005 men in market households each farmed an average of 2.6 distinct plots. This figure declined slightly in 2005 to 2.1 before rising in 2006 to 3.2. Their farm productivity per hectare was all over the place, ranging from $170 per hectare in 2004 to $190 in 2005 before falling to $150 in 2006. The chaos in men's agricultural incomes cannot be attributed to a new engagement with wage and commercial opportunities that took their attention away from their farms. Men's annual wage and commercial incomes fell from $360 to $135 between 2004 and 2005 before slightly recovering to $155 in 2006. Men's wage and commercial activities fell from 40 percent of their total incomes in 2004 to 20 percent in 2006.

The trends in women's livelihoods in market households are quite different. Their reported average income shot up from $220 in 2004 to $520 in 2005 before falling back to $420 in 2006. This trend is closely related to the amount of land they were farming. In 2004 the average woman in these households farmed .3 hectare. This farm size shot up to 1.62 hectares in 2005 before falling back to .73 hectare in 2006. The farms of women in market households became somewhat more disaggregated after the

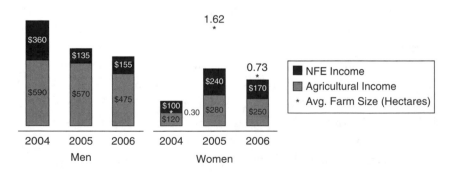

Figure 7.4 Chart illustrating the different outcomes for men and women within market households

construction of the road. In 2004 each of these women farmed a single plot. This jumped to two plots in 2005 before falling back to 1.5 (a somewhat elevated figure, as four of the six women farmed only a single plot). Their per-hectare productivity went from $400 in 2004 to $170 in 2005 before climbing back to $340 in 2006. At the same time, women's wage and commercial incomes also rose parallel to their agricultural incomes. In 2004 women reported an average wage and commercial income of $100. This figure rose dramatically to $240 in 2005 before falling back to $170 in 2006. Unlike their husbands, women in these households maintained a steady blend of agricultural income with wage and commercial incomes across the two years after the construction of the road, where agriculture was 55 percent of total income and commercial activities made up nearly all the remaining 45 percent.

Understanding what was going on with women and men in these households helps explain the outcomes I observed after the road was constructed. First, it is clear the overall decline in household income in actuality reflected a significant decline in men's income. It appears the men, many of whom told me in 2004 they would seek out wage opportunities in the coming years, were a bit overconfident. In 2005 they scaled back the size of their farms and began to intensify their focus on tree crops in anticipation of wage employment that would take them away from their farms. As the data clearly show, however, this did not happen. Jobs were not as plentiful as the men had expected, and therefore they ended up with smaller farms and reduced agricultural incomes, without any increase in wage or commercial income to offset this change. These men largely gave up on the wage labor market after 2005, returning to intensive agricultural labor as the backbone of their incomes.

This interpretation is consistent with the trend toward the greater disaggregation of these farms. First, men in these households were planting more tree crops than ever before. As tree crops could not move with the men as they opened up new farms, the plots of previous farms planted with these trees continued to receive attention as part of these new farms. Second, as men in these households became more reliant on their farms for their incomes, and for control over their households, they paid more attention to the management of environmental uncertainty, especially precipitation, in their farm layouts. Third, as men shifted away from wage and commercial activities, they had more time to dedicate to their farms, making greater disaggregation of the farms possible. Where such disaggregation would have previously resulted in lost (scarce) labor time as these farmers traveled between plots, this time constraint became less of an issue as men shifted their focus to agriculture.

Women's outcomes were greatly shaped by men's expectations and outcomes. The explosion in women's incomes in these households was closely tied to the size of their farms. In 2005 men were so confident in their ability to earn wage and commercial income that they reduced the size of their own farms and allowed their wives to take up the land they were not farming. This resulted in considerable increases in the size of women's farms. These women could not farm all this area as intensively as their previous, smaller plots, and their per-hectare productivity declined. However, their much larger farms enabled larger surpluses for market sale, which gave women much more cash income than in previous years. This income was, in part, plowed back into commercial activities, such as petty trading and food preparation, resulting in the expansion of commercial income among these women.

Because of these dramatic improvements in women's incomes, in 2005 their average earning in these households was 75 percent that of their husbands (up from 23 percent in 2004), and much of that 75 percent was coming from commercial activities, such as petty trading, not directly tied to land access. In short, the changes in women's incomes between 2004 and 2005 put great stress on men' abilities to maintain control over their households. Men moved to correct this situation in 2006, cutting the size of their wives' farms by more than half. This was not a knee-jerk reaction but rather a closely calculated effort to manage the incomes of their wives to ensure the subsistence needs of the household were met without enabling challenges to male control. Despite a remarkable reduction of 56 percent in their farms' sizes between 2005 and 2006, women's agricultural incomes dropped only 10 percent, from $280 to $250. Their wage and commercial incomes, though, fell 30 percent, from $240 to $170. Men were cutting their wives' farm sizes down enough to limit investment in non-farm activities while still enabling women to meet the subsistence needs of the households.

This reaction is consistent with the disaggregation trends on women's farms. In 2005 women were able to farm more disaggregated plots because of the increased amount of land they were allotted. However, they were then greatly constrained by the loss of nearly half of this land in 2006. The reduction in the number of plots also reflects the efforts of men to keep their wives from planting tree crops. In 2005 several women began to plant crops such as acacia, palm, and coconut. In 2006 these were far fewer on women's farms, suggesting these crops, when planted by women, were not allowed to mature.

In summary, the loss of income seen in these households and the increased engagement with agriculture, as opposed to wage and commercial activities, were the outcomes of household-level efforts not only to meet the material needs of the household but also to preserve the prerogatives of men in those households. Men chose to reduce the overall money available (recall that they indirectly control a good portion of their wives' incomes) to ensure that their social status remained intact.

In households adopting the diversified strategy a different pattern emerged. The average reported income for these households was $325 in 2004. This rose to $345 in 2005 before increasing sharply to $920 in 2006. This growth in income is directly tied to the growth of agricultural incomes in these households. However, this spike in income came as those households shifted *away* from wage and commercial activities. First, the average diversified household's farm rose from 3.10 hectares 4.46 hectares between 2004 and 2006. Second, whereas wage and commercial income made up around 35 percent of the household income in 2004 and 2005, this income fell to 15 percent in 2006. Third, per-hectare farm productivity exploded in 2006. Whereas it had hovered around $70 per hectare in 2004 and 2005, productivity jumped in 2006 to $175 per hectare.

While this overall trend appears positive in terms of household income and productivity, the fact that these households turned away from wage and commercial activities runs against expectations. Distinguishing between the actions of men and women in these households helps us to understand the causal connection between the road and these improving incomes as well as the reasons why these households did not see greater engagement with wage and commercial activity. Once again, these are not trivial questions that inform an esoteric academic debate. Disengagement with wage and commercial activity reduces the resilience of these household incomes, making the households more vulnerable to some shocks (such as irregularities in rainfall) while reducing exposure to shocks in the economic sector. The choices these households make now will affect their ability to deal with ongoing climate change and economic transformations.

The men at the head of diversified households saw their incomes rise dramatically, from $170 in 2004 to $650 in 2006. However, the composition

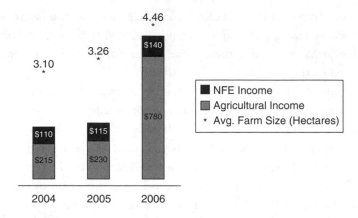

Figure 7.5   Chart illustrating the livelihoods outcomes of diversified households

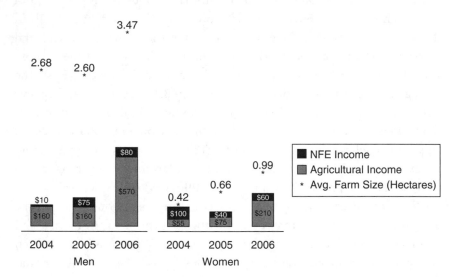

Figure 7.6   Chart illustrating the different outcomes for men and women within diversified households

of their income followed a pattern similar to that of men in market households. While wage and commercial income rose from only $10 in 2004 to $75 in 2006, this change did not reflect a sustained engagement with wage and commercial activities. In 2004 these activities made up only 7 percent of their income. This jumped to over 30 percent in 2005 before falling back to 13 percent in 2006. The real story here is the massive jump in men's agricultural income, from the fairly steady $160 per year of 2004 and 2005 to $570 in 2006. Part of this jump is related to an increase in men's farm size. In 2004 and 2005 the average man's farm was 2.6 hectares. This figure jumped 35 percent to 3.5 hectares in 2006. Another part is related to a change in the crops these men were growing. They began to emphasize cassava, acacia, and palm and introduced coconut and orange to their farms across this period. Finally, as men scaled back their overall engagement with wage and commercial activities, they paid more attention to their farms and cultivated them more intensively. Taken together, these three factors resulted in a jump in farm productivity, from $60 per hectare in 2004 and 2005 to $160 per hectare in 2006.

Women in diversified households also saw significant increases in their incomes. They reported total incomes of $155 in 2004. This fell to $115 in 2005 before rising to $270 in 2006. This change in income took place as women restructured their livelihoods. In 2004 nearly 65 percent of their incomes came from NFE. In 2005 the percentage of NFE in their incomes fell to 35 percent, and by 2006 these activities made up just over 20 percent of their total incomes. At the same time, agricultural incomes were rising, from $55 in 2004 to $75 in 2005 before rising sharply to $210 in 2006. These increasing incomes are closely linked to increasing farm sizes, which rose steadily from .4 hectares in 2004 to nearly a hectare in 2006. As is the case with men in these households, in 2006 women were much more productive per hectare than before the improvement of the road. Their average per hectare productivity hovered around $120 in 2004 and 2005 before rising dramatically to $210 in 2006. This is partially explained by a shift out of commercial activities, which took time and attention away from farm labor.

The other part of this explanation is, however, significant for understanding livelihoods in these households. In the two years after the construction of the road, women shifted their agricultural production from a subsistence focus to a market focus. In 2004 women in diversified households identified only two crops, garden egg and pepper, as being more for sale than for consumption. This is to be expected, as their principal agricultural and social roles are to meet first the needs of their households. It would have been surprising if they had been planning to market the majority of the harvest of more than one or two crops each. These two crops took up about 15 percent of the area on an average woman's farm in that year. In 2005 these women identified three crops—maize, orange, and palm—as more for sale than for consumption. These three crops took up 41 percent of their farms. Clearly, these women were shifting from a subsistence-first role toward more of a market-first role like that seen for the women of market households. By 2006 women identified maize, acacia, and palm as more for sale than for consumption. These three crops took up 59 percent of their farms. In short, by 2006 women in these households were no longer principally subsistence-agriculture producers. The idea of a diversified agricultural strategy that incorporated distinct market and subsistence producers was fading from these villages entirely.

In these households a very different dynamic explains the relationship between road construction and observed outcomes. It is clear the men in diversified households, like those in market households, gambled on access to wage and commercial activities in 2005. Many managed to secure at least a little bit of income from these activities. However, the financial return on that employment was clearly not what these men expected, and so by 2006 they had withdrawn from that market to focus on their farms. In their exuberance over anticipated wage and commercial opportunities, men in these households allowed their wives to farm roughly 50 percent more land in 2005 than in 2004. As demonstrated earlier, even a tenth of a hectare of extra land can have an immense impact on the ability of women in these households to produce a marketable surplus. Thus, this extra land allowed these women to start producing a surplus, which accounted for their rising agricultural incomes. However, this increased agricultural productivity did not fund increased commercial activities. Instead, it appears the extra land came at the expense of commercial income. That women's incomes were allowed to rise in this manner makes a great deal of sense, for while these incomes were rising, they were more focused on agricultural production, which men could control through access to land. Rising commercial incomes, on the other hand, might result in female incomes and independence that men could not check. Further, men's exploding incomes made an increase in their wives' agricultural incomes less threatening than it might have been a few years earlier.

This interpretation of the different trends in men's and women's incomes puts something of a different spin on how some might view the rising incomes in these households. First, these rising incomes have come at the cost of income diversity. There is less wage and commercial income in these households than before the road improvements, making them more vulnerable to environmental shocks. This loss of wage and commercial income appears to be a combination of weak wage-labor markets, which drove men back to their farms, and intrahousehold bargaining that encouraged women to shift out of commercial activities and into agricultural production. Second, the agricultural production of these households is less resilient than it was before the road was improved. Where once these households blended subsistence and market production to account for various sorts of economic and environmental shocks, now men's and women's farms are both oriented toward market production and contain many of the same crops. This loss of agricultural diversity makes their production less resilient in the face of potential shocks. In other words, the sharp rise in income observed in these households between 2004 and 2006 may have come at the cost of future stability and well-being.

For female-headed households, the post–road-improvement trends seem overwhelmingly positive. Reported annual income rose from $60 in 2004 to $70 in 2005 before jumping to $240 in 2006. This trend is, however, disproportionate to the growing size of their farms under cultivation. While female-headed households farmed 30 percent more land in 2006 than in 2004, the increase in real terms was only .14 hectare, or an area roughly 40 meters square. Thus, access to more farmland is only part of the story in these households. The increase in incomes also appears related to a shift in emphasis away from commercial activities. In 2004 commercial activities comprised nearly 25 percent of the incomes of women in female-headed households. This fell to 4 percent in 2005 and only 3 percent in 2006.

As these women focused more of their attention on their farms, they also shifted toward market agricultural production. In 2004 they identified only two crops, pepper and tomato, as more for market sale than for household consumption. These two crops made up only 8 percent of the average farm's area. In 2005 these women dedicated roughly 10 percent of their farms to three market crops: pepper, garden egg, and tomato. In 2006, 15 percent of their farms were dedicated to three market crops: okra, oranges, and plantains. Women were also using their limited farmland much more intensively. In 2004 each planted an average of five crops. This rose to six crops in 2005 and nearly ten crops in 2006. This gradual shift toward increased market production, the increased intensity of land-use by these households, and the increased time these women were spending on their small farms were rewarded by a sharp jump in productivity, from $170 per hectare in 2004 to over $600 per hectare in 2006.

Many of the changes in incomes and livelihoods for female-headed households can be traced to the reallocation of land from men to women in other households. Recall that the women heading households are nearly

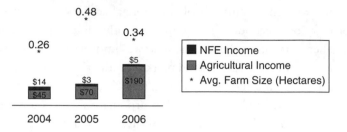

Figure 7.7   Chart illustrating the livelihoods outcomes of female-headed households

completely dependent on uncles and fathers for access to land. It appears these women, like married women, benefited from a pervasive belief among the men of Dominase and Ponkrum that men would be shifting into wage and commercial activities. As men reduced the sizes of their own farms, they gave some of this land to their wives. It appears they also allocated land to women heading households. However, when the employment hopes of these men did not play out as expected, they took this land back, and these women saw their farm size contract—though to a size still 30 percent larger than in 2004. Otherwise, it appears that these women were responding to the road improvement in the manner that planners might hope. They diversified their farms and engaged with market production. They likely benefited from increased access to transportation, as the remarkable increase in reported per-hectare productivity cannot be completely explained by farm size, strategic shifts toward market production, or new crops. Instead, it seems likely these women took less time to transport their crops to and from market, allowing them to avoid lost days in the field.

At a glance, the changes in Dominase and Ponkrum appear transformative, the mark of significant social and economic progress. Today, there is far greater intracommunity equality of income than in 2004, especially at the household level. The poorer "diversified" households now earn roughly as much as the once wealthier "market" households, suggesting progress toward the eradication of poverty in these villages. Women earn substantially more than in 2004, and even the poorest households, those headed by women, have seen substantial increases in income since the construction of the road. This might be read as progress toward greater gender equality in the wake of the road improvements.

Yet, the return of globalization to Dominase and Ponkrum has not been the transformation it outwardly appears to be, and is far more problematic than this simplistic read suggests. For one thing, the trends described above do not in any way reflect a change in the role of women in this society, even as these livelihoods strategies and outcomes have shifted. In 2006 women were still seen by everyone in these villages as domestic laborers whose principal responsibility was meeting the needs of the household. These women still farm some crops for subsistence but now complement these activities with the sale of surplus crops for cash income. Men still withhold their incomes from the household, and women still spend nearly half their incomes on "men's expenses." Women may be somewhat better off materially than in 2004, but they have no greater control over their incomes or life choices than they did before the road was constructed. These changing incomes are not indicators of progress toward gender equity. They mask the remarkable durability of women's roles and position in this society.

The continuity of gender roles can also be seen in the composition of men's and women's farms two years after the road improvements. Men's farms emphasized tree crops that have greater value at market, and which require special dispensations in the local land-tenure system to allow for the continuous farming of the same plot of land for a long time. Women's farms, on the other hand, were still dominated by crops such as pepper, tomato, and garden egg, which tend to be less valuable at market and vulnerable to fluctuations in rainfall. While some women started to introduce tree crops to their farms, those with such crops are still a small minority belonging to the wealthiest households in the villages.

The situation of female-headed households also provides a sharp reminder that the land tenure system remains as gender-biased as ever. Though their incomes have increased, they still farm tiny plots of land that do not enable incomes that achieve self-sufficiency. They cannot access larger plots without husbands and so remain largely stuck where they are with regard to income and opportunity. Women in married households, despite increasing incomes, face a similar problem. Men in these households allowed their wives' incomes to increase over the two years after the improvement of the road. However, they allowed this to happen only when (1) it was not so large as to challenge the income of the male head of household, and (2) if the increase was largely seen in the area of agricultural production, because men could relatively easily choke off this production and the income associated with it by withdrawing access to land.

In addition, it is unclear that the shifts in income and livelihoods strategy are really moves away from poverty in either the short or the long term. While the income gains reported by the majority of residents in these villages are important for improving their well-being, these gains are not transformative. Even if residents are underreporting their incomes by 50 percent (which is probably generous), married households in 2006 earned roughly $2,000 per year beyond subsistence. The average monogamous household contains 6.33 people, which means this income really equates to $0.87 per person per day. This is a lot more than before the road was improved, but hardly an amount that will transform the lives of the residents of Dominase and Ponkrum.

In addition, household incomes are not likely to increase in the near term. It is clear that men in market households are capping their wives' incomes and likely pushing the boundaries of their own agricultural efficiency, which means these incomes will not improve much in the near term. Because one of the goals of these livelihoods strategies is to maintain men's control over their households, any increase in household incomes will have to include increases in men's incomes proportionate to those of their wives. The most likely avenue for such income is through wage and commercial activity outside these villages. It is not clear how long it will be before men try to gain access to this opportunity after the failed experiments of 2005. However, without a strong regional labor market, there is little likelihood of significant increases in men's incomes in the near future. Further, it is unlikely that men will encourage their wives to intensify their participation in commercial activities, because such income can free women from the constraints of the land-tenure system.

The shifts in income are not only well short of transformative but may also mark a transition to new forms of vulnerability in Dominase and Ponkrum. All married households in these villages are largely dependent on the maximization of income for their livelihoods. However, men are capping their wives' incomes, limiting their commercial activities and, at least in market households, their overall incomes. Further, virtually everyone in these households is more dependent than ever on their farms for their livelihoods. Therefore, all these households have far less resilience in the face of environmental shocks. Significant problems with rainfall, such as continuation of the trend toward a single rainy season or the larger-scale trend of diminishing precipitation in West Africa, could result in recurrent crises in these households, greatly limiting their ability to improve their material situation.

The return of globalization to Dominase and Ponkrum via transportation development was not a harbinger of doom. Nor did it solve all that has ailed those living in these villages. Instead, it created a set of opportunities, such as access to wage labor employment and markets for their crops, which various people in the villages tried to leverage to their advantage. The outcomes of these efforts are complex and not easily understood in terms of universal human motivations, such as income-maximization. The people of these villages responded to locally specific social imperatives and economic factors. The outcomes of these responses are mixed; the appearance of improved incomes and greater equity, both across households and even in some cases within households, obscures the facts that gender inequality remains pervasive and these households may, despite greater incomes, be more vulnerable than ever to the sorts of uncertainty that characterize everyday life in these villages.

≈ ≈

We can see how the current situation of those living in Dominase and Ponkrum is not the result of a lack of development or inadequate connection to global markets for their goods and the goods they might purchase. Instead these conditions are the result of 170 years of engagement with global markets and development activities, as well as the decisions of these residents in the face of that changing engagement.

What does this story mean for our broader understanding of development and globalization? The obvious challenge to drawing any broad conclusions from the story of Dominase and Ponkrum is the argument that these are unique villages with unique experiences not representative of the majority of people living along globalization's shoreline. This is the story of how global politics and economics came into play in a particular part of the world at a particular time. Further, this story addresses the decisions made by a relatively small community in Ghana, only one of many countries in West Africa. It is a place-specific tale.

Yet, the point is not to come up with a new formulation of how globalization or development works. Instead, I have presented an anecdote about two villages and their experience of globalization and development via contact, colonialism, and development. The power of this anecdote lies in its underlying theme, which is very different than that advanced by the dominant stories of globalization and development that circulate in the public discourse. In Dominase and Ponkrum globalization and development are more than 170 years old, and the interaction of the residents with these efforts has produced many of the lamentable conditions of life that outsiders might seek to remedy through development. Further, the late twentieth-century experience of globalization and development in these villages was anything but triumphant, and there is clear evidence that residents sometimes chose to disengage strategically from broader economic networks in an effort to maintain their social position and well-being. This story cannot replace the dominant tale of globalization with a new one. Instead it serves to call into question our current understanding of this process and to open the possibility of examining our assumptions about it.

Dominase and Ponkrum show that globalization and development are neither solutions for what ails the global poor nor the principal cause of their ills. Globalization plays out in different ways in different places, creating place-specific opportunities and challenges. These opportunities and challenges do not determine the way people behave. Instead people leverage these challenges and opportunities to advance their own goals, which may have little to do with what we understand as development or progress. If we want to understand how globalization works, we need to become humble in a way that has been unthinkable in development for six decades. We have wasted decades assuming we knew how people would behave, to the point that many development experts become frustrated when people do not behave "as they should." This is backward. Sixty years of trying to make a people—their motivations, and their actions—fit into our beliefs about how people should behave has gotten us nowhere, and it has done tremendous harm. Dominase and Ponkrum present a single story that clearly illustrates this point. The experiences of those living in these villages are a call for change in how we think about globalization and its impacts in the developing world.

Chapter 8

Scaling Up: Why the Lessons of Dominase and Ponkrum Matter to the World

The case of Dominase and Ponkrum calls into question many prevalent but not ubiquitous assumptions about globalization and development. The current conditions in which the residents live are not the result of an absence of development. Instead, they are closely tied to more than 150 years of engagement with global markets and various development interventions intended to facilitate that engagement. These interventions, and the resultant engagements with global markets, have not resulted in sustained prosperity or improvements in the quality of life in these villages. If anything, their history of globalization and development is one of ever-increasing instability and uncertainty in the residents' day-to-day lives.

When we see globalization and development as historical processes that have shaped the current situation, the belief that through more development and more globalization we can address the challenges that face the residents of Dominase and Ponkrum seems a bit absurd. The residents themselves know this is not a workable solution. In their efforts to manage economic and environmental shocks, they have at times intensified their connection to global markets and at other times pulled back, as their situations warranted.

Dominase and Ponkrum call into question the *universality* of our assumptions about development and globalization. Certainly there are places along globalization's shoreline where a sustained engagement with global markets is associated with improvements in people's lives. However, Dominase and Ponkrum illustrate that the outcomes of development and globalization hinge on local conditions that vary widely across globalization's shoreline. As a result, there will be a wide variety of outcomes for those who engage with global markets via these avenues. Sometimes local conditions will align with our broad assumptions, and the outcomes of our projects and policies will be as expected. At other times local conditions will run contrary to expectations, leading to unexpected policy and project outcomes. Viewed from this perspective, the complex, contradictory outcomes of development projects and economic policy are no longer inexplicable or idiosyncratic. Whether we are discussing the ways in which a new road through a village in Ghana raises incomes but also raises the vulnerability of the population to economic and environmental shocks, or how a single economic policy creates both expected and unexpected outcomes in different communities in the same country, we are dealing with the outcomes of locally specific opportunities and challenges that emerge from a project or policy. When we ignore this reality and operate with broad policies and projects founded on the assumptions that globalization and development produce regular, universal, and therefore predictable outcomes, we are going to get it wrong much of the time.

Why does the fact that we get it wrong matter? Certainly it matters greatly to those along globalization's shoreline. No matter how well-intended they might be, policies and projects based on misguided assumptions about globalization and development often fail to deliver expected or desired outcomes. As the history of Dominase and Ponkrum illustrates, misguided development projects and economic policies often result in greater uncertainty and challenges to the well-being of those living on globalization's shoreline rather than in improvements in the human condition. This uncertainty is heaped upon the challenges created by other global-scale processes, such as climate change, which already influence their vulnerability. When we get it wrong, the world's poorest and most vulnerable suffer.

If, however, we focus only on the ways in which our misunderstandings impact those who are living on globalization's shoreline, we limit the arguments for creating alternative understandings of globalization, development, and life in that area. Generally speaking, concerns for the well-being of those along the shoreline are couched in the language of victimization and framed in moral terms, or in terms of historical debts to the places that gave us the resources upon which the wealthiest parts of the world built their success. I agree with most of these arguments since, indeed, they are implicit in the story of Dominase and Ponkrum. After all, the agroecology of these villages was reworked repeatedly to accommodate the cash crops required by various colonial governments. The transportation network of the area rose, fell, and rose again in response to global and national demand for resources such as tropical hardwoods. The purchasing power of the residents still fluctuates in response to shifts in global markets for cocoa and gold. In their small way, the residents of these villages have helped keep the price of various global goods low for consumers in advanced economies. Unfortunately, in playing that role for those of us living in advanced economies, they have paid a price in the quality of their lives. I certainly feel we owe them something for the role they have played, however small, and the rather large price that so many of them have paid in playing that role.

I find that arguments about our responsibilities and debts to the global poor are not enough to spur action among those of us living in advanced economies. Like commercials for various aid agencies that showcase poor and often dirty children, these arguments capture the reader for a minute or two, but for most people they are ultimately dismissible and forgettable because we fail to see our self-interest in the conditions of life in places that seem so distant. Even the story of Dominase and Ponkrum seems to represent the connection between these faraway villagers and the rest of the world as one of victimization, a history of what the world, and certainly the advanced economies, have done to the residents of two faraway villages. Living in a world permeated by this storyline, we can be forgiven for asking, "What's in it for me?" when the plight of the global poor comes up in conversation or in the media.

The answer to that question, as it turns out, is: "Quite a lot." Our misunderstandings and failings are not only causing problems for people living far away, on globalization's shoreline, but also have left *everyone on the planet* extraordinarily vulnerable to economic and environmental shocks. For years these assumptions have underlain policies and projects that are putting us on a path to economic and environmental disasters out of which even advanced economies will not be able to buy their way. The entire world has long relied on the natural resources along globalization's shoreline to regulate the global climate and fuel the global economy. The conditions of life along this shoreline are such, however, that the residents are being forced into decisions that may make these roles unsupportable in the near future.

Although we have not always understood the relationship as such, those living in advanced economies have long counted on globalization's shoreline to play various roles for us—roles we either did not want to play or could not play. The first of these is as regulators of the global climate. As we in the advanced economies cut down our own forests to make way for agricultural lands to feed our growing populations and used more and more fossil fuels to power our economies, we created ever-rising concentrations of atmospheric CO_2 and other greenhouse gases. As our emissions rose and our forests declined, we became more and more dependent on various parts of the natural environment along globalization's shoreline for regulation of the global climate. For example, research conducted by a multinational team and published in the journal *Nature* estimates that tropical forests, virtually all of which are located along globalization's shoreline, absorb roughly 18 percent of all CO_2 emitted by burning fossil fuels.[1] Everyone on Earth needs those forests to help limit the concentrations of greenhouse gases in the atmosphere and thereby reduce, and eventually control, the rate of global climate change. Without the carbon uptake of these forests, carbon dioxide concentrations in the atmosphere will rise even more rapidly, speeding the rise of global temperatures and the scope of climate disruption around the world. This is the key point: Events on globalization's shoreline will result in climate disruptions *around the world*, not just on the shoreline.

Climate disruptions are the real problem of climate change. For most people, increased temperatures are not likely, in and of themselves, to be a directly significant problem. Three or four degrees Celsius are not, in most settings, going to push human beings past livable thresholds. For crops and other plants, though, this level of temperature change alone can reorganize habitats and change the places in which they can grow, upsetting our supplies of food and other plant resources. Further, increases in temperatures are usually accompanied by other shifts. An increment of a few degrees Celsius, while relatively insignificant to human comfort, represents an astonishing amount of energy stored within the climate system. This energy will reshape wind patterns, ocean currents, and precipitation patterns. Therefore, in many locations rising temperatures will be accompanied by increasing or declining amounts of precipitation, which will greatly reshape habitats for plants and animals.

While we cannot be completely sure what form future climate changes will take in every part of the world, the models we do have suggest significant disruptions in the way of life for people in *every part* of the world. For example, the most recent IPCC report notes that nearly all climate models show southern Africa's dry season becoming much dryer and the rainy season starting later and later over the next hundred years. This change in precipitation, coupled with expected temperature increases in the range of four degrees Celsius, is expected to create significant problems for the growing of maize, perhaps *the* staple crop of the region. Staple crops will also suffer in the advanced economies. New reports emerging from The Nature Conservancy[2] and a team of researchers from North Carolina State University and Columbia University[3] argue that current warming projections suggest declines of between 30 percent (in the best case) and 82 percent (in the worst case) in yields of corn (maize), soybeans, and cotton grown in the American Midwest by 2100. Even in the best case, yield-loss has the potential to destabilize the entire agrifood system of the United States, which is heavily reliant on cheap and abundant corn and soy as sources of food, not only for humans, but also for poultry and livestock.

The difference between globalization's shoreline and the advanced economies lies not in where climate disruption will occur, but in the different capacities for dealing with these changes among the populations of these two regions. In the advanced economies, our concerns for climate change are largely couched in terms of the cost of new infrastructure to address emerging challenges, such as droughts and changes in seasonal river flows. These economies, however, have the resources to adjust, at least initially, to minor disruptions. On globalization's shoreline the story is quite different. Here most residents are much more directly dependent on the immediate environment for their livelihoods, and they have far fewer resources for manipulating that environment (e.g., via irrigation) to manage emerging changes in climate. Therefore, along globalization's shoreline the effects of climate change are felt much more immediately and more directly than in advanced economies. More and more, as both climate change and economic change impact their capacity to raise the food and money they need to get through each day, residents of this shoreline find themselves forced into trade-offs they would rather not make.

For example, most of the farmers in Dominase and Ponkrum agree that deforestation lowers the agricultural productivity of their farms, due to both the loss of local precipitation that accompanies deforestation and the loss of shade that enables the growth of sensitive crops, such as cocoa. At the same time, the sound of chainsaws can still be heard around these villages every once in a while, as a head of lineage allows someone from town to cut down one of the few remaining trees in the area for a one-time payment of a few hundred dollars. These heads of family know that in allowing the cutting of trees they are mortgaging the future productivity of this land, but they see little other choice when crops do not come in as expected or jobs are hard to find.

From a global perspective, this example may not seem that dire. After all, when one tree falls, the impact on the global carbon cycle is minuscule. However, if similar stresses and decisions result in the cutting of thousands of trees each day, the impact can be significant. All along the shoreline, people are forced into this sort of trade-off every day, and in their decision-making the long-term conservation of needed natural resources usually falls by the wayside.

This problem can be dealt with most effectively by addressing the well-being of those living on globalization's shoreline. Indeed, there may be no other way, as existing alternatives appear to be unworkable. There are, however, those who believe we must protect these resources from the very people who live in and around them; and that this must be done by locking away from human use carbon sinks and other areas that serve as habitats for various endangered or otherwise important species. This "fortress conservation" mentality is ethically problematic and in practice unworkable. The vast majority of areas that, under this sort of scheme, would be walled off from human use, are located along globalization's shoreline, such as in the Amazon Basin. Ironically, the problems these areas solve, ranging from the uptake of carbon dioxide to the preservation of global biodiversity, are problems principally caused by the lifestyles and living standards of those living in advanced economies. The United States and the European Union together produced 34 percent of the globe's carbon emissions in 2008. If we want to offset some of these emissions by locking away the Amazon rainforest from human use, we are asking the people of Brazil, Venezuela, Colombia, Ecuador, Peru, and Bolivia—who generate a combined 2.2 percent of the globe's carbon emissions—to leave these forests untouched. In short, fortress conservation demands that the world's poorest continue to sacrifice their own economic growth to clean up the mess made by the world's wealthiest. We cannot sell that argument globally.

As a result, fortress conservation is unworkable, even if its ethical problems could be overlooked. Governments along globalization's shoreline have neither the incentive nor the ability to enforce such conservation measures. In the 12 months I spent in Dominase and Ponkrum between 1997 and 2000, I never once saw an agent of the state in these villages—be it police, fire, military, or anyone from a ministry or government office. Between 2004 and 2006 the Ministry of Health sent teams there once a month to weigh young children so they could identify early cases of malnutrition. Therefore, even after the improvement of the local road network, the reach of the state barely extended to the people of these villages, and they live just three miles from the nearest highway! Imagine the lives of those Ghanaians in the northern parts of the country, where population densities are much lower than around Dominase and Ponkrum and infrastructure is much more limited. In the rainy season some of these areas are completely cut off from the outside world by flooding, effectively isolating them for months each year. Under these conditions there is simply no way to enforce draconian conservation regulations.

Market-led solutions offer an alternative to the coercive methods of fortress conservation; this approach pays people who own key natural resources, such as forests and/or biodiversity, to protect those resources. The general idea is that the owner of a key resource, such as forested land, can calculate the environmental value of that land—for example, in terms of the amount of carbon the land takes up via photosynthesis each year. That value is then redeemed by selling a credit for that amount of emissions to a carbon emissions-producing company or individual who wishes to offset those emissions. The assumption is that a market in these offsets will determine a carbon price (calculated as price per ton of CO_2) high enough to provide landowners with a financial incentive to protect and preserve their forested areas, and with a steady source of income that can be drawn upon to improve their well-being. This basic idea is moving in specific ways into implementation via various intergovernmental/international initiatives, including Reducing Emissions from Deforestation and Forest Degradation (REDD) and three protocols of the United Nations Framework Convention on Climate Change (UNFCCC).

The key to these projects is the notion of a win-win-win outcome in which investors make a profit on these projects, local owners and communities living in and around the resource receive money and other benefits for their participation, and the world shares the environmental benefit. The first and third of these "wins" are well-analyzed and developed. The profit potential of these projects has been carefully researched, as this information is a key part of any investment plan or business model. The global environmental benefits of a particular project are calculable in terms of environmental impact (such as in a measurably lower amount of greenhouse gases in the atmosphere) or economic benefit (largely framed in terms of the savings created when we do not have to address water shortages, crop relocations, or disease outbreaks that appear likely under future climate scenarios).

The likely outcomes for the well-being of affected communities are nearly always predicated on an implicit market function whereby a fair price for the conservation of the resource will be established and the payments for the conservation of that resource will result in satisfied communities and the safety of the resource. These assumptions about the outcomes for affected communities are, however, just some specific instances of the broader assumptions I have called into question regarding globalization and development. As with the outcomes of globalization and development, the translation of payments into well-being is complex and locally specific and is not best understood as an outcome that is predictable through universal assumptions about human behavior. If we are to make any payment scheme actually work, we need to know what each community might see as a benefit (and *who* in each community will benefit), what they see as barriers to their well-being, and how they are currently addressing their own needs and managing existing challenges.[4]

The lack of such knowledge is a stunning omission endemic to these projects. If local communities do not receive benefits from these projects, the result is de facto fortress conservation, with all the attendant ethical and practical problems. From a business perspective, this is a disaster, as such situations greatly increase the likelihood of project-sabotage by affected communities. Members of these communities will realize rather quickly that if the conservation project fails, the investors will leave and the communities will regain access to the reserve area. In the academic literature on the creation of national parks and reserves there is plenty of evidence of this sort of behavior. Who can blame these communities, as they lose access to needed resources in the name of global environmental problems created by other people? No intelligent investor should risk money on a project that provides so little guarantee against this problem. That none of the projects I have seen treat the understanding of local challenges and their mitigation as a central point of concern suggests a real blindness to what is really taking place every day along globalization's shoreline.

Therefore, if those living in advanced economies want to share in the benefits provided by resources located on globalization's shoreline, everyone must work together to improve the quality of life for those living on

Box 8.1   Managing Acacia

Those in favor of fortress conservation tactics to preserve environmental resources overlook the fact that the residents of globalization's shoreline usually know how to manage their local environments and have the tools to do so even in the absence of formal environmental protection laws. Proponents of fortress conservation do not understand these local systems of management, often because they work from a fundamental assumption that these local systems are inferior to the scientific management with which they are familiar. As a result, the lessons that particular communities living in particular places have learned through long experience are lost.

I have a particularly clear understanding of this problem because I was guilty of this sort of thinking in my 2005 analysis of charcoal production and acacia growth in Dominase and Ponkrum. Charcoal is an important source of fuel for cooking in Ghana, and the government and various conservation organizations have expressed concern for the impact of charcoal production on existing stands of trees in rural parts of the country. Though there are few suitable trees around Dominase and Ponkrum, residents have long engaged in charcoal production by using as raw material the woody shrubs that overgrow fallow farm plots. These shrubs, however, produce relatively small pieces of charcoal that have a limited value at market.

Since the mid-1990s farmers in Dominase and Ponkrum have addressed this problem, and augmented their incomes, by planting a species of acacia tree (*Acacia polyacantha*) on their farms to improve their charcoal products. Acacia is a dryland tree optimized for environments with little rainfall. This particular species, when transplanted to the much wetter surroundings of these villages, can grow at tremendous rates. Over a seven-month span in 2000 I watched a newly planted stand of acacia grow more than eight feet tall. The trees require no real attention as they grow, freeing the farmers to focus on their food crops. After two years the trees can stand twenty-feet high and have trunk diameters of four inches. Trees of this size can be harvested to produce large charcoal pieces that command a premium at market. Further, harvesting does not kill these trees. Cutting the tree down resulted in the sprouting of two or more new trunks from the remains of the first trunk. These new trunks then grew as rapidly as the first.

Therefore, acacia appeared to be an ideal source of sustainable charcoal, and its cultivation spread through men's farms rapidly (it is still unusual for women to raise acacia in these villages). As they left fields to lie fallow, farmers would plant acacia on them (they are nitrogen-fixing trees, and therefore this seemed to be a good idea from an extension standpoint). The introduction of acacia to these farms appeared to be the latest remarkable adaptation of the local agroecology to the economic needs of the residents of these villages. By 2004, however, it had become clear that something was wrong. Farmers reported that nothing would grow on fields planted with acacia. Simply put, the extensive, shallow root systems of these trees were sucking up all of the available water that fell near them, depriving all other plants around them of needed moisture. Further, removing the trees proved more easily said than done. Short of digging up the extensive root system of each tree, the farmers had no way to completely kill the trees. Acacia had completely taken over the fallow plots on which it had been planted, and there was no option to farm on them again.

Assuming that the farmers did not understand the stress that acacia cultivation was placing on their farming system, I ran an analysis of the area under acacia and the total agricultural area around the villages in 2004. When I returned to Dominase and Ponkrum in 2005, I proudly presented my findings, complete with maps, to the heads of the families in charge of distributing and managing land around these villages. I knew that if this agroforestry practice was to change, these were the people to whom I had to make the case. I was startled when four of these family heads not only agreed with my analysis of the problems being caused by acacia but also noted that they already knew this was a problem and had banned the further planting of acacia on their family lands. These heads of family had already been engaged in a form of data collection on this issue, listening to the various members of their families report back on the effects of this tree on the land. From this information they were able to piece together the problem and convey their findings to other family members. Because the land belonged to entire families, not to single individuals, most families had decided that it was not in their interest to allow individual farmers to profit from these lands for a short time in a manner that ruined their productivity for the larger family over the long term. Further, because the land belonged to entire families, many people policed the activities of each farmer. In short, the residents of these villages had already gathered their own data on this environmental challenge and had used their own institutions to decide how to address the challenge and enforce their collective decision about future land use.

Rather than catalyze changes in agroforestry practice around these villages, my analysis helped to consolidate the changes already decided upon by these heads of families. Those in favor of banning acacia proceeded to tell the more recalcitrant members of their families that my measurements supported their point of view, which lent their decision greater legitimacy for some members of the community. Thus, my analysis contributed, in a small way, to the management of this challenge, though not in the way I had envisioned.

that shoreline, removing the conditions of deprivation and uncertainty that lead to the trade-offs that will eventually decimate these resources. A sustainable future begins with the achievement of this goal, broadly speaking. How we go about improving the quality of people's lives, however, must remain flexible and sensitive to local needs and situations.

While we rely on globalization's shoreline to regulate the global climate and protect the global environment, we also have close economic ties to this shoreline, ties that will only tighten over time. An excellent example of these connections is in the area of agriculture. The United States produces substantially more food than is needed to feed its population. This production has not only provided food directly to Americans but also has enabled the raising of cheap livestock and poultry as well as the provision of inexpensive sweeteners for our food. Indeed, our entire food supply, from what we eat to how much we pay for it, is predicated on our current means of growing food and raising animals. These agricultural and pastoral techniques, in turn, rest upon current environmental conditions in various food-producing regions of the country. It seems unlikely, under current scenarios, that these environmental conditions will remain stable enough to facilitate this sort of production over the next 50 to 100 years.

Beyond the warming of the Midwest, there are concerns for the unsustainable drawdown of underground water supplies, such as the Ogallala Aquifer beneath the American Great Plains states. The Ogallala Aquifer feeds an astonishing 27 percent of the total irrigated land in the United States and, if climate models are correct, as temperatures rise farmers in South Dakota, Wyoming, Colorado, Kansas, New Mexico, Oklahoma, and Texas will need to draw even more water from the aquifer to enable continued agricultural production at current levels. This will likely result in a more rapid drawdown of the Ogallala Aquifer until such time as its use is not practical. The intersection of climate change and a reliance on unsustainably irrigated agriculture is slowly choking to death a major portion of the American food supply, and there may be little we can do to avoid this outcome. In the long term, the preservation of our food supply may require expensive infrastructural investments and complicated, expensive, and ecologically problematic genetically modified crops. The costs of these efforts will be borne initially by farmers—whose small margins may disappear entirely—and, ultimately, by consumers in the form of rising food costs.

This does not mean, however, that we are doomed. It simply means we will have to rethink the majority of our food as a globally sourced commodity. While important environmentally sustainable farming efforts are taking place in the United States, in the near term these efforts may not become widespread enough to supply the needs of a rapidly growing population. Instead we will need to buy food from other places. If we start buying our food from globalization's shoreline, we have the chance to create a win-win situation: We get the food we need at more or less the prices we pay now, while the residents of the shoreline get access to global markets and acquire new financial resources, on terms they find productive.

How might this happen? Quite simply, by dropping our protectionist subsidies and tariffs on agriculture. In 2007 member countries of the Organization for Economic Cooperation and Development (OECD), all advanced economies, spent $365 billion on agricultural subsidies.[5] Citizens and residents of these countries paid this bill via their taxes, in effect paying for their food twice—once at the point of sale, and once via their tax bills. These people have also paid the bill for tens of billions of dollars in agricultural aid to people living along globalization's shoreline each year, in a remarkably paradoxical process whereby we encourage people to grow more food, more efficiently, and then refuse to let them sell us that food. While obtaining our food from places such as Africa will require expensive shipping that would drive up the price of these goods, these increased costs will be offset by two sources of savings.

First, the cost of agricultural production is significantly lower along globalization's shoreline than it is in the advanced economies. The farm-gate price of an orange in Dominase and Ponkrum is around ten cents, and an egg is less than seven cents. Thus, the point-of-production costs are much lower. In addition, in many cases these oranges and eggs are raised without hormones, fertilizers, or pesticides, attributes that many in advanced economies find desirable and are willing to pay a premium to obtain. Second, if we were to drop our own trade barriers and pass that savings on to taxpayers, we would save money on our annual tax bills, a second source of savings. The elimination of subsidies—and the subsequent global sourcing of food supplies—has almost no net impact on the cost of food to consumers, according to colleagues working at the FAO of the United Nations.

In other words, at no cost to us, we could move a significant portion of our food supply to a more sustainable location and at the same time contribute greatly to the well-being of those growing that food. Even by conservative estimates, such as those of the World Bank, the removal of the advanced economies' barriers to the trade in agricultural products would generate a tremendous flow of capital into places such as sub-Saharan Africa. One World Bank report suggests such a move would generate a flow of roughly $23 billion dollars into Africa.[6] Other estimates are much higher and rival the entire global aid budget for countries on globalization's shoreline. While there is no guarantee that these new markets, and the flows of capital they would generate, will be without problems, distortions, or negative effects—for at least some African producers—under these new economic conditions it might become possible to drop our aid budget to these countries and let the residents of globalization's shoreline decide how best to use these new resources to better their situations, another potential savings.[7]

There are those who see danger in this scenario, in that people living in advanced economies becoming dependent on globalization's shoreline for our food might run the risk of having food used as a weapon against them. This argument fails to grasp the extent to which everyone on the planet is already tightly interdependent. The United States is heavily dependent on China for its financial well-being, as China has historically bought up a great deal of U.S. debt and has continued to buy that debt even during the global downturn. Indeed, China could render the United States insolvent simply by calling in at one time all the debt it is owed. Few people talk about this when discussing the global or national economy, and for good reason. China has no interest in collapsing the American economy, as much of its own financial stability rests on the confidence that the United States will continue to pay off that debt, with interest, into the future. By destroying the economy of the United States, China would effectively destroy its own economy.

A similar situation would exist for food. By opening our markets to agricultural products from globalization's shoreline, we will create unprecedented flows of wealth to the poorest people in the world. For many, these new resources will enable real changes in the quality of their lives and new hope for their future. Once the residents of globalization's shoreline start seeing improved food security, shelter, and certainty about their economic and material future, they are unlikely to be willing to surrender these advantages except in the most dire of circumstances. There is simply no way, without very good cause, that a farmer in Ponkrum would be willing, after earning ten dollars each day under a new global trade regime, to return to living on two dollars per day. Petty global politics are unlikely to be sufficient motivation for any farmer I know, and any government foolish enough to deprive its citizens of this income for any but the most serious of reasons would in short order likely find itself out of power.

New market access will create new demands on these farmers and their production. These demands might lead to changes in agricultural strategy and agroecology, much like those seen over the history of Dominase and Ponkrum. The principal difference will likely be that, instead of having new crops forced on them, the farmers will finally have the leverage to decide what they want to plant. While farmers all along the shoreline have proved remarkably adept at such adoption and at the management of challenges that emerge with new crops, we cannot expect that all new adoptions will go smoothly or that all responses to global markets will result in sustainable agricultural practices. Thus, it will be in everyone's interest to work together to ensure the well-being of others in the world.

To reiterate, the well-being of those living along globalization's shoreline is central to the economic future of everyone in the world, including those living in advanced economies. If the poorest on the planet have their most basic needs met and the resources at hand to address the many challenges they face in their everyday lives, everyone in the world can benefit from a stable, sustainable source of food that preserves quality of life well into the future.

In the end, the only real way to guarantee the safety and security of the various resources we all need—natural, agricultural, and otherwise—is to address the specific needs and desires of those who own those resources and live near them. To do this requires *working with* the residents of globalization's shoreline through a reorientation of development practice and economic policy-making. I begin this reorientation by exploring how the data we use to understand globalization's shoreline do not tell us what we need to know, and thereby allow thousands of Dominases and Ponkrums to go unobserved or misunderstood.

Chapter 9

Losing the Signal in the Noise

How we measure globalization, development, and human well-being has important implications for how we understand the human condition around the world and the likely economic and environmental future toward which we are moving. Contemporary development policy, like economic policy, is grounded in a tremendous amount of empirical data. For example, global trade patterns are analyzed via a variety of measures. Some are well known, such as the Gross Domestic Product (GDP). Others are far more esoteric; for example, the Baltic Dry Index, a measure of shipping costs for commodities. In the months leading up to the economic collapse of 2008, this database recorded a precipitous decline in the cost of shipping, as the supply of ships greatly outstripped the number of goods being shipped, warning of the collapse to come.

The measurement of globalization, development, and human well-being is significantly more complicated than most people understand or acknowledge. There are major technical obstacles to measuring such things as economic growth and human well-being. There are also significant conceptual challenges to these measurements. We are pretty good at addressing the technical issues, but we largely overlook the conceptual problems at the heart of these measures. As a result, we often refine ways of measuring the wrong information and, therefore, obtain ever more accurate measurements of variables that do not tell us what we need to know about the world around us.

To illustrate some of the technical and conceptual challenges behind the measurement of globalization, development, and human well-being, I turn to GDP. Simply put, the GDP is an estimate of the value of all goods and services produced in a country in a given year. GDP is most commonly represented as a measure of economic production per person in a particular country—in short, we take the GDP and divide it by the population to get a per-person measure of productivity (which many economists take as a representation of the per-person wages paid). According to the World Bank, global GDP in 2007 was $54.5 trillion.[1] This means that if we add up the value of every resource extracted from the environment (for example, oil, lumber, fish), the value added to these resources when they were manufactured into products (for example, cars, computers, books), and every service provided (for example, the salaries of teachers, lawyers, and wait staff), it was all worth $54.5 trillion. Dividing this figure by the entire world population reveals a global per capita GDP of roughly $8,300. This measure simply means that in 2007 the average human being generated $8,300 worth of economic value, which he or she (theoretically) collected in wages.

GDP is a common and enormously influential measure of economic productivity and development. We often look to GDP to tell us about the state of the economy. If the GDP of the world is rising, this suggests we are producing more economic value, which is generally interpreted to mean greater wealth and opportunity. Even more important is the per capita GDP figure. If the per capita figure is rising, then we know the increase in wealth is not simply a product of more and more people working but is also an indicator that people are working ever more efficiently, and therefore generating more value. This additional value is assumed to translate into rising wages, which are assumed to create more wealth and opportunity. Examining Ghana's GDP we find it rose 303 percent between 2000 ($4.98 billion) and 2007 ($15.1 billion). Across this same time frame, the population of Ghana rose 16.4 percent. Thus, at least for the past several years Ghana's overall production of economic value has grown, both as an absolute number and as a per capita average (from approximately $250 to $650). This rising per capita figure suggests the people of Ghana are becoming more economically productive, perhaps more economically efficient, and more affluent.

There are some standard technical criticisms of GDP as a measure of wealth and well-being, and a few are worth quickly reviewing to illustrate their character. GDP is an aggregate figure that makes it hard to see variation in economic productivity and wages. For example, we know that economic productivity is not evenly distributed around the world. Sub-Saharan

Africa produced $847.4 billion of economic wealth in 2007, which resulted in a per capita GDP of roughly $1,060. In South Asia this per capita figure was $950. In Latin America per capita GDP reached $6,450. Compare these figures to that of the European Union ($37,870) or the United States ($45,600), and we quickly realize that economic productivity and wealth are not evenly distributed around the world. So a global figure for GDP or GDP per capita oversimplifies the picture of economic production and wealth generation. It hides the fact that some people are much more economically productive, and much better paid, than others.

This argument can be scaled down to the country level, where national growth rates can obscure important differences within the country. Typically, urban areas have much greater economic productivity than rural areas, a key difference that is erased by a national GDP figure. Further, in small, poor countries a single economic sector can distort the national economic picture. Take, for example, the case of Equatorial Guinea, which in 1998 had a per capita GDP of around $1,000. The next year its reserves of oil came on line, and oil companies began to pay the government a share of the profits. These profits were so massive that in two years the country's per capita GDP increased to $2,000, a jump of 100 percent. However, for those living on Rio Muni, the mainland portion of the country, nothing about their everyday lives changed as members of President Teodoro Obeng's government skimmed off most of this wealth instead of reinvesting it in the country.

GDP has long been criticized for failing to measure significant flows of economic value created by both overseas investment and remittances. Remittances are funds migrants and immigrants transfer to families and friends back in their countries of origin. Global flows of remittances are giant, amounting to $318 billion in 2007. In Senegal, for example, these remittances were equal to 7.6 percent of the 2006 GDP.[2] Because these funds are generated through goods and services produced elsewhere, they are not captured in GDP. Ignoring such a large flow of money, especially when it is the source of from 30 percent to 70 percent of the typical Senegalese household budget,[3] makes little sense when trying to understand human well-being in that country.

These are largely technical issues that have been addressed in various methodological ways. For example, GDP is now complemented, if not replaced, by Gross National Income (GNI), which takes into account overseas investment and remittances as parts of the economic value circulating

within a country. To capture the unevenness of economic growth and production, we can use tools such as the GINI coefficient, a statistical measure
that when applied to income data measures how dispersed those incomes
are. Generally speaking, the higher the GINI coefficient, the more dispersed, and therefore the more unequal, incomes are in a given country.
Thus, if a country has a rising GDP or GNI but also a rising GINI coefficient, it is likely that the increased economic growth is concentrated in
the hands of a relatively small portion of the population or in a handful of
economic sectors.[4] Alternatively, rising GDP/GNI and falling GINI coeffi-
cients suggest rising economic productivity with benefits that are reaching
a greater and greater portion of the population. In Ghana, GINI dropped
from 40.8 in 1998 to 39.4 in 2005–06.[5] While this is not a huge drop, it
does suggest that Ghana's economic growth is not merely consolidating
wealth among the wealthy.

Therefore, while the signal of economic growth might be a bit difficult
to discern from the noise of data measurement and interpretation issues
related to GDP, ongoing efforts refine our understanding of these figures. However, this solution presumes that the data itself is valid. In many
cases this is a problematic assumption. Problems with data quality range
from the straightforward to the complex. The straightforward cases are
easy to illustrate. For example, in 2000, while I was conducting fieldwork
in Ghana, I was counted in the Ghanaian census—twice. Thus, I can say
definitively that the Ghanaian census of 2000 overstates the population by
at least two people, and the population of both Ponkrum and Cape Coast
by at least one person each.

While my participation in the Ghanaian census is somewhat humorous,
it speaks to larger problems with data collection related to economic and
population data. Every census in the world runs into problems counting
the entire population of a country. Even in the United States, where we
have tremendous financial and human resources behind our census, we
cannot do anything about the fact that sometimes people are not home
when the enumerators arrive, or that some enumerators will not go into
areas such as public housing projects. As a result we systematically under-
count portions of our population in each census. Those who go uncounted
are disproportionately poor.

In Ghana such factors as the absence of house numbers and fixed
addresses for nearly all residents compounded these basic problems. There
are no street numbers on buildings in cities, towns, or villages. Nobody

lives at 123 Kotokoraba Road in Cape Coast; instead they live in the building with an internet café on the first floor, about 150 meters down the Kotokoraba Road from the market, on the right side. To address this problem in Ghana, enumerators marked each building with paint after they had completed counting all the occupants.

Despite the work of dedicated people in the Ghana Statistical Services and the aid of population and census experts from around the world, the enumerators ran into situations that led to people being counted more than once or not at all. This is not to disparage the Ghanaian Census of 2000. Having at least some information about the population is substantially better than having no formal information at all. However, people tend to take the results of a census as absolute and ignore all the caveats about the data and the figures that are included in the census documents. It is much easier simply to say that in 2000 there were 19,727,000 people living in Ghana, 82,563 people in the metro Cape Coast area, and 211 people in Ponkrum, although none of these figures is absolutely accurate. At the level of tiny villages like Ponkrum, the miscount is probably only a few people. In Cape Coast and other towns, the likely miscount ran into the hundreds. For the entire country the margin of error was many thousands of people. The figures we work with are approximations and need to be treated as such.

If population data are a bit tricky to gather, obtaining information about the economy of Ghana is inordinately difficult. The majority of the population is engaged in agricultural practices much like those described in Dominase and Ponkrum and, therefore, calculating their economic productivity is an arduous task. My own measurements of their productivity are based on self-reported income figures. This self-reporting is well-known to represent a massive underestimation of income (and a significant overestimation of expenses).[6] After more than 18 months in these villages, I would hazard that in interviews the residents typically underestimated their incomes by about half.[7] Further, I have not measured the value of the crops they consumed for subsistence, though those crops do have a value that can be calculated from market prices. To get that information I would have to measure the portion of each crop from its own farms the household ate for subsistence, then find out the local market price for each crop eaten and multiply the amount consumed by the market price to get a value for the subsistence crops. This sort of calculation takes months of observation and multiple rounds of

interviews or surveys. Even if the government of Ghana had the inclina-
tion to make these calculations, it lacks the resources to conduct such
measurements.

To address this problem, governments and agencies sample various parts
of a country to find out the value of their agricultural production and labor.
These figures are then extrapolated across the rest of the rural population
through various statistical means in an effort to gain a sense of the level of
economic production within the country, and of any trends in that production. While this is a reasonable, cost-effective method for addressing a data
need that cannot be met otherwise, it is not accurate. Therefore, when the
World Bank reports Ghana's 2007 GDP to be $15.15 billion dollars, the
Bank is reporting an estimated figure with a substantial margin of error.

All this means that the numbers I presented with regard to Ghana's
GDP growth, population growth, and growth in GDP per capita are, in
fact, all estimates with compounded margins of error. For example, if GDP
growth was overstated by 5 percent in 2007, and the population was underestimated by 3 percent, per capita GDP drops to $600. While this is only a
change of $60 per person, it means that the average Ghanaian is getting by
on 10 percent less income and resources than we thought. When you make
less than $2 per day, this is a serious amount of money, and the lower value
reflects a significantly different material situation for many Ghanaians. By
the same token, underestimating the economic value produced by subsistence farmers might mask even larger growth in economic productivity in
the country and greater declines in the GINI coefficient—which together
would paint a bright picture for Ghana's future. In short, on the shores of
globalization it can be hard to discern the signal of economic trends in the
noise of everyday data collection and analysis challenges.

These technical problems receive most of the attention from those who
question how we understand development and globalization. The assumption behind this focus is that we will be able to understand what is happening in these economies and societies if we can get the measurements right.
However, this argument presumes that what we are measuring actually
reflects anything about what we want to know. I have no objection, in
principle, to these technical fixes. They help to refine these measurements
and to better interpret the patterns we see in the figures over time. These
efforts improve the signal-to-noise ratio in the data all the time. Yet, none
of these technical fixes addresses whether or not the variables being measuring reflect the changing well-being of those living along the shores of

globalization. This, fundamentally, is where we are losing the signal in the noise. There is no technical fix for data that do not measure the issue in which we are most interested, and much of the data we gather do not measure what we think they do.

The reason we are gathering the wrong information, I argue, has everything to do with the assumptions about globalization and development the first part of the book questions. First, most efforts to measure human well-being along globalization's shoreline assume that such places lack development and lack adequate connection to global markets that might "bring development" to them and thereby improve their lives. Second, these measures carry an assumption that a growing economy is the same thing as improving human well-being. This belief is so strong that those who suffer far more challenges than opportunities under development and globalization are often dismissed as collateral damage to be sacrificed for the greater good of society, rather than as outcomes of the normal workings of globalization and development whose plight must be addressed through economic and environmental policy. Third, there is a strong belief that globalization and development directly create changes in human well-being, and that this process can be measured through universal variables such as GDP.

These assumptions are all-important because they serve to justify the types of data we gather, where we gather them, and how we interpret them. Yet, as I argue in the first section of this book, along many parts of globalization's shoreline these assumptions are fundamentally incorrect. As a result, the data we gather about these areas, no matter how technically refined, are often not relevant to the situations of those living along that shoreline. Therefore, our interpretations of that data inevitably misrepresent what is happening on the ground.

To illustrate my point, I turn to one source of information about life on globalization's shoreline: Poverty Environment Indicators (PEIndicators).[8] PEIndicators are variables selected to help project planners and policy-makers better evaluate the linked social, economic, and environmental effects of particular projects or policies. For example, as an indicator of the relationship between poverty and the environment in a particular community, one might use a calculation of how far members of households must walk to gather firewood. This indicator captures something about the local relationship between poverty and environmental quality if we assume that those who walk farther either (1) live in a degraded environment that requires them to walk longer distances to find needed fuel, (2) lack the resources to purchase alternative fuels, or (3) are dealing with a combination of these two factors.

Using a single measure, such as the distance walked to gather firewood, to stand in for a whole suite of local issues ranging from household income to the quality of the local environment is not, in and of itself, a problem. The purpose of an indicator is to create a means of rapidly and cheaply assessing a particular situation in a particular place. When interpreted correctly, changes in such indicators can help us understand when significant challenges or opportunities exist in particular places, and they can spur efforts to help people maximize the benefits and minimize the costs associated with those changes.

Of course, for a particular measure (or sets of measures) to function as an effective proxy for particular relationships, we must interpret that measure in a manner relevant to those living in the place in question. If, to better understand the relationship between poverty and the environment in a particular place, we measure the distance walked for firewood, then we assume that our interpretation of what this distance indicates will meaningfully illuminate some aspect or aspects of the connection between poverty and the environment in that place. It is easy to envision settings where a changing distanced walked to collect firewood would not. For example, if it turns out that people living in an arid area with little vegetation simply prefer firewood to other forms of fuel for cultural reasons, then going a long distance to gather firewood may simply indicate a strong cultural preference for firewood that has always been scarce in the area; it would neither indicate poverty (as they are buying firewood and taking the time to send someone to go get it) nor a degrading environment (scarce vegetation is not a new challenge). Simply put, even indicators, which are meant to be rapid, cost-effective proxies for complex local relationships, require some local context in their interpretation. If we were to apply the common interpretation of this PEIndicator to the community in the more arid setting, we would misunderstand what was taking place in that community and likely would respond inappropriately.

This point is well-known among those using poverty-environment indicators. Some authors even go so far as to make this point in reports that employ such indicators. In practice, however, the selection, measurement, and interpretation of PEIndicators often fail to take serious stock of local context. Instead, the selection and interpretation of these variables seem predicated on the idea that globalization is something new to the areas under investigation, that the areas under measurement are in need of development and globalization, and that increasing levels of globalization and income are positive trends in poverty-environment relationships. As I laid out in the first section of the book, none of these assumptions holds up all the time, which undermines the foundation upon which much PEIndicator interpretation rests.

A concrete example shows where the interpretation of PEIndicators can go wrong because of these assumptions. In a World Bank–funded study of PEIndicators in Nigeria,[9] a key indicator was "rural per capita cereal production." The author of the report took rising per capita yields to mean there were positive environmental conditions resulting in increased food production, which in turn provided food and income that increased human well-being in Nigeria. At first glance, this interpretation appears completely reasonable. It should, because it speaks directly to many of our implicit understandings of globalization and development. In Nigeria, cereals are often export crops, so a rising per capita production of cereals suggests rising engagement with global markets and, therefore, greater access to global circuits of wealth. Under the assumptions about globalization that seem to dominate economic and development policy, rising per capita production of cereals likely means greater wealth, and greater well-being, in the study area.

However, as the story of Dominase and Ponkrum has shown, our assumptions about globalization and development are often inappropriate when applied to particular places and situations. If the assumptions about globalization and development upon which an interpretation of the indicator rests are not universally applicable, then we may have to consider alternate interpretations and rule the inappropriate assumptions out in order to produce a rigorous analysis. For example, high per capita cereal production can be an indicator of rising food insecurity. The well-being of those who rely on export cereals for much of their income is closely tied to global commodities markets for these crops. If the market declines while the price of food rises, the selling price of this crop might not be high enough to enable adequate food purchases. Therefore, to interpret this indicator we need to consider the relative income gleaned from increased cash cropping versus the cost of food to be purchased with that income.

In addition, rising per capita figures for cereal production are likely obscuring uneven levels of production across households, communities, and countries. It is possible for farmers to consolidate a great deal of land by buying it from distressed neighbors who need the money to make ends meet, and then plant this land with cereal crops (instead of the mix of cereals and food crops commonly seen on small farms). This scenario would result in a rising per capita figure for cereal production but would overlook the fact that the income was concentrated in the hands of a few wealthy farmers while many others suffered.

These two scenarios can be combined into a third scenario that has played out numerous times, most notoriously under the "green revolution" in parts of Southeast Asia. When global markets for their crops fell, small farmers found themselves unable to pay off loans needed for fertilizers, pesticides, and food. To make ends meet, some of these farmers were forced to sell off part of their landholdings to wealthy farmers who were not under the same stress, creating a situation where the green revolution inadvertently consolidated wealth within communities, making the rich richer while the poor got poorer.

A similar interpretive problem arises for a second PEIndicator in this same study of Nigeria: the percentage of the agricultural area that is irrigated. Here the clear assumption is that a rising percentage of irrigated area will maximize the potential of the environment to produce crops, enabling either larger supplies of food crops or greater amounts of cereal crops for export. Both outcomes would improve human well-being in Nigeria, either by assuring local food supplies or by raising local incomes through engagement with global markets.

However, this interpretation rests on flimsy assumptions about how globalization and development work in particular places. If the overall percentage of irrigated area is large, then a rising percentage of irrigated land might indeed be an indicator of an improving poverty-environment relationship. In this situation much of the population already has access to irrigation, and the extension of irrigation capacity is likely improving the overall productivity of farms throughout the country. However, if the overall percentage of area under irrigation is small, a rising percentage of irrigated area may be an indicator of wealth-consolidation and of a significant decline in the well-being of the majority of the population. In a situation where there is relatively little irrigated land, it is likely that only a few farmers control it. When compared to their rain-dependent compatriots, those with irrigation have livelihoods that are more resilient in the face of environmental shocks, such as drought, and more amenable to forward planning of crops in relation to market prices. Therefore, farmers with irrigation are likely to have more money, and be less stressed, than those without irrigation. In the event of a drought or other shock, these few farmers will experience less of an impact on their farms, incomes, and well-being than will their rain-fed neighbors. Those failing farmers will begin to seek out income and food. If the shock is severe and lasts months, those with irrigation and money will be able to purchase land from their desperate neighbors at cut-rate prices, thus increasing their landholdings and prompting the extension of irrigation systems into their new land.

In both cases we could address these interpretive challenges relatively easily with a common technical fix—the GINI coefficient. By examining the GINI coefficient for agricultural producers over time alongside the trends in per capita cereal production and irrigated area, we could figure out whether rising figures indicate consolidation of wealth or a broad-based rise in well-being among Nigerian farmers. The author of this report did not do so. To be fair, this may have been because the GINI data was not readily available for agricultural producers and, therefore, might have required significant expenditures in time and money for organization and analysis.

Even if the author obtained the GINI data and employed it, this technical fix would not have addressed another significant technical problem: the scale of investigation. This report lumps together data for all of Nigeria and then analyzes them as a whole. However, Nigeria is a country of nearly 150 million people living in six different agroecological zones. In other words, this report grouped agricultural practices associated with different environments and crops under a single measure. Further, the report lumps three different general approaches to land tenure under each indicator. As we have seen in Dominase and Ponkrum, the local agroecology and the means by which people gain access to farmland are critical factors that shape the crops grown in particular places, how those crops are grown, and the amount of land available to individual farmers to grow them. For example, in a communal land-tenure system that recirculates land back to the larger lineage after a year or two of use, a farmer has little incentive to invest in irrigation as he or she would soon lose access to those improvements. As a result, this farmer is unlikely to grow crops requiring irrigation in the first place. Therefore, to interpret these two PEIndicators meaningfully, at the very least one has to understand the local combination of agroecology and land tenure.

In our examination of PEIndicators, Nate Kettle, Andrew Hoskins, and I found that, at the coarsest level, Nigeria could be divided into at least 13 zones of distinct agroecology and land tenure (see figure 9.1). These zones do not adhere to existing administrative boundaries in the country. Therefore, the data we need just to interpret PEIndicators meaningfully—about agricultural production, area under irrigation, and incomes—have not been gathered in a manner that maps to the zones for which we need those data. To correct this spatial mismatch will take significant time and money, but a correction is necessary if we are ever to use these indicators in a meaningful way.

I believe many of the problems I have identified with this report went unaddressed because the interpretations of these data rested on the same deeply held, largely unquestioned understandings of globalization and development—understandings called into question throughout this book. When interpretations of these indicators largely confirmed the author's (and likely many readers') assumptions, they reinforced his understanding of how the world worked, and *appeared* valid, if not self-evident. This is a case of confirmation bias—the author found what he was looking for because his findings, predicated on unquestioned assumptions about how the world works, largely confirmed those assumptions.

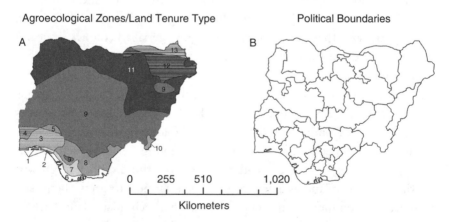

Figure 9.1 Maps illustrating the challenge of employing poverty-environment indicators in a meaningful manner in Nigeria reprinted from *International Journal of Sustainable Development and World Ecology*, 16(2), Edward R. Carr, Nathan P. Kettle, and Andrew Hoskins. "Evaluating Poverty-Environment Dynamics" 87–93. Copyright 2009, with permission from Taylor & Francis Ltd.

Box 9.1   Poverty-Environment Indicators in
Dominase and Ponkrum

The use of PEIndicators to understand trends in environment and development along globalization's shoreline is made even more complicated by the very different experiences of everyday life *within* particular communities. Take, for example, the experiences of Efua and Abena (not their real names), two women who live in Ponkrum. Efua's husband works part-time as a truck driver, and they have invested a lot of his income in land around the villages, which they have planted with acacia and palm. As a household operating under the market-oriented livelihoods strategy, they have a relatively large, fairly stable income each year. Abena is a widow and supports her elderly mother. She relies on two of her sons to supply her with a few acres of land each year to plant, and she is completely dependent on the production of a small surplus of food crops for any income beyond subsistence.

Although both these women have livelihoods anchored in agricultural activities that take place in nearly identical environments, the challenges they face are very different. Efua's landholdings are scattered around the village. She has to walk several kilometers to get to some of her acacia holdings, from which she gathers firewood or charcoal that she and her husband have burned. Therefore, Efua's relatively long journey to collect firewood is a product of her highly secure access to this resource, which also grants her household a sizable annual income. In contrast, Abena has no acacia holdings and either purchases charcoal or gathers firewood from the fallen branches of trees that ring the edge of the village, next to her house. Her short trip to collect firewood is a product of her lack of access to firewood on her farm and her reliance on limited firewood supplies from fallen branches at the edge of the village.

When we examine the trend in distance walked to collect fuelwood over time, the situation on the ground makes this indicator even more problematic. Because Efua is collecting her fuelwood from an acacia plantation belonging to her household, and because acacia is a durable tree that produces significant amounts of new wood every year, her journey to collect firewood is not likely to change anytime soon. Though we might interpret this trend as a stable poverty-environment relationship, this does not take into account the negative environmental impacts of acacia on that land and perhaps the land surrounding that plantation, which might compromise food crop production and drive down the quality of the local environment.

In contrast, one of Abena's sons recently planted several acres of acacia on land near Dominase, roughly half a kilometer from Ponkrum. Although he plans to make charcoal from this acacia, he also plans to let his mother gather some firewood or charcoal from these trees as they get larger. Thus, as these trees mature, the distance of Abena's journey to collect firewood will increase. Rather than indicate either a problem with her existing sources of firewood or increasing poverty that prevents the purchase of adequate charcoal or fuelwood, this increasing travel actually results from a situation in which her fuelwood supply is becoming more stable and secure over time.

If we were to aggregate the two trends represented by Abena and Efua into a single measure—for example, using the distance traveled to collect firewood to capture a linked poverty-environment trend in these villages—we would likely interpret the overall increase in travel time to gather fuel as a sign that something about the poverty-environment relationship in the area was changing for the worse. However, this change in the average distance these two women have to walk to obtain fuel and firewood is detached from negative changes to the local environment and their incomes. Instead, the individual with the increasingly long walk to collect firewood is the one with an ever more secure source of fuel and well-being, and the woman with the stable walk for such fuel may be engaged in agroforestry practices that are not sustainable over the long term.

This case illustrates why we must rethink our assumptions about how development and globalization work, because if we do not, we will continue to gather data that have little bearing on actual events on the ground along globalization's shoreline. Such assumptions make it hard to see that these data are not particularly valuable. Indeed, because they are somewhat detached from the processes and events that really matter on the ground, they become easy to interpret—through our current, flawed understandings of globalization and development—without actually calling either into question. The result is an echo chamber of misunderstanding with regard to life and events along globalization's shoreline. We expect the world to work in a certain manner. Therefore, we gather data to measure expected workings, and we analyze those data through frameworks founded on the same understandings of the world they are meant either to affirm or to challenge. In addition, by our choice of data and our means of analysis, we end up affirming that the world does indeed work the way we thought it did. This handcuffs any effort to understand and improve the well-being of those living on globalization's shoreline.

To break out of this echo chamber we need to find a new way to learn about life and events on globalization's shoreline. We cannot do this by employing the ideas and assumptions of the advanced economies alone. We must engage those living on globalization's shoreline as real partners in this endeavor. We have much farther to fall if we do not.

Chapter 10

The Long Emergency on the Shoreline of Globalization: It Is Not Their Problem

The global economic downturn that began in 2008 wrought spectacular damage on the global economy. In June 2009 the International Monetary Fund projected a contraction of the global GDP by 2.9 percent for the calendar year 2009. However, if we disaggregate the IMF's statistics on the global economic downturn, we find its effects are not really global. The only economies that are actually losing value are the "advanced economies," for example, the United States and the countries of the European Union, which the IMF projected in July 2009 will lose 3.8 percent of GDP that year. The economies in the developing world, along the shoreline of globalization, continue to grow. For example, the GDP of sub-Saharan Africa is expected to increase by 1.5 percent in 2009, after successive years of growth in the 5–6 percent range. While this slowdown is certainly significant, it is also important to note that in the midst of this economic crisis, economic growth is continuing in Africa and other developing areas.[1] The 2.9 percent contraction in the global economy is actually a product of a massive downturn in developed economies, not in all economies in the world.

The economic devastation wrought by this crisis in the advanced economies is well documented and is a significant concern for those living in those economies. Yet, organizations such as the World Bank and the IMF have tried to highlight the impact of this crisis on those living along globalization's shoreline, at least in part to prevent the abandonment of aid commitments. Some analyses of this crisis' impacts on economies along this shoreline are straightforward, and somewhat depressing. For example, in the February 20, 2009, issue of *IMFsurvey* magazine, the IMF argued,

> Before the global financial crisis, some African countries had started to attract new investment inflows and had begun borrowing on international capital markets. Research by the IMF in September 2008 identified eight countries, beyond South Africa, which could become emerging or frontier markets: Botswana, Ghana, Kenya, Mozambique, Nigeria, Tanzania, Uganda, and Zambia. All these countries had experienced a takeoff in growth, led by the private sector, and had public policies in place that embraced market-led growth, as well as financial markets that attracted foreign investors. Today, less than half a year later, the outlook is more bleak. With the expectation of a more pronounced global downturn, weaker commodity prices, and pressure on capital flows, the IMF expects growth in sub-Saharan Africa to slow from about 5 ¼ percent in 2008 to about 3 ¼ percent in 2009, about 3 percentage points less than projected just four months ago. And for the time being, investor interest in sub-Saharan Africa has cooled off.

Other commentaries touch a note of crisis in conveying the severity of the impacts of this downturn on these populations. In an op-ed published in the *Financial Times* in January 2009, Robert Zoellick, the president of the World Bank, argued for a vulnerability fund to protect "the hundreds of millions who are victims of a crisis not of their making." In a *New York Times* op-ed published around the same time, Zoellick wrote, "Support for a vulnerability fund can help limit the depth and length of the international downturn, prevent the contagion of social unrest and help save a generation from a new poverty trap." Some of the hue and cry about the impact of the downturn on those living on globalization's shoreline is highly pitched. For example, World Bank economist Shanta Devarajan, on his blog (http://africacan.worldbank.org), noted, "If Africa experiences a growth deceleration that is typical of the past, we estimate that an additional 700,000 infants will die before their first birthday."

Throughout this book I have argued that we cannot simply treat either development or globalization as causing anything to happen directly. Instead development and globalization create opportunities and challenges that are mobilized and managed by individuals with reference to particular needs in particular places. Therefore, as well-meaning as these officials' efforts to keep the plight of the poor in the spotlight might be, we cannot simply say that growth deceleration will directly lead to 700,000 additional infant deaths in sub-Saharan Africa. Instead we need to link the downturn (itself a manifestation of globalization) to place-specific opportunities and

challenges if we want to understand how economic slowdown can be translated into infant deaths, social unrest, or poverty traps.

Generally the arguments linking the economic downturn to impacts on
the residents of globalization's shoreline boil down to four key challenges
(there is little, if any, discussion of opportunities arising from the downturn). First, the downturn will reduce private capital flows to the shoreline
of globalization, preventing the construction of needed infrastructure and
the integration of local production into global markets. Second, the funds
migrants living in the developed world send back to the shoreline countries
are projected to shrink. This loss of capital is implicitly expected to impact
the ability of those living along the shoreline to meet their material needs.
Third, the downturn will result in reduced aid to those countries, which
will have an effect similar to that of reducing the flow of private capital.
Fourth, the rapid decline in global commodity prices, driven by reduced
demand for all sorts of commodities in the face of the economic crisis, will
negatively impact economies along the shoreline of globalization, as these
are the economies most dependent on the export of commodities for their
revenues. These lost exports will negatively impact producers, those who
provide services to producers, and governments that can no longer collect
tax revenues on these exports.

Once we understand these four points framing how the global economic crisis contributes to problems on the shoreline of globalization, we
can see how these points are employed time and again, in whole or in part,
in public statements linking the challenges of poverty reduction and development to the global economic crisis. For example, in a February 2009
op-ed published in *The National*, a paper in the United Arab Emirates,
Dominique Strauss-Kahn, managing director of the IMF, stated, "Weak
global growth is shrinking export markets, and many commodity prices
are plunging. The combination of tighter credit conditions in the advanced
economies and dimmer economic prospects in low-income countries is hit-
ting investment flows. And workers' remittances, which now eclipse aid
as the biggest financial flows to low-income countries, are also falling."
IMFsurvey, in its April 24, 2009, issue, quoted Antoinette Sayeh, director
of the IMF's African Department, as saying, "Demand for African exports
has weakened and prices for most commodity exports have fallen. Tighter
global credit and investor risk aversion have led to a reversal of portfolio
inflows, are discouraging foreign investment, and have made trade finance
more costly. Also, remittances flows may be weakening."

I have no doubt the various officials quoted here are concerned with the impact of the global economic downturn on those living along globalization's shoreline. However, the arguments they are making for increased aid are distressingly flimsy. For example, the decline in flows of private capital (and foreign aid and government revenue) will no doubt reduce the amount of infrastructural development taking place in countries such as Ghana over the next year or two. Nevertheless, the failure to build something that people never had in the first place will not cast them *deeper* into poverty. Further, the assumption that infrastructural development, or similar efforts, would necessarily spur economic growth, improve health outcomes, or otherwise reduce the vulnerability of particular communities within Ghana rests on the idea that development projects actually create these outcomes, as opposed to providing opportunities and challenges that might be mobilized into these outcomes. Simply put, we cannot say, in a general way, what the overall impact of the economic downturn will be on globalization's shoreline. The claim of 700,000 excess infant deaths in sub-Saharan Africa is based, in the end, on correlations between economic growth and infant mortality that tell us little about the *causal* relationship between the two. The number 700,000 is just a guess. In addition, the attribution of these deaths to development that will not happen is an even more dubious guess. Neither speculation points to the cause of excess infant deaths, which is what we need to know if we are to address this problem.

It is useful to return to Dominase and Ponkrum to consider the claims being made for the impact of the downturn on their lives. First to be examined are remittances. Only one or two households in these villages receive significant remittances. Further, in these households these remittances occur only when the male heads temporarily migrate to another country to work. For example, one man regularly travels to Abidjan in neighboring Côte d'Ivoire to work as a baker. In cases such as this, the loss of remittance is not an absolute loss, because the person who would have been remitting wages is still resident in the household and can contribute to farm labor and other means of meeting the household's needs. Thus, the decline in remittances will have little effect in these villages. This is not to suggest that remittances are not important aspects of livelihoods and well-being anywhere along the shoreline of globalization, but rather that this importance varies dramatically depending on location.

Next to be examined is the issue of commodity price instability. Such instability has been a fact of life in these communities since their inception. Perhaps the first commodity price collapse they endured was the declining value of palm oil across the late nineteenth and early twentieth centuries, as competitor products steadily eroded the market share of this commodity. The collapse in global timber prices led to the end of local logging in the late 1960s and to the subsequent end of the local transportation network. Cocoa price instability triggered the collapse of the cedi in 1999–2000. Therefore, while a new round of declining commodity prices is bad news for those living in Dominase and Ponkrum, this sort of event is nothing new to these communities.

As with remittances, the residents have only a limited engagement with export crops. As a result, the direct impact of commodity price fluctuations on the livelihoods and well-being of those living in Dominase and Ponkrum is mostly one of comfort, not life or death. While incomes are more closely linked to the market sale of crops than ever before, few crops on these farms cannot be eaten by the household in the event that market prices fall too far. Once again, this is not to say that these price fluctuations will have no effect along globalization's shoreline, but that such effects will be uneven and place-dependent. Even along parts of the shoreline that are heavily committed to export-crop production, such as Kenyan communities that contain coffee and tea growers, price fluctuations will not directly cause particular outcomes, such as rising rates of infant mortality. Instead, price instability will create opportunities and challenges—for example, for tea and coffee growers—that they will understand and address through locally specific lenses. So even in those parts of the shoreline dominated by export crops, the outcome of this instability is going to be uneven.

The impact of the loss of private capital investment as well as foreign aid and government revenues is also questionable. For example, it is clear that reduced flows of capital and aid will reduce the financial resources available for infrastructural development. Even if we assume these funds would have been funneled into infrastructural projects that the residents of Dominase and Ponkrum might access regularly (and this is quite unlikely), we cannot assume that infrastructural development will result in short- or long-term benefits across the community. As illustrated earlier, the construction of the road through Dominase and Ponkrum had a complex set of outcomes. Certainly, it appears that local efforts to take advantage of opportunities that emerged in the context of the new road resulted in increased household incomes and greater engagement with local agricultural markets. These changes can be captured as parts of a rising GDP. This rising economic productivity has, however, come at the cost of lost resilience in their liveli-hoods, as people now rely more heavily on market sale than on subsistence production to meet household needs. In turn, this tighter engagement with markets makes households more sensitive to economic fluctuations that might impact agricultural prices in local markets.

While male heads of household in Dominase and Ponkrum tried to take advantage of potential new opportunities afforded by the road, at the same time they addressed the risk of increased women's empower-ment in such a way as to reinforce existing gender inequality in their households. This outcome makes it likely that local birthrates will remain high, which in the longer run will mean more and larger households that need access to land. Thus, road construction may have produced some-what larger incomes in the short term, but has done little to improve the long-term sustainability of those livelihoods. Because of the ways in which the residents of these villages viewed the opportunities and challenges stemming from the construction of the road, a rising GDP goes hand-in-hand with lost resilience, new risks and shocks, and likely long-term environmental degradation. It is possible to argue that the road was critical to short-term economic growth. However, to argue that the failure to build this road—because of lost financing—would have compromised the long-term well-being of these communities requires overlooking the long-term negative outcomes associated with this road-construction project.

Framing the global economic downturn's impact on those living on globalization's shoreline around these issues does not really explain exist-ing trends across this part of the world, nor does it serve as a terribly use-ful foundation for projecting what will happen going forward. Instead, this framing and these projections seem much more oriented toward those parts of the shoreline found in the boardrooms and lobbies of five-star hotels of Africa, Asia, and Latin America. This wealthier part of the shore-line requires foreign investment capital to grow, often needs the data and transportation infrastructure that aid dollars and government revenues can finance, and may rely heavily on high commodity market prices for par-ticular resources to ensure profits and growth. This way of framing of the downturn and its impacts makes sense only for those who focus on this relatively small part of the shoreline of globalization.

However, these concerns are still predicated on the idea that the economic downturn is taking away from growth that was going to happen but now will be delayed. This, in turn, presumes an even larger belief, namely that the economic growth seen along the shoreline of globalization would eventually transform this large, complex global region into a place where the material standard of living is similar to that enjoyed in the advanced economies. Thus, the global economic downturn is framed as a problem because of the ways in which the downturn slows growth and prevents people from achieving this larger goal of prosperity. The problem with this argument is that this growth was never, in the long term, going to raise the material standard of living along globalization's shoreline to that seen in the advanced economies.

There are just not enough resources on planet Earth to allow every single person to live at the same material standard of living seen in the United States, or in the advanced economies more generally. While the calculation of per capita resource use is complex and contentious, an examination of two key resources illustrates the point adequately. The first is petroleum. Whether or not we have reached "peak oil" (the highest point of oil-field production before the inevitable steady decline as we draw these fields down), we have certainly reached a point where consumption is catching up to production. If the Chinese and Indians alone raise their per capita automobile use to the same level as that of the United States, the annual global consumption of petroleum would more than triple what we currently pump out of the ground, likely exceeding our ability to produce or refine enough fuel to enable such levels of automobile use.[2] Rising affluence along the shoreline of globalization will have much the same effect, pushing the number of automobiles and miles driven higher and higher. This pressure, in turn, will drive petroleum consumption up, first beyond our refining capacity and later beyond our production capacity. We have already seen hints of what this pressure will look like in the United States, most recently when Hurricane Ike struck Houston in September 2007. Precautionary shutdowns and relatively minor hurricane damage to these refineries took nearly 25 percent of American refining capacity out of operation, triggering fuel shortages and spectacular spikes in price as demand greatly exceeded supply.

A second, less-often considered resource is land. We require land to grow our food, to provide raw materials for our livelihoods, and for living on. On the other hand, we also require land, and the vegetation it supports, to regulate our climate—for example, by taking carbon out of the atmosphere via photosynthesis. We need land for trees, which are used to build shelter, burned for fuel, and converted into paper. Therefore, land is one of the resources that serve as foundations for our livelihoods, whether we live in an advanced economy or along the shoreline of globalization. Estimates of how much land we require to support our various lifestyles are tricky to calculate but include the area required to farm all of the fruits, vegetables, and grains we consume; the land required to raise the livestock, fish, and fowl (and to manage their waste) that we eat; the amount of forest or other land-cover required to take up our carbon emissions generated from driving, flying, heating our houses, and powering various electronic devices; the land required to produce the ores and other raw materials that go into our houses and devices; and the land required to dispose of the waste we generate. While there are several estimations of individual "footprint," or land required to sustain a particular lifestyle, most suggest that in the advanced economies our levels of consumption are so high that it would require three or more Earths' worth of land to support the entire global population at this level of affluence. Obviously, we do not have any more Earths to mine for resources or on which to grow crops and raise animals. This means it is simply not possible, under current manufacturing, agricultural, and energy-generation regimes, to elevate the standard of living of the entire globe to that of the advanced economies.

Another way to put this: We in the advanced economies live the way we do because billions of people along the shoreline of globalization do not. There is no way to perpetuate historic rates of economic growth in advanced economies if the entire world, or even a significant percentage of the world, consumes resources at the same rate as the advanced economies. If the consumption of those living along the shoreline of globalization were to rise toward levels of consumption seen in the advanced economies, the shortages and price spikes this consumption would trigger would significantly increase the cost of raw materials, shipping, and finished goods around the world. As these increased costs are passed on to consumers in the form of higher prices for goods, consumption would slow. This, in turn, would slow the growth of the advanced economies.

The implication of this problem is that development is impossible, at least if we conceive development as raising people's standard of living to that of the advanced economies. Connecting people to global markets will not enable this outcome, because this outcome cannot occur. Oddly enough, the global economic downturn, which has reduced the size of the advanced economies' GDPs while only slowing the growth of those in emerging and developing economies, has done more to equalize global economic productivity and incomes than did the last 60 years of development.

Another way to think about this is in terms of what some are calling the "long emergency," the coming changes in society and economy that some expect in the wake of declining petroleum supplies. Much has been written about this coming period, in most cases evoking a Cormac McCarthy–esque world in which central authority breaks down, economies become hyperlocal, the population size collapses, and the world returns to something resembling the agrarian landscapes of early nineteenth-century America. These scenarios are best guesses at what might be ahead, but oddly enough they make no reference to the majority of the world that already lives under conditions similar to the long emergency. The long emergency is neither a fiction nor a completely conjectural situation that will arise in the future. Versions of the long emergency are in play all along globalization's shoreline right now.

Those living along the shoreline of globalization are already squeezed by the same resource shortages that are projected for the rest of the globe. Petroleum is neither easily accessed nor affordable, even in places that produce petroleum. In Ghana gasoline routinely tops $5 per gallon. While that price is quite high, consider that Ghana's per capita GDP figure suggests that wages in the country average only $2 per day. A gallon of gasoline therefore costs two and a half days' wages for the average Ghanaian. A gallon of gasoline here in the United States, even at the relatively high rate of $3 per gallon, costs only 2 percent of an average day's wages of $144.68.[3] To put this in perspective, if gasoline in the United States were as expensive, in terms of average daily wages, as it is in Ghana, it would cost $361.70 per gallon.

As key resources such as petroleum start to dwindle, the rising prices of key commodities like gasoline are expected to lead first to economic and then to societal collapse in the United States and other advanced economies. Yet, Ghana's economy has grown under this kind of stress. The reason is that, as with globalization and development, resource shortages do not cause economic collapse or social unrest. Instead these shortages create challenges, and even some opportunities for innovation that those living with these shortages negotiate as best they can. The result, at least along globalization's shoreline, has been myriad innovations that improve the efficiency of petroleum use. The clearest example is discussed in chapter 2: the taxicab system in towns and cities in Ghana. While it is possible to hire a cab to deliver you to a precise location at a particular time, much as one would in an advanced economy, this option is extraordinarily expensive and well beyond the means of the average Ghanaian. The driver of the taxicab has to pay for the gasoline, maintenance of the vehicle, and a few bribes for traffic police each day before he (it nearly always is a man) can begin to make a profit. Therefore, if you hire a cab, you personally have to absorb a share of all those costs associated with taking you to your destination and for the driver to return to find another fare. This situation is much like that expected to exist during the long emergency.

Further, the Ghanaian urban and rural landscapes are not particularly conducive to public transportation. Accra, the capital, sprawls over nearly 80 square miles. Even Cape Coast, a much smaller city, has sprawling residential development taking place at its edges. Much like the American landscape, this sprawl is difficult to service via centralized bus routes and is dispersed enough to make walking to jobs and markets in the city from outlying residential areas impractical. For those writing about the long emergency in America, such a landscape will become an insurmountable barrier to social connection as people lose access to transportation, leading to the abandonment of suburban subdivisions.

However, though Ghana currently displays fuel pricing similar to that expected under the long emergency and shares some of the landscape constraints expected to become disasters for us in the future, the Ghanaian economy has not localized and society has not collapsed into smaller, nucleated communities. Villages several kilometers from cities continue to grow—there is no abandonment of Ghana's equivalent of the suburbs in the face of these pressures. People still travel between villages and cities regularly. In Cape Coast, which is home to more than 80,000 people, thousands of commuters ride in taxis every day, heading to work, school, market, or home. Since 1997, when I first started working in Ghana, the number of cabs and passengers has increased, not only in cities such as Cape Coast but also in the rural hinterlands. This long emergency is not playing out as expected.

The reason these outcomes are unexpected is because claims about the long emergency rest on the idea that there are no practical ways to address the challenges created by our landscape and transportation needs. However, standing along any major road in Cape Coast, one can see the solution to this problem. Every minute dozens of cabs pass. If a full cab is considered to hold four passengers (in cities the number is four; on less policed rural roads this number can rise to six, with people riding on one another's laps), one can count more than a dozen cabs, between 75 and 100 percent full, passing every minute. What you are witnessing, in this moment, is an astonishingly efficient transportation system. These are shared cabs, with each passenger paying separately and only for the distance he/she travels along a fixed route. In Cape Coast these routes follow every major road in and out of the city. In Cape Coast proper, you are never more than a quarter-mile from a route that cabs ply regularly. Therefore, to get from one place to another, you use the cab system much like a subway. For example, in Cape Coast, if you are at the university and need to get to Kotokoraba Market in the center of town, you would pick up a shared cab from the university over to Pedu Junction 1.8 miles away. In 2006 this ride cost 2,000 cedis, or about $0.22. Once in Pedu Junction, you get out of the cab and walk across the road and down Jukwa road, a trip of about two hundred yards. Here you can catch another shared cab directly to Kotokoraba Market, another 2.2 miles away, for 1,200 cedis, or $0.13. Your total cost for the trip is $0.35, and the total travel time is probably about ten minutes longer than if you hired a cab to take you the whole way. This is cheaper than every major subway system in the advanced economies.

The key to this system is efficiency and low labor costs. The shared cab at the university will not move until it has four paying passengers. When the cab reaches Pedu Junction and you get out, someone will immediately step in and take your seat. The taxi you catch at Pedu Junction, headed to Kotokoraba Market, will likely be letting a passenger out at that same stop, so you are stepping into that empty seat. The cabs are nearly always full. Thus, for the trip from the university to Pedu Junction, the driver is collecting around $0.88. Assuming his cab is running with any sort of fuel efficiency (let's assume a very low 15 miles per gallon), the gasoline for the trip costs around $0.60. Mileage costs are low in Ghana because the cost of labor, even auto mechanics, is low—probably less than $0.05 a mile, for a total of $0.09 per trip. For each run to or from Pedu Junction, this driver accrues costs of $0.69 and collects a total fare of $0.88, leaving $0.19 profit. Over the course of a day, a driver might make 20 or 25 round trips from the university to Pedu Junction, for an overall daily profit of between $7.60 and $9.50. If the driver is in good standing with the local traffic police, he likely has to pay only a small bribe of roughly $0.45 per day to prevent further harassment or troubles. At the end of the day, then, the driver has a profit of $7.25 to $9.05. If he is not the owner of the car, he will have to pay the owner between a half and two-thirds of these earnings (though in these situations the owner often foots much of the bill for maintenance), leaving the driver with between $4.33 and $6.32.

The efficiency of this system is astonishing. However, it is also precarious. An accident or need for major repair can put a driver or owner out of business immediately. Even so, most of my Ghanaian friends argue that driving a taxi is one of the better jobs in the country because of its earning potential. While daily wages of $4 to $6 seems like a paltry sum, consider that the per capita GDP of Ghana in 2007 was slightly less than $645. The cab driver, who will work nearly every day of the year, can earn between $1,400 and $2,000 per year, much more than the average Ghanaian. In addition, considering that my estimate of fuel efficiency and number of runs per day is conservative, actual profit margins are typically higher. Even better is to be a car owner collecting a percentage of the revenues of your drivers each day. In other words, there is development and investment potential in this shared-cab system, though these potentials are relative to the local economic context.

The lessons from this case are twofold. First, the long emergency may be much less of an emergency than many expect. Human beings are innovators and find ways to make things work in even the most difficult of circumstances. Anyone who has truly visited the shoreline of globalization (and not merely its hotels) knows the residents of this expansive part of the world are capable of adapting to nearly any circumstance and finding ways to identify and exploit opportunities in any change. We are no different. However, we are perhaps less adept at such adaptation, as we have not been required to think about the world in this way, or under this kind of duress. Those living along the shoreline of globalization are, perhaps, better prepared than we are for coming changes in environment and economy, because they are already living under the conditions of deprivation that we fear most.

Second, things are not going to get substantially worse for most people living along the shoreline if globalization pulls back and development goes away, because neither was doing all that much for the majority of those living in this region in the first place. Further, neither development nor globalization has long-term potential to really change the standard of living for the majority of those on this shoreline because there are not enough

Box 10.1 Joe Dadzie's Short Emergency

In 1999 and 2000 the economy of Ghana collapsed in dramatic fashion. As I recounted in chapter 4, across little more than fifteen months the cedi lost roughly 65 percent of its value against major currencies, and the citizens of Ghana lived through rampant inflation and rapidly decreasing access to imported goods, an economic experience similar to one that might result from the dramatic collapse of global trade. This economic crisis, however, did not result in significant negative health, nutrition, or educational outcomes for the residents of Dominase and Ponkrum. I was living in these villages during part of this collapse (February–August 2000), and in all that I saw, the villagers' experience of this crisis is perhaps best captured in the story of Joe Dadzie's quest to buy a new roofing sheet for his house in July 2000.

In 2000 Joe was a thirty-two-year-old husband and father of an infant daughter. When in Ponkrum, Joe worked on his farm to earn a living. However, every few years Joe would travel to Abidjan, in neighboring Cote d'Ivoire, to work as a baker. While in Abidjan, Joe would save up as much of his wages as he could. After a few months he returned to Ponkrum with money, which he invested in housing improvements, furniture, and other needed items. Joe was also a member of my field crew in 2000, and therefore he had a source of steady income that he was saving to buy a new asbestos roofing sheet for his house. Because he knew that the pricing of these sheets had become unstable, Joe planned this purchase carefully. To avoid losing wages by taking unnecessary days off from work, he sent someone to Elmina to inquire about the going rate for roofing sheets the day before he planned to go to market. This allowed Joe to keep working and get the latest price for these sheets. After receiving this information, and confirming that he had enough money for the purchase, Joe came to me and requested a day off to go buy the roofing sheet. He left early the next morning, walking through Sanka and Bronyibima to Elmina. He did not return until it was nearly dark, and when he did, he was empty-handed. When I asked him what had happened, he told me that the price of roofing sheets had gone up overnight, leaving him well short of what was needed for the purchase. He had spent an entire day walking to and from market and lost a day's pay, only to come up empty.

This story captures the experience of living through this sort of economic collapse while on the rural parts of globalization's shoreline—one of inconvenience and frustration, but not necessarily of crisis and catastrophe. Joe did not *need* a new roofing sheet. His existing roof was functional, but since it was starting to fall into disrepair, he was trying to plan ahead and make the purchase before it became a necessity he could not put off. Further, Joe did not have to purchase a machined roofing sheet to shore up the roof of his house. Many residents of Dominase and Ponkrum use bamboo shoots as roofing material. It is cheap and available in several stands around the village. When assembled correctly, a bamboo roof can keep out even the most intense rainfall in the peak of the major rainy season. So Joe's family was in no danger of going without adequate shelter, even without this new roofing sheet. Shelter aside, Joe had plenty of food from his farm to feed himself and his family, and I was adjusting his wages in an effort to keep up with inflation. He had adequate resources to keep himself and his family clothed, sheltered, and reasonably well-fed. In short, this economic crisis produced significant inconveniences for Joe and the other residents of Dominase and Ponkrum, but it did not pose a fundamental challenge to their immediate or long-term well-being. Like everyone else, Joe had to wait out the unstable economy before he could make this purchase, but eventually he did get his roofing sheet. When I returned to Ponkrum in 2004, his house had a new roof.

resources out there to make that kind of change possible. Globalization, as it exists, is simply not in the interest of those living along its shoreline. They cannot benefit from it as much as those of us in advanced economies because we already take up too many resources to allow for tranformative growth and change along globalization's shoreline. Without radical transformations in how we raise our food, manufacture our goods, dispose of or reuse our waste, and generate our energy, globalization will never be in the interest of the majority of those living at its shoreline. Engagement with global markets can only fuel continued consumption by the advanced economies and, perhaps, a select few along the shoreline. The majority will be left to deal with the tide coming in and out, the occasional flood, and the inevitable recession of the floodwaters. To claim otherwise is disingenuous. Unless the way we create and distribute wealth on this planet changes dramatically, the current global economic downturn will be nothing more than the newest convenient scapegoat for rationalizing the inevitable failure of development and globalization to deliver promised changes in human well-being along the shoreline of globalization.

Chapter 11

Understanding the World Anew

The world is not the same place it was only a few years ago. The ongoing economic crisis has cost the advanced economies a tremendous number of jobs and a great deal of wealth. Global assessments show the environmental cost of human economic growth is too high to bear for much longer. In addition, globalization's shoreline is no longer a place we can think of as being detached from our lives or our fate. Our standard of living and rate of economic growth have been predicated on a particular form of globalization, and the access to resources (both natural and human) that allowed for the accumulation of material wealth and goods in advanced economies. Yet, we have operated with very little sense of how globalization, as a process, played out along globalization's shoreline, or what the implications of various changes along this shoreline actually were, not only for people living there but also for those living far away in seemingly isolated advanced economies. Our professed concern for that shoreline was charity, or perhaps pity. Now, we must recognize this concern is in our own self-interest.

We know many of the ways in which our current means of generating economic growth lead to environmental degradation. We can develop technical, political, or social means to address these problems. It is what we do not know—and there is a great deal—that is most worrisome. As previous chapters have demonstrated, in our efforts to learn about what is happening on globalization's shoreline we are often gathering inappropriate data on the economy, environment, and society, and those data are being framed in a way that makes it difficult to learn anything new or useful from them.

To overcome these problems, we need locally specific data. The material presented in this book is grounded in data, but data about two communities in a particular place throughout different points in time. While the experiences of these communities are instructive for thinking about globalization and development, I am not suggesting that the particular intersection of social, economic, and environmental processes in these communities always will be mirrored in other communities. The outcomes of development and globalization are not universal. They create locally specific opportunities and challenges that, in turn, are managed and leveraged by residents with reference to their local social, economic, and environmental needs. It would, therefore, be a mistake to argue that the challenges and opportunities laid out with regard to Dominase and Ponkrum—the ways their people view and deal with these challenges and opportunities, and the outcomes of these processes—are somehow representative of a broad swath of the population living along globalization's shoreline. Each place is different. Therefore, to truly grasp what is going on in the world, we need to know a great deal about a significant sample of these places.

How can we acquire such information in a practical way? The data and lessons presented in the first part of the book were gathered over nine years of study and research, of which 18 months were spent in the field. These time frames are too long for the sort of urgent action required in the face of global economic and environmental change. Further, this kind of research is relatively expensive. Obtaining free data from the World Bank or the United Nations FAO and running national, regional, and global analyses from an office in a developed economy can be done fairly cheaply. It costs quite a bit more to send a trained researcher into the field for six months or more and then pay that person for additional years of research and write-up. On one hand, given the staggering estimated cost of factors such as climate change over the next century (at least 5 percent of Global GDP, according to the *Stern Review on the Economics of Climate Change*), the cost of this sort of research (perhaps $100,000 per year per researcher) seems paltry. On the other hand, I do not want to make yet another argument that we can do this sort of work because it is relatively inexpensive. There are two reasons for this. First, I think these arguments are profoundly unrealistic, as previous efforts to sell this point in the broader context of poverty alleviation (such as Sachs's *End of Poverty* and related events such as the "Live 8" concert) have failed woefully. Second, this argument reproduces the idea that only we living in the advanced economies can do this sort of work, and that those living along the shoreline of globalization need us to do that work for them. Just as they do not need globalization, they do not necessarily need experts (including me) to gather and transmit this information to the larger world. After 60 years of failure resulting from projects and policies designed by experts for those living on globalization's shoreline, it is time to give those living there the opportunity to devise their own solutions, either alone or in concert with the experts who have dominated development thinking for so long.

People are students of the places in which they live. They know better than any outsider ever will about changes to these places and the challenges and opportunities that arise from them. They understand the logic behind particular efforts to manage challenges and leverage opportunities. In short, those living along the shoreline of globalization constitute a vast, untapped database on the changing world. If we are to address the data challenges that lie in the way of productive policy, we need to engage this database.

Note that I did not say we should tap or mine that database. I am fundamentally uncomfortable with the idea of extracting information from those living along globalization's shoreline, especially in a world where that information will benefit the rich as much as the global poor. This sort of activity tends to strip knowledge from people much in the way that mining physically strips minerals from the earth. I am not interested in establishing a new extractive industry along globalization's shoreline. Those living there have had quite enough of extractive industries and processes. Instead we have to build a process of engagement that is both transparent in its goals and practices and provides something tangible to those who participate.

To facilitate this engagement, I suggest we build a network of information, constituted by those on globalization's shoreline and those in advanced economies, that facilitates the flow of information about changes, opportunities, challenges, and responses (failures and successes) to all participants. Rather than just another effort to solve a development or environmental problem through the application of technology, this network could be a means of facilitating the discovery and communication of the many solutions that already exist in communities along globalization's shoreline. In other words, the network is not the solution to our problems. The value of this network is not in the technology, but in how the technology might be used to help us see the world differently.

For those on globalization's shoreline, the most tangible benefit of such a network is access to information about the larger processes, politics, and projects in which they find themselves caught up. In many communities there is little access to information about these processes and, therefore, little understanding of the factors that shape the uncertainty and vulnerability they face every day. Instead, local experience is confined to addressing the manifestations of these processes, such as uncertain rainfall or currency collapse. For the most part residents of globalization's shoreline are left to react to events rather than plan for their management, and as a result the scope and capacity of their efforts to maintain or improve their standard of living are greatly limited. Make no mistake, many people along globalization's shoreline are aware of this problem and yearn for a solution. In 1999 I was at the Sammo Lodge (the Cape Coast guesthouse that was my principal residence when not in the village) watching a report on Ghana Television about the falling price of cocoa. At the time none of us watching the report had any idea of the chaos this falling price would unleash on Ghana's economy over the next year and a half. In the course of a report, a government minister made a vague statement about the falling price of cocoa, and a Ghanaian watching with me stood up and started shouting at the television, "Don't tell me the price is falling! Tell me *why* the price is falling!"

A little knowledge spread through this network of information would go a long way toward building and sustaining the network. Once communities along the shoreline start to understand their position vis-à-vis larger economic and political processes, the hunger will be strong for information about these processes (as well as about their manifestations in other parts of the world). I have seen this hunger at work in India. Colleagues working for TARAhaat, a business and marketing enterprise attached to the Indian nonprofit organization Development Alternatives, working in concert with One World South Asia and British Telecom, are running a project called Lifeline India. The idea behind this project is simple: to provide rural farmers access, via mobile phones, to an agricultural-techniques database maintained by trained experts. Volunteers bring the phones to villages, and for a small fee they can call a number and record their questions. Each farmer receives a reference number for the query and can call back in a day using that reference number to access the reply. The project promises and delivers rapid replies to queries (less than 24 hours) and provides information of great value to farmers. As a result, use of the network has exploded. Where only a few hundred farmers used the network when it came on line in October 2006, within a year the network was receiving around 3,500 queries a month. The number has continued to rise since then, and in January 2009 handled nearly 6,500 queries.

As Lifeline India demonstrates, when communities feel they are receiving information valuable for their daily lives, they will engage. Mobile phones are a key means of making this happen, even along globalization's shoreline. When I arrived in Ghana in 1997, there was virtually no access to mobile phones. This was true through 2000. When I returned in 2004, they were everywhere, and by 2006 it was possible to buy a new, basic phone with a SIM card and a reasonable stock of pay-as-you-go minutes for about $35 in any reasonably sized town in the country. Kiosks selling recharge units for these phones sprang up everywhere, to the extent that wherever I traveled in the country I never worried about finding somewhere to buy them.

Engagement with the envisioned network, though, would be somewhat different than engagement with Lifeline India. Where Lifeline India links individual farmers to a database of agricultural knowledge and a set of experts who provide responses to individual queries, the database I envision will link communities to one another as well as to experts in other parts of the world. This will allow communities in various parts of the world to learn from one another much more directly and rapidly than is possible when such knowledge must first be gathered, organized, and made available through a typical research program or policy initiative. Further, it will allow these communities to tap the experiences of other communities that have tried "expert advice" or are engaging with a particular organization. Ideally, with this cross-community conversation communities will better understand whom they are dealing with when interacting with experts or organizations, and they will have a sense of the community-level view of the benefits and drawbacks associated with a particular solution to their problems. This, in turn, will create healthier negotiations among communities, experts, and organizations as development projects and policies are designed and implemented.

We must also ask what the advanced economies stand to gain from such a network. Someone will have to pay, at least initially, for the design and setup of the interface, for the organization of information-transferal, and must somehow create a situation whereby those living along globalization's shoreline can afford the necessary technology, from phones to computers,

Box 11.1 The Mobile Phone Comes to Ponkrum

When I first arrived in Ghana in 1997, there were almost no mobile phones in the country, and these did not work outside the largest cities. By 2004, though, mobile phones had become common. Upon my arrival in Ghana that year, I borrowed a phone from Bossman Murey, a friend and colleague in the Department of Archaeology at the University of Ghana; purchased a SIM card and some calling minutes; and for less than ten dollars had a phone number in Ghana.

Having a number in Ghana, however, was not the same thing as having a number in Dominase and Ponkrum. In 2004 nobody in these villages owned a mobile phone. This was, perhaps, for good reason. To get a signal in Ponkrum, I had to climb the rather steep hill behind my house and stand in the direct, blazing sun. Even then, the signal sometimes faded out, and my calls were often dropped. When I complained about this to Julius Fobil, a colleague in public health at the University of Ghana, he reminded me that in his village in the north of Ghana people had to climb a tree for a similarly poor signal, and he suggested I stop complaining.

Service improved extremely rapidly between 2004 and 2006, and by the latter year I had a signal in Ponkrum. At the same time, the cost of both phones and minutes dropped due to competition between several new carriers. As a result, a few people in Ponkrum purchased mobile phones, which they charged on car batteries. Walking between Eguafo and Ponkrum in June of that year I saw a farmer put down his machete and take a call while standing in the field next to the path.

These phones have enabled remarkable changes in people's livelihoods and facilitated their efforts to take charge of their own development. Francis Quayson, my long-time research assistant, finds himself in search of wage-paying jobs whenever he is not working on one of my projects. Before, news of such jobs passed by word of mouth, often arriving after the opportunity had passed. Now, Francis receives calls from friends who let him know about opportunities in a timely manner, helping him secure jobs more frequently. Further, Francis and I continue to work together on aspects of my research, and efforts to improve the well-being of those in Dominase and Ponkrum, via phone. For example, since 2006 I have been trying to coordinate the construction of a nursery school in Ponkrum at the request of the women living in both Dominase and Ponkrum. Francis keeps me apprised of progress on the school and calls me if and when progress stalls. With this information I, in turn, can make phone calls to relevant friends and colleagues to keep the project on track. Thus, one resident of Ponkrum uses mobile telephony as a means of securing his own livelihood and negotiating the challenges that emerge from a particular development project in Ponkrum.

to enable their interaction. The overall start-up costs of such a network are relatively small, probably less than $20 million for five years of inception and implementation that could reach several hundred communities and generate a critical mass of communication that would become self-sustaining. Costs will drop dramatically as time goes on, for the interface and database are meant to be open-source and evolving, attracting users so that ongoing costs eventually can be distributed broadly across network users and volunteers. Ideally, the database and interface would eventually be run and maintained by the users themselves—much like Wikipedia, the computer-operating system Linux, or the computer office productivity suite OpenOffice—with voluntary payments from users who are able to afford it, and in-kind contributions from experts in the community of users largely sustaining these initiatives.

It is no small thing to ask for $20 million for a network that nobody will own and that nobody will "profit" from in the classic business sense. However, two key contributions to development initiatives that this network might offer could make such contributions not only possible but likely. First, this database will present an opportunity for connecting development-project design to local needs in a manner that improves outcomes for targeted communities and increases the efficacy of development organizations. The literature critiquing the current project planning and design process within multilateral, bilateral, and nongovernmental organizations is extensive and detailed. In general, the literature argues that this process is not driven by the priorities of the recipient community, but rather is heavily driven by the priorities of the donor constituents to whom these various organizations are beholden.

The most problematic of these situations emerges in the case of bilateral organizations whose funding is directly tied to electoral politics, such as the United States Agency for International Development (USAID). These organizations frequently are pressured by elected officials to enact projects that will benefit individuals or companies in key constituencies and thereby improve their electoral outlook. For example, if an official from a constituency with a factory building turbines for hydroelectric dams is concerned about the long-term prospect of that factory and its employees, the legislator might pressure the development agency to set up a dam-building project somewhere and consider that factory for acquiring the turbine. In such a situation those working for the agency find themselves in a bind. It is unwise to upset an elected official, as an agency's annual budget might come under severe stress the next year in retaliation. However, adding a dam project to the annual budget without first having identified a need for it risks creating a rushed process and the inappropriate introduction of this project into a place that does not need or want it. This sort of political juggling makes it difficult for bilateral development agencies to actually help people improve their standard of living along globalization's shoreline. Contrary to those who blame the failures of development on the quality or avariciousness of the staff of these agencies and other organizations, this highly politicized planning requires strategic and tactical thinking that would stymie the best ideas from the smartest, most altruistic people.

Even though this process of planning and funding is an embarrassment, it is unlikely to change anytime soon. However, the database-and-interface approach I have advocated can work with this system and improve, at least incrementally, how planning and budgeting play out in practice. The evolving database will provide various agencies with information about existing development efforts and needs that can be matched to donor priorities, thus creating a more consistent match between project design and actual on-the-ground needs in communities around the world. By participating in this effort, these organizations will see greater rates of project success and, by extension, more effective use of their resources than is usually seen in current project planning. This does not solve the front-end political problem behind budgeting and planning in development, but it does provide a tangible benefit to a host of agencies that justifies at least some of the start-up cost.

A second way this information can be used is to refine and "ground-truth" early warning systems. Numerous programs seek to predict such events as drought and famine. For example, the Famine Early Warning Systems Network (FEWS NET) aggregates data on seasonal precipitation, vegetation cover, and prices for key food crops in particular places, and evaluates how and when the intersection of various trends, in these and other measures, might result in abnormal food shortages. The results of these exercises are published as reports, briefing papers, and even as maps that indicate where famine is taking place or is likely to take place in the near future.

Programs such as FEWS NET face two fundamental challenges. First, they must identify and measure appropriate indicators of the hazards for which they seek to provide warning and organize these indicators into an appropriate framework or index. Thus, these organizations face the same challenges laid out in chapter 9. By connecting these programs to an evolving database of information about globalization's shoreline, especially the aspects of the database focused on adaptation needs and emerging problems, they will be able to evaluate the relevance of their indicators to the experiences of those communities dealing with a particular hazard. Further, this information will provide a basis against which to measure the organization and analysis of indicators within these programs.

The second challenge facing these organizations is verifying that a predicted hazard is, in fact, taking place and the prediction is not a false alarm. By accessing an evolving database of information about events and processes on globalization's shoreline, organizations will gain entrée to specific, local, experiential information about the projected or modeled hazard. This will allow these early warning systems access to a form of rapid "ground-truthing" of their models and indices, whereby they can cross-check the predictions of their models against actual events on the ground. This is more than a learning exercise that will improve the quality of warnings from these systems. When notifying appropriate aid organizations of predicted crises as they emerge, ground-truthed data on crises are much more effective than modeled projections.

In other words, there is a constituency in the development community for this sort of approach to impacts and outcomes on globalization's shoreline. Asking the various organizations engaged in development planning or early warning systems for the initial investment to get this sort of approach off the ground is not at all unrealistic. Over the long haul, they will gain far more in new and valuable information than they spend to set the network up. Further, for those agencies engaged in development planning, the savings associated with greater rates of project success will likely repay the cost of any contribution in relatively short order. We can do this.

However, building this database does not fundamentally address the conceptual issues with globalization and development that result in our misunderstandings of life on globalization's shoreline. Data alone do not bring a new perspective to the table. Instead, we must learn from this database how globalization and development actually play out in particular places, and new approaches based on this new knowledge must be created. Three principal opportunities for this learning come to mind.

First, we will develop meaningful understandings of the causal pathways through which globalization and development are translated into particular livelihoods and environmental outcomes that simultaneously affect the well-being of those living along globalization's shoreline and those living in advanced economies. As argued previously, this is the central knowledge gap associated with understanding events on globalization's shoreline. This is not to say that the topic is completely ignored in development work. In fact, there is quite a bit of information out there that examines these pathways, either directly or indirectly. However, much of that information is buried in the project reports of organizations engaged in development. These organizations are often so busy with project implementation that they have no time to systematically examine the various specific lessons they learn from particular projects. As a result, most successful organizations have a well-developed understanding of the social issues that are likely to emerge around a particular project in a particular place and have worked out means of addressing these immediate issues. However, these tend to be based on a "best practices" model of what has worked in the past, as opposed to systematic understandings of the social impacts of these adaptations.

Without a systematic understanding of the social impacts associated with particular interventions, these organizations cannot reliably employ their "best practices" across contexts; they will face difficulties in translating the experiences of one community into another, and will find themselves vulnerable to the implementation of projects that, while addressing an immediate need, are not sustainable in the long term and, therefore, do not further community adaptation. By contributing their project-specific knowledge to the database, these agencies and organizations can crowdsource the broader analysis of these data. This will allow development practitioners in these organizations to remain focused on implementation of projects and policies, while the organization's practices will benefit from lessons gleaned from the systematic analysis of its data, and the data of other organizations, at low or no cost.

Second, we will be better able to connect local needs to the policymakers who shape economic policy and development projects. For decades development projects have been plagued by a disconnect between what development professionals (including academics) think is important to local communities and what local communities consider important. Despite a relatively recent push to include community voices in project design, development projects continue to suffer from this disconnect between professional knowledge and local knowledge. Often this shortcoming becomes apparent in development practice only when a project runs into crisis, often a late stage at which point recovery is impossible.

Accessing the massive human database along globalization's shoreline provides a unique opportunity to explore what communities will prioritize if they do not feel they have to meet the needs of outside experts in order to receive desired benefits. After all, if a proposed project will bring a well to a community, the residents will likely answer questions about their needs in a manner that ensures the delivery of the well, even if water supply or quality was a relatively low priority issue in the community. We have no idea what these actual needs will look like, as no network has ever existed that allowed a broad set of communities to articulate their concerns outside the context of a particular project or policy that might shape their responses. This database would provide an opportunity to better understand what factors such as climate change, adaptation, and development mean to these communities, and how our understanding of these ideas can be better aligned with the understandings of the people we seek to help.

Third, by gaining access to detailed information—for example, on livelihoods and land use in a multitude of communities—we will be able to assess meaningfully the cumulative impacts of multiple, heterogeneous efforts to manage or leverage globalization- and development-induced changes in particular places. Local adaptations are taking place throughout particular regions, or even the world, that produce biophysical outcomes. In some cases these impacts aggregate into significant impacts on regional and global scales. In other cases impacts might offset one another. Therefore, it is not enough to presume that if an adaptation is sustainable on a local scale (that is, does not deplete the local resource base), it is appropriate and should be supported. Indeed, the potential for aggregation and offset suggests there is no such thing as local sustainability, since an adaptation that does not deplete local resources might alter larger-scale processes via, say, locally increasing net carbon emissions. Such changes will, over time, contribute to climate changes that do deplete local resources. Therefore, in order to better grasp the impact of local processes on global and regional processes related to climate change, we need a better understanding and measurement of how the impacts of particular adaptations accumulate and offset. Such information will be invaluable to global and regional organizations as they develop adaptation strategies, and it will be a critical tool for communities as they evaluate various adaptation options and their likely outcomes.

To ensure productive learning outcomes from this network—which will facilitate not just data collection but also, and more important, a new view of globalization and development needed to make that data meaningful—we must make it open-source and outside the purview of any single organization. Control of this database by a single user or group of users would likely be disastrous. This is not to suggest there are specific nefarious actors out there who will somehow grab control of the database and interface and turn the information gained through that information to evil purposes. Instead, I am concerned about the ways such control can inadvertently affect the process of learning and engagement critical to the success and sustainability of the network. When a single actor, such as a large multilateral organization, captures this sort of effort, institutional politics and pressures come into play. The questions and answers that are prioritized are often determined by political considerations that have nothing to do with good science, good policy, or the needs of other users of the database. Under these conditions there is a greatly increased likelihood that assumptions about development and globalization, such as those challenged in the first part of this book, will begin to drive both research and policy at the expense of the data coming from the database, with the result of pulling this entire effort into the echo chamber. When questions and answers are driven by institutional politics and founded on assumptions about development and globalization that are not appropriate to globalization's shoreline, the value of the information returning to the communities often becomes tangential, at best, to their needs. This lowers the value of participation and eventually leads to the collapse of the interface and the loss of access to the database.

The only way to avoid this outcome is to prevent such capture. There are two simple ways to do so. First, build the interface via open-source methods and grant all users access to the interface code and SDK so they can build locally appropriate applications that facilitate engagement with the larger database. The shoreline of globalization is an especially fertile site for such application-development, as the limited data capacity of local mobile phone networks has created unique challenges for designers and, therefore, unique competencies. For example, in 2008 the *New York Times* reported on the emergence of Kenyan programmers of mobile phone applications. Rather than focus on high-end, high-bandwidth applications, these programmers were developing unique design skills for applications that had to run on very simple phones at extremely low bandwidths.[1] This is precisely the sort of competency needed to make this network initiative work—competency that comes from the shoreline of globalization. Second, create (or encourage the creation of) mirror versions of the database in various sites around the world. In this manner it will become difficult for a single institution to capture the database and then constrain discussion and learning to its own interests. These two simple techniques to avoid capture of the database can create an environment of constant challenge wherein ideas are tested and accepted or rejected on their merits, not on their political usefulness or institutional origins.

This network could be a tremendous opportunity to change how we view and understand the world. Putting the production of data in the hands of those living along globalization's shoreline will empower them to represent their world to us in ways that are relevant to their needs and experiences. Further, it will enable them more easily to accept or reject the ways we talk about their lives and experiences, and the ways we propose to help them. However, how we build policy from these data requires a fundamental rethinking of policy-making and public participation.

Chapter 12

Truly Participatory Development

To address the challenges that events on globalization's shoreline present to the world, it is not enough simply to build a network from which new and much-needed information can emerge. Information can frame policies and projects, but without the help of those living along the shoreline, we will simply continue to fail where we have failed before. Until now, those living in advanced economies have attempted to guide and control, directly or indirectly, activities along globalization's shoreline in an effort to both maximize the benefits we receive and mitigate the challenges emerging from this part of the world. However, as illustrated time and again in this book, these benefits and emerging challenges have such complex, and locally specific, causes that their centralized management is impossible.

Our crude and inaccurate conceptualizations of globalization and development result in policies and practices akin to grabbing a handful of sand. As we limit our understanding of globalization and development to certain expected, regular outcomes, we tighten our conceptual fist, and more and more of the information we hope to gather and interpret flows out. I fear we have reached a point where most of what we are trying to understand has in fact been squeezed out by our misconceptions, and we are left holding only a few, largely unrepresentative, grains of information. The centralized management of development projects, economic policy, environmental challenges, and environmental policy operates in a similar manner. Distilling the complexity of particular events and processes into a general set of events and processes squeezes out the very local particularities that serve as causal explanations for what we see taking place along globalization's shoreline.

If we truly hope to address the emerging environmental and economic challenges along globalization's shoreline in a manner that creates the best possible future for everyone, those living in the advanced economies must not succumb to the temptation to dictate project and policy design to the rest of the world. Practically speaking, we cannot control the myriad decisions, events, and actions along the shoreline that, in aggregate, result in global-scale economic and environmental impacts. People living in advanced economies do not know best what is happening along globalization's shoreline, nor do we know how best to address the events we do see taking place there. Those living along this shoreline must be brought into the process of policy-making and project design if we hope to create policies that address the challenges to people everywhere.

While this seems to be a relatively straightforward argument, creating circumstances in which people can participate in the creation of policies and projects that affect their daily lives is difficult. For many years now, it has been nearly impossible to discuss development planning or policy without addressing participation, but project and policy failures are still commonplace in development. This is not because participation, in and of itself, does not work. The problem lies, instead, in how participation is used in the planning and design process. There is no universal standard for participation in development practice; different projects and policies engage target communities in very different ways. A growing body of literature suggests that, as a result, "participation" has become a word that means whatever the project designer or organization wants it to mean.

This conceptual flexibility becomes a problem in the context of development practice specifically, and environmental and economic policy in general, because there are significant barriers to the meaningful participation of those most affected by these policies and projects. Therefore, participatory development, whether in the design of a village-level project or in the construction of a national poverty-reduction strategy, tends not to be very participatory. Often, participation is so constrained that the voices of those living along globalization's shoreline cannot be heard in the echo chamber of larger political concerns and misguided understandings of globalization and development (misunderstandings that are ever present in project design and implementation). In the worst cases, participation becomes a means of legitimizing a problematic project or unexpected and unwanted project/policy outcomes.

The warping of participation in development and policy-making is often unintentional and poorly understood. The participation of communities can be constrained by the point in project or policy design at which they are consulted, the questions they are allowed to answer, or the ways in which they are encouraged (intentionally or otherwise) to answer. For example, much development planning that incorporates a participatory component employs surveys of affected populations to gauge community interest and concerns related to the project.[1] Surveys are convenient tools for this sort of work. They can be used to reach a large number of people in the community. The responses tend to be standardized, making the organization and analysis of data relatively easy, but designing a survey to elicit community concerns and ideas is difficult. Given that the complex social situation in Dominase and Ponkrum is quite common in communities along globalization's shoreline, designing a survey to capture the different concerns and ideas circulating within a community requires a detailed understanding of that community. Of course, if that sort of understanding were available, there would be no need for the survey, but without this level of comprehension, the risk of inappropriate questions or options for response is high.

Limiting the possible concerns of the community to a set of preselected choices may constrain the answers of community members to relatively low-priority concerns. Simply providing an option for an "other" among these responses is not enough to ensure that this does not occur. In many cases communities being surveyed know they are likely to receive some form of material benefit from their participation in the project, and they are not willing to provide answers that could upset project planners or undermine the basis for the project. People know what the "right" answer is, even when that answer has nothing to do with what they really think. If the organization on hand is interested in clean water issues, the community members will likely prioritize water in their responses to any needs assessment from that NGO, whether or not they see water as a real problem. There is no intent here by the organization to constrain the participation of the community in this project, but the very structure of inquiry around this hypothetical project has this result de facto.

It is worth considering two illustrations of participation gone wrong to illustrate the scope of the challenge at hand. The Millennium Village Project (MVP) is an excellent example of how participation can go wrong at the project level, handicapping even the best-intentioned plans. The MVP emerged from a much larger program framed around the Millennium Development Goals (MDGs), a UN-led initiative to address extreme poverty by identifying key problems, setting targets for solving at least some aspects of these problems, and making a timetable to meet these targets. For example, goal number one of the MDGs is to eradicate extreme poverty and hunger. A key problem identified under goal one is the number of people living on less than a dollar per day. For this key problem the target is to cut the number of people living in this circumstance by half. Like all Millennium Development Goals, this is to be achieved by 2015.

In 2002 the UN evaluated progress being made toward the MDGs and found that many people living along globalization's shoreline were not likely to see the achievement of these goals by the 2015 target date. In response to this finding, Secretary-General Kofi Annan initiated a three-year advisory effort called the United Nations Millennium Project to find practical means of achieving the MDGs on schedule in all countries. Developed by the United Nations Millennium Project and the Earth Institute at Columbia University, the MVP is an initiative aimed at understanding how best to achieve the MDGs in practical ways at the village level.

The MVP has three main goals.[2] First, according to the Millennium Villages Project Web site (www.millenniumvillages.org), it seeks to provide "rigorous proof of concept for integrated, community-based, low-cost interventions" that will serve as a practical means to achieving the MDGs in rural Africa. Second, the project tries to identify means of scaling up these interventions to support regional and national development strategies focused on the MDGs. Third, the project seeks to expand its efforts over ten years to examine further sites in Africa and other parts of globalization's shoreline.

The project takes as its starting point the MDGs in the framing of all local projects. For example, the Millennium Villages Project Web site contains the following description of community participation:

> An open dialogue [between MDG-trained teams and groups or committees of villagers] will cover topics such as local problems as related to the MDGs, constraints and opportunities for achieving the MDGs at their village level, initial discussions on possible solutions and approaches for achieving the MDGs, and general impressions/consensus on being included as a Millennium Villages Project site.

In this way villagers are encouraged to frame their concerns in terms of the MDGs, which allows for the framing of cross-village understandings of the efficacy of particular interventions in achieving a shared set of goals, and potentially serves as a means of making village-level concerns intelligible to the national-level policy-makers who use the MDGs as a framework for development policy.

However straightforward and practical this project may seem, its very foundations present significant challenges for meaningful community participation in the projects that will take shape in these villages. Simply put, the MVP begins from preconceived notions both of what constitutes a problem to be dealt with in a particular place and how to deal with that problem. The project has no clear means of accounting for how its preconceived frameworks and understandings of problems and solutions will align with, or obscure, local identification of problems and solutions.

The problem of preconceived challenges and solutions pervades the MVP. Jeffrey Sachs, a globe-trotting development economist, writing with John McArthur, argues that the MVP is built upon the "core truth" that there are "known packages of effective and generally low-cost interventions" that can and should be applied to the challenges of extreme poverty.[3] In other words, the MVP is a proving ground for the selected packages of interventions that its leaders have more or less called foolproof. This is a dubious claim. If, in fact, there were such packages, they would be in common use, and we would have little problem achieving the Millennium Development Goals. Indeed, the very presence of the MVP calls this assertion into question, as the MVP, itself, is an effort to get the world back on track to achieving the MDGs. The subtle implication here is that we know how to fix poverty, but we choose not to do so. I suggest this stance is a rather unfair reading, and perhaps a significant misunderstanding, of development's failures over the past six decades.

The idea that we already know how to address poverty and other development challenges, however, has significant implications for participation. On one hand, the project has an interest in validating the problems identified in the MDGs and the interventions of the MVP. On the other hand, the project is supposed to develop locally appropriate interventions in concert with the villagers, such as in the following claim on the MVP Web site: "The list of candidate interventions derived from the U.N. Millennium Project serves as a template from which the villages can begin their assessment and project planning. The project team will encourage inclusion of other actions identified by the villagers." In many cases this dual focus of the project will result in a conflict of interest on the part of project workers when local concerns do not align with either the MDGs or preconceived interventions. In such situations it is not possible to support both

the MDG-oriented interventions of the MVP and locally identified problems. It is unclear how such conflicts will be resolved. The long history
of development strongly suggests that any resolution will not be in the
villagers' favor.

The MVP faces another challenge to participation in its surprisingly
simplistic representation of the communities, hypothetical or real, in
which it is working. The project seems to have little sense of the diversity
of people and, therefore, little sense of the diversity of problems that will
be encountered, at the village scale. Consider the following description
of needs-assessment and community engagement from the Millennium
Village Project Web site, a description representative of the limited literature on this project:

> Members of the Millennium Villages Project team will visit selected villages
> and conduct one to two needs assessments with the villagers. During this
> visit, the project team will discuss the MDGs with the villagers and will
> work with them to identify specific problems in the village, reasons for these
> problems, and attempts by the government, village or other groups or indi-
> viduals to address these problems.

What I find surprising is the way the project seems to treat villagers as
an undifferentiated group whose concerns can be captured as a whole.
The examples of Dominase and Ponkrum have made it clear this approach
will overlook the complex, varied experiences of life along globalization's
shoreline in every community, no matter how small. We cannot simply
lump the residents of these communities together, disregarding their social
status or role, and hope to understand their behaviors in a meaningful
way. Unless the MVP examines the heterogeneity of village society and
implements some means of identifying and bringing forth various voices
in a given village, it is likely the project will identify and focus only on the
problems of the powerful at the expense of poorer members of the community, with their limited rights and capacities, such as the women heads
of households in Dominase and Ponkrum. The needs and desires of the
wealthiest households in these villages have little to do with the issues of
land tenure and gender roles that compromise the well-being of women
heading households. Therefore, interventions that do not critically consider this situation could result in damage (for example, to the resilience
of livelihoods crucial for the management of a particular local problem by
these women). For example, the privatization of landholding in Dominase

and Ponkrum would greatly empower wealthy households, while doing little for women heading households, who can make no claim on newly privatized family lands and have no savings from which to purchase such land. In the long run, privatized landholding would likely result in disaster for all households. In the short run, such interventions would do nothing to address the needs of female-headed households and, indeed, might create more problems than they solve for these women, and perhaps for the larger population.

What, then, does participation mean for the MVP? It is clear that those working on the MVP intend to integrate community input into project design and implementation, with the goal of creating more successful and sustainable improvements in the standard of living in participating villages. However, the structure of the project, from its initial assumptions about the problems facing those living along globalization's shoreline to its belief in the efficacy of particular packages of interventions, makes it unlikely the voices of those living in these villages will be heard in a meaningful way. Telling villagers how to phrase their problems and asking them to choose from a short list of possible solutions do not constitute participation. These are exercises in getting people to tell you what you want to hear.

Why does the issue of participation matter in the context of the MVP? In short, without significant participation and project flexibility, the MVP is nothing new in development. It is just another project, like so many that have come before, presuming to tell people what their problems are and how to solve them. As a result, I have no faith that these projects will work, in the long run. I find it telling that the Millennium Villages Web site (www.millenniumvillages.org) contains only two reports from villages. One, from Sauri, Kenya, the first Millennium Village, is for 2004–05. The other, for Koraro, Ethiopia, dates to 2005–06. Nine other villages are covered in the 2006–07 MVP annual report. All these reports are year-one summaries. There are no longitudinal data for project progress for any of these 11 villages. All have been in operation for at least two full years, and Sauri has been running for nearly five years. There has been enough time to see clear trends in well-being that might speak to the efficacy of the "known packages of interventions" being applied in each village.

If these trends were positive and provided support for the MVP's approach, they would be highly visible. Instead they are inaccessible. There are vague summaries of "intervention highlights" for each village on the Millennium Villages Web site, but these summaries do not present an overall picture of how the lives of those in these villages are being meaning-fully transformed by engagement with the project. Virtually all the results listed under these highlights could have been achieved by pouring aid into the villages under any standard development project. I believe the MVP is failing, at least in part, because it does not meaningfully incorporate those living in the villages into the project design.

The above issues with the MVP are evident to many who work on ques-tions of poverty, development, and environment along globalization's shoreline. One must ask, then: What has allowed this project to gain fund-ing and support? While it is to some extent a product of the personalities associated with it (for example, Jeffrey Sachs and Bono), the appeal of the MVP also stems from the ways in which it fits into the existing thinking on development, including participation in the formation of development policy and projects. In short, the MVP is not a uniquely problematic proj-ect, but rather an example of how participation falls apart in development practice, allowing the echo chamber of globalization and development to persist intact.

The MVP gains traction in the development community because it operates in nearly the same manner (and with the same assumptions) as broader development policy. Consider Poverty Reduction Strategy Papers (PRSP), an effort by the IMF and World Bank to facilitate the creation of country-specific poverty-reduction policies.[4] The PRSP approach, introduced in 1999, is framed around five principles. First, the papers are supposed to be produced by the governments of par-ticular countries in concert with civil society. This process is meant to be broadly participatory. Second, the papers are to be results-oriented, focused on outcomes that benefit the poor, as opposed to the dogmatic application of particular approaches to poverty (here the PRSP process runs contrary to the MVP). Third, PRSPs are meant to address poverty as a multidimensional phenomenon, instead of as a singular problem. In other words, the IMF and World Bank recognize that it makes little sense to treat a community that has inadequate safe drinking water, sig-nificant malaria problems, and little access to education as one that is suffering from "poverty." Instead, any policy aimed at alleviating the conditions of poverty in this community have to deal specifically with each of its constituent problems. Fourth, the resultant policy document is meant to foster partnership between donors, governments, and the people of a given country. Fifth, these policies are to take a long view of addressing poverty reduction, building solutions that are sustainable over a long period of time.

PRSPs are not merely documents, but are the end result of an effort to build participation into policy and project development. Yet, a more careful reading of the purpose behind PRSPs, and the process through which they are developed, suggests significant barriers to participation that sound rather similar to those arising in the context of the MVP. PRSPs are not merely about poverty reduction. They are also policy documents created as requirements, conditions, for receiving aid funds or debt relief from the IMF and World Bank. In short, they are documents that enable governments to access needed loans and aid. This is a perfectly reasonable requirement. By mandating PRSPs as a condition of receiving needed loan funds, the IMF and World Bank can put significant pressure on national governments to increase the levels of citizen participation in the creation of poverty-alleviation policies. However, it is not enough that a country works up a poverty reduction strategy and formalizes that policy in a PRSP. The IMF and World Bank assess the document and have the power to reject it if it does not provide "a credible framework within which the Bank and the IMF can design their assistance programs."[5] Despite the careful disclaimers that precede this statement—including the fact that the IMF and World Bank do not have to agree with all analyses, targets, and public actions in the plan or even believe that the plan is the best possible strategy for the country—this is still a serious instance of constraint. No matter what the disclaimers say, in practice the PRSPs must align with the broad philosophies of the World Bank and the IMF to be accepted and for the aid and loans to be released. Thus, in the end the IMF and World Bank still decide, in a broad philosophical sense, what constitutes an appropriate policy for poverty reduction in a particular country, even if the government and people of that country disagree with this overarching philosophy.

This constraint, while apparently broad, significantly impacts the practice of poverty alleviation. Both the World Bank and the IMF take a broadly market-led approach to development, which means that a PRSP that advocated price controls on key foods or protective tariffs on key industries to protect worker jobs would not contain recommendations upon which acceptable assistance programs could be designed. Thus, a whole suite of policy options are taken off the table in the PRSP process, without regard for the appropriateness of those options in the country at hand. This takes on special urgency when one considers that since 1950 the only places that have transformed themselves from developing to advanced economies—for example, South Korea, Taiwan, and Singapore—greatly restricted trade, protected domestic industries as they matured, and generally operated under less than democratic political structures until such time as they could compete in global markets and these restrictions were phased out. In short, it is impossible to get a PRSP approved without taking the only successful model of contemporary development off the table.

This process creates a terrible conflict of interest for the governments of these countries. These documents and policies are meant to be country-owned and developed through a broad participatory process that engages the general citizenry of the country. However, if the citizenry does not propose or agree with policies and projects that generally mesh with the development philosophy of the IMF and the World Bank, the government will not be able to produce a paper that enables access to needed aid or loans. In these situations what is a government to do? For all the rhetoric in official policy documents of the IMF and World Bank about the importance of democracy and citizen participation in their national political processes, these two massive organizations are not simply going to revise their philosophies to better suit the desires of the poorest people in the poorest countries. Because the IMF and World Bank will not back down, national governments often find themselves caught between the desires of their citizens and the philosophy of the IMF and World Bank. In these situations governments have a powerful inducement to suppress the participation of their citizens.

These problems with participation are already manifest in the PRSP processes of several countries. For example, in Zambia[6] the PRSP process has had a mixed set of outcomes. On the positive side, what was once a weak set of citizen organizations was, in the context of the PRSP process, organized into an NGO network called Civil Society for Poverty Reduction (CSPR). Because of their participation in this process and the government's willingness to engage them in the context of policy-making, these organizations and the citizens they represent have higher expectations for participation in the development process, including increased oversight of the release and use of aid funds and an increased voice in the decision of the government to take on new loans. Thus, the PRSP process has fostered participation in policy-making and project planning.

At the same time, the Zambian PRSP process highlights the limits to this new participation. The Zambian government largely sees the PRSP process as a means of mobilizing aid resources and gaining debt relief. This approach makes the stated goal, poverty alleviation, a secondary consideration to the adequate fulfillment of a requirement for access to aid and loans. The citizenry and citizen organizations, on the other hand, expect the PRSP process to focus on poverty reduction. The result has been ongoing debate between the government and its citizens over the shape of poverty-reduction policy and the implementation of projects aimed at the goals laid out in the Zambian PRSP. In its most problematic moments, this tension has resulted in clear constraints on citizen participation as the government reaches the limits of what it will tolerate in terms of oversight. For example, the Zambian government suspended a monitoring and tracking team in which citizen organizations had a voice after the team reported abuses of poverty-alleviation funds unlocked by the successful completion of the PRSP process.

Taken together, the MVP and the PRSP process illustrate the pervasive problems with participation in development. I believe that both of these initiatives were designed with the best of intentions, and participation was included as a good-faith effort to bring a broad set of voices into the planning of projects (the MVP) and policy (PRSPs). Neither initiative set out to disenfranchise those living along the shoreline of globalization. However, both operate with significant, but completely unacknowledged, constraints that make real participation difficult if not impossible to achieve. Because of their considerable policy baggage resulting from their institutional ties, participation falls apart and both projects become efforts to control highly complex, heterogeneous situations through a set of standardized philosophies (PRSPs) and interventions (MVP). Inadvertently, the message of both projects becomes "You can participate, as long as you say what we need you to say." The right to agree is not the same thing as participation. What we are left with is the same development-planning process as before, only now with a veneer of participation that makes it more difficult to see where these projects go wrong. And they are going wrong.

So what do we do? How can we overcome a problem that has plagued even the best-intentioned, well-funded, and well-staffed projects? There are a few points of intervention where this might be possible. First, let's return to the idea (presented in the previous chapter) of the database-and-interface model of learning about, and learning from, those living on the shores of globalization. One of the principal reasons I insist that this whole approach be open-sourced and not dependent on a single source of funding is to prevent the very conflicts of interest that plague the MVP and the PRSP process. If the constraints created by institutional philosophies and politics are removed, many of the conflicts among those living on globalization's shoreline, their governments, and outside organizations disappear.

However, this does not solve all our problems. The emergent forms of information and knowledge that will likely characterize the interface-and-database model of interaction will provide new ideas about how to improve the material standard of living for people around the world; how to manage the various manifestations of climate change and economic transformation that mark the world today; and how to achieve better understandings of the lives of those who seem distant but are, in fact, closely tied to us and our well-being. But these ideas and information, like the information on Dominase and Ponkrum presented earlier, will often run contrary to existing understandings of how the economy, the environment, and indeed the world work. These ideas will encounter significant resistance in policy circles, development organizations, and national governments because they call into question policies and projects of the past and present. This will exacerbate existing tensions, for example those between the citizens of Zambia and their government over the use and oversight of funds aimed at poverty alleviation. These problems cannot be overcome through reliance on new institutional structures as much as they can be overcome by a change in the philosophy determining what we think participation is.

The geographer Katharine McKinnon has suggested that a way forward for participation in development is to give up on a universal definition of the term, an idea I find intriguing for two reasons. First, it is a somewhat terrifying vision that gives up on the idea of a standardized notion of participation that might be applied or measured across contexts. Second, it is also a thrilling vision because it actually might work, especially in the context of an interface-and-database approach to the shoreline of globalization.

McKinnon argues that a universal definition of "participation" is impossible because it means different things in different places and at different times. Rather than take this as a moment of despair, she sees an opportunity. If participation can never be defined outside a specific project or policy-design process, then it must be defined by those affected in the context of a given project or policy. In other words, the very idea of participation becomes a matter of political negotiation at the outset of a project or policy process; and a shared definition of participation, agreed upon by those affected by the project or policy, becomes a prerequisite to further movement.

The problem is, that by the time it becomes apparent there are competing views of participation, project and policy development are generally beyond a point where this participation can be productively negotiated, leading to breakdowns in communication and to the dominant organization's, or actor's, interpretation winning out. For example, in the case of the Zambian PRSP, the citizen organizations saw participation as meaning they would get to help shape poverty-reduction policy to better suit their needs, monitor the use of the funds aimed at poverty reduction, and contribute to decisions about future loans and aid. The Zambian government saw participation as a process of input into a document that would facilitate its acceptance by the World Bank and IMF, thereby unlocking needed aid and loans. The government had no intention of allowing citizen groups any meaningful oversight of the use of the funds or a real voice in decisions about loans and aid. However, by the time the citizen organizations came to understand this clearly, they had already participated in the PRSP process, legitimizing the government's claim to the needed aid and loans. They had given away any leverage they might have had over what participation means within the context of poverty-alleviation policy and projects in Zambia, allowing the government effectively to marginalize their concerns, at least until the next round of PRSP development.

At this point in development policy and practice, arguing against participation is a bit like arguing against clean air and water—it is politically infeasible. Therefore, participation will remain a significant component of project and policy approval going forward, giving those in affected communities a tremendous amount of leverage *if they are willing to argue about what participation means before they agree to participate*. If the residents of Sauri were unwilling to participate in the MVP until there was agreement over the terms of participation, those working on the MVP would have been left with two choices: abandon work at Sauri, and in so doing concede they are not that interested in local participation; or negotiate with the community over what participation means, creating real opportunities for local voices to be heard even when those voices say things that do not support the general philosophy or the specific interventions supported by the MVP. If citizen organizations in Zambia had refused to participate in the PRSP process until there was a formal, negotiated agreement over what shape that participation would take, the government would have been

Box 12.1   Participation in Dominase and Ponkrum

I often tell people that the outcome of my entire research program in Dominase and Ponkrum can be traced to a single day and a single exchange during my first field season in 1997. On our first day of mapping (see chapter 5), I chose to start with the occupied part of Dominase because that part of the village would not require a lot of work with machetes. As Francis, Samuel, and I began to pull tapes and measure the corners of houses, Ekow Ackon emerged from his house. In Dominase, Ekow was one of four living brothers who were the grandchildren of the last chief of the village. I had met with and discussed my research project with the other three brothers, but Ekow had not been in Dominase during the week. He introduced himself, and it became clear that he spoke English (unlike everyone else in Dominase) and that he had an education. He asked several pointed questions, and I could tell that he was skeptical of my plans. Unsure of what to do, I proceeded with the mapping under his watchful eye.

A few minutes later Francis, Samuel, and I came to the remains of a partially collapsed house that had been abandoned, and we began to map it in. Ekow wandered over and asked me why I was mapping an abandoned house. I explained that I needed to map the remains of every structure I could find so that I could develop an understanding of the changing landscape of the village over time. "Well," said Ekow, "if you are mapping fallen houses, there was one right there." He pointed to a low mound of dirt so eroded that I had mistaken it for a slightly uneven portion of his yard. After I asked Ekow if he could remember where the corners of the house were, he walked over and pointed them out. I immediately mapped the remains of the house and asked him if he could remember where the doors and windows had been located. He told me, and I drew them onto my map. Ekow broke into a wide smile and began to trot around the village, pointing out every structure he could remember and volunteering everything he could about each structure. Simply by listening to him, and taking him seriously, I had gained access to a wealth of information about this landscape I would have otherwise overlooked.

This is not to say that this initial exchange converted Ekow into my unquestioning ally. Instead he became one of the most challenging people I worked with in these villages. Because he knew I was listening to him and that I had a genuine interest in trying to answer his questions, he would press me about what he considered to be the real challenges facing residents of Dominase and Ponkrum, and he asked how my research would address those challenges. He questioned my conclusions and my motivations all the time, and though I could not always answer him to his (or my own) satisfaction, we developed a trust and respect that I know he communicated to other residents. In short, he participated in my research project, but on his own terms. As a result, he made me constantly consider my own motivations and goals in conducting my project, which enriched my research questions and results.

At the same time, I also had to negotiate my relationship with Ekow constantly. In 2006, as I worked with colleagues from the University of Cape Coast to plan a project that would benefit as wide a segment of the community as possible, Ekow, like all the other men in the village, largely ignored project ideas that might address the specific challenges faced by women in their everyday lives. Although he and I spoke about the needs of the residents, Ekow's distinctly gendered view of those challenges did not include such things as the strains of domestic labor or the particular challenges associated with crops grown predominantly by women. To his credit, when I pushed him on these issues, he would acknowledge them and sometimes discuss them at length. He was rarely dismissive of women's issues, but they were not at the front of his mind in our conversations. Thus, fostering Ekow's open and constantly renegotiated participation in my project did not mean that I had to uncritically accept his claims, or those of any other member of the community, no matter how well meaning they might have been. If I had simply listened to Ekow when trying to identify an appropriate community project, I would never have realized how important the issue of child care was to many of the households in the village, and that option might not have been offered to the villagers for their selection.

unable to access the aid and loans it wanted without first giving its citizens a significant voice in the process and its outcomes.

A network that links communities to one another could enable the sorts of conversations that allow citizens and communities to know that they can argue about this and learn about strategies for making the sort of arguments that were effective in other places and contexts. This is not to suggest that the people working on the MVP or those in the government of Zambia are bad people who do not care about the ideas and experiences of those living along the shoreline of globalization. I am advocating negotiation over the idea of participation because it forces even the best intentioned people to consider, and make explicit, their own ideas about participation, development, and life at the shoreline of globalization. It is impossible to question one's own beliefs and biases until you have confronted them in an explicit manner.

Here, the proposed database approach to understanding globalization's shoreline takes on an important role as communities anywhere in the world can contact one another to discuss how to start such negotiations, what to negotiate for, and what sort of results other communities have had in their negotiations. This will create a process of negotiation in which both sides are well informed about the intentions of the other and both sides will have to address the other in a serious way. In this sort of negotiation, policy-makers and practitioners who might otherwise be unable or unwilling to move beyond their assumptions about how globalization and development work along globalization's shoreline can approach the emergent information about life along this shoreline flowing out of its residents' massive, open-sourced database of experiences and information. Further, this database of information can become a critical negotiation tool, a source that communities and citizenry can use to support claims about their needs, experiences, and capacities. This database can become the site through which these communities, in their negotiations over participation and their experiences of globalization, development, and environmental change, can become more than exceptions to the rule; they can become particular expressions of how life really works along globalization's shoreline.

Chapter 13

Two Futures (Out of Many)

We have choices. One is to continue to get globalization and development wrong and, in turn, keep failing in our efforts to build a sustainable future. The other is to build a different future founded on new ways of gathering data, on new sources of information, and on new forms of collaboration between those in advanced economies and those living on globalization's shoreline. Continuing on our current path meets with the least amount of resistance. For decades we have invested in ideas, studies, and solutions that have slowly but steadily refined information that does not tell us what we need to know or bring about the outcomes we hoped to see. Each study, measurement, and idea builds upon those that came before and informs those that come after. The assumptions at the heart of the entire practice of development and the perceived benefits of globalization have been reiterated so many times and in so many venues that they no longer seem to be contestable claims about the world so much as they are considered simple, self-evident, descriptive statements about how the world works. For those who live their professional lives in this world, it is extremely difficult to deal with cases that run contrary to these apparently universally held beliefs about development and globalization. The very idea that development might actually be part of the problem, and that globalization might systematically produce significant negative issues among the many populations it is meant to benefit, appears irrational. Thus, cases such as Dominase and Ponkrum, which call these assumptions into question, are dismissed as outliers, as unique exceptions that exist outside the *real* story of globalization and development.

Yet, a brief step outside this echo chamber and into the places where real people live real lives calls all these assumptions into question. In many cases apparent exceptions are, in fact, the real story of globalization and development. Dominase and Ponkrum, and thousands of communities like them, bear witness to the fact that globalization and development do not always work as we think they work. When you are standing with a farmer in his field of failing corn, it is nearly impossible to tell him his experience is not real, or representative, or all that important in the grand scheme of global progress. If we can accept that globalization and development are much more unruly processes than we typically imagine, and that they are not, in any organized way, leading toward a future we want to occupy, we all have a chance to rethink our engagements with one another, from how we share information to how we build projects and policies, and build that future.

The question, then, is whether governments, development agencies, and international organizations will try to see what is happening on the ground in communities around the world and deal with that reality, or continue to live in their self-imposed echo chamber. This choice will have substantial impact on the future in which we will live. To illustrate this impact, I present two scenarios of future Earths. One plays out under business as usual, with development and economic policy carrying current assumptions into the future. The other envisions a world wherein these policies begin to respond to, and engage with, those living on globalization's shoreline. These scenarios are merely two plausible futures from many possible pathways. The course of global environment, economy, and politics is shaped by far too many factors to make realistic predictions possible. Both a seemingly small event, such as a routine election in an advanced economy, or a highly visible terrorist attack, can have tremendous cascading effects that can reshape future pathways, not only of national and global politics, but also of global environmental and economic outcomes. The futures I offer in this chapter are grounded in state-of-the-art knowledge about the changing global climate and environment captured by the Millennium Ecosystem Assessment (MA) and GEO-4. My scenarios have much in common with some of the scenarios posed in these two assessments, but mine speak more clearly to how our policies will shape these futures and therefore point a clearer path to the sorts of policy change that can create an alternative outcome.

The scenarios extrapolated from the experiences of Dominase and Ponkrum concretely illustrate how certain assumptions will play out for real people along globalization's shoreline. Global predictions about the future state of the economy, environment, and politics are implicit in these scenarios. Those interested in the global ramifications of the events described here should refer to the MA and GEO-4.

Both of my scenarios rest upon a set of shared assumptions. The first is that current regimes of agricultural subsidy and protection in the advanced economies will come to an end before 2020. The convergence of environmental necessity and global-trade pressure makes this outcome a near certainty. The second assumption is that Ghana's offshore oil reserves will come online in 2011, and that the country will not succumb to unchecked corruption and attendant challenges often seen in petro-states. Third, current trends in regional precipitation and the overfishing of the Gulf of Guinea will continue following current trajectories (and in the case of the Gulf of Guinea until the fishery collapses). The long-term trends in precipitation in West Africa are not certain, but for the purposes of this exercise I will extend the current trend into the future. The fourth assumption is that the logic of livelihoods decision-making in Dominase and Ponkrum will not change dramatically in the face of new shocks. This does not mean livelihoods will not change, but any change in livelihoods will follow the dual logic of maintaining the authority of men over their households while meeting the material needs of the household. If these two goals come into conflict, the maintenance of authority will be the overriding factor. In both scenarios I use data reported in the Millennium Ecosystem Assessment and GEO-4 to inform the timing of economic and environmental events.

The principal distinction between these scenarios lies in how we believe globalization and development work In the first scenario, which represents business as usual, both economic policy generally and development policy specifically will continue to operate with many of the same beliefs about globalization and development that shape such policy today. Specifically, policy-makers will continue to ignore the long histories of globalization and development along globalization's shoreline and act as if more development (connecting more places to global markets), is the best path toward an environmentally and economically sustainable future. Further, they will continue to believe that globalization and development make things happen directly and predictably. They will continue to see globalization as inevitable and irreversible, and to treat cases where globalization leads to negative outcomes as outliers, at least for the next few decades. Policy- and development-project design processes will be based on the same problematic data and will engage local participation largely as a box to be checked in the planning and design process. In this scenario the voices of those living along the shoreline will not rise to the level of those making policy or designing projects, unless those voices are reporting events or data that support established assumptions about globalization and development. Thus, there will be little learning from mistakes and little ability to see what is actually happening along globalization's shoreline. In this scenario, the potential for unpleasant surprises in terms of environmental and economic change is, therefore, high.

In the second scenario, I envision a world in which development and economic policy are generated with reference to actual events on globalization's shoreline, and created in the recognition that the well-being of those living there is a critical component of the well-being of those living in advanced economies. Under this scenario large development agencies such as the World Bank will generate a more realistic (as opposed to dogmatic) view of globalization and development that allows for the reconsideration and rethinking of policies and projects in light of previous failures. Further, the policies and projects flowing from these organizations will be aimed at fostering locally specific understandings of well-being, with an eye toward maintaining the natural resource base upon which the global economy and human society are built. New sources of data will be considered, as old metrics fail to capture information critical to the design of projects and policies that can bring about productive outcomes for people and environments along globalization's shoreline. The design of both projects and policies will recognize that globalization and development are catalysts for local change and, therefore, project outcomes will be framed more in terms of desired trends and general outcomes, rather than specific outcomes measured in predetermined ways. The voices of those living along globalization's shoreline are critically important to the creation of projects and policies and to the monitoring of their outcomes. As a result, both projects and policies will become much more efficient in improving the quality of life for residents of globalization's shoreline.

The principal difference between these two scenarios lies in how we perceive the workings of globalization and development. However, this small change in perception can flow into two very different futures, with important divergences appearing in the very near future.

Scenario 1. Business as Usual: Living in the Echo Chamber

In 2011 Ghana's large offshore oil reserves came online, flooding the country with revenue via rising oil prices as the global economic recovery drove increasing demand for petroleum. With little refining capacity of its own, however, Ghana remained dependent on the importation of refined fuels to meet its transportation and energy needs. To compensate for rising prices, the government used the sale of some of its oil revenues to subsidize the price of gasoline and keep transportation costs manageable for the average Ghanaian. The use of taxis and tro-tros continued to grow rapidly as shared transportation reached further and further into rural Ghana.

For the residents of Dominase and Ponkrum, the beginning of oil revenues and the subsidization of gasoline were a boon. The government, awash in revenues and carrying relatively little debt, invested heavily in infrastructure, bringing electricity to these villages in 2012 and surfacing the local roads with tarmac in 2013. Transportation to and from Dominase and Ponkrum was abundant and cheaper than at any point in their history. The declining cost and increasing availability of transportation improved the efficiency of agricultural marketing for the residents of these villages, driving agricultural incomes up.

What truly transformed life in these villages, though, was the explosion of the Ghanaian economy in the wake of the new oil revenues. Having learned from the mistakes of other oil-rich countries, such as nearby Nigeria, the Ghanaian government managed to avoid the rampant corruption that plagues so many petro-states by quickly investing its new revenues in infrastructure—for example, a reliable electrical grid and new solar generating facilities in the Upper East and Upper West Regions. This rapid spending, while temporarily increasing the country's national debt, prevented the accumulation of large, tempting cash reserves resulting from the new oil revenues. Such reserves had, in other states, invited corruption. At the same time, this infrastructure created a favorable climate for business development, and international investment began to flow into the country, spurring the growth of the overall economy. Jobs in construction and in unskilled areas opened up rapidly. The residents of Dominase and Ponkrum, newly connected to these labor markets via their improved roads, were able to take advantage of the demand for wage labor.

Men were the principal beneficiaries of this economic surge, taking up many unskilled job opportunities. Because these jobs kept them away from their farms, these men changed their agricultural strategies. They reduced their farm sizes and focused on the cultivation of low-maintenance tree crops. At the same time, their greatly increased wages and reduced farm sizes allowed women to take up land, enlarging their own farms and their farm incomes. Rapidly growing towns such as Elmina and Cape Coast drove food prices up, increasing women's incomes throughout these villages. Many women were able to diversify into petty trading, though profits from this activity fell off a bit once everyone was able to get to and from markets in Elmina and Cape Coast easily and cheaply.

In 2017, under pressure from the World Trade Organization and a surprisingly coordinated push from the G-77 coalition of developing nations, agricultural markets in advanced economies opened to nearly unrestricted imports from those living on globalization's shoreline. The paramount chief of the Eguafo Traditional Area, having experience dealing with European buyers for citrus products from the villages under his leadership, set up an agricultural collective, creating a pool of crops large enough to attract the attention of agricultural exporters. In Dominase and Ponkrum maize and citrus prices skyrocketed. The surge in citrus prices benefited men, who were already planting this tree crop on their farms as part of their shift in agricultural strategy. As prices for citrus rose, these men used the profits to obtain saplings and plant new plots of citrus each season, augmenting their rising wage incomes with now-rising agricultural income.

This had a dual impact. First, land under tree-crop cultivation did not rotate into fallow, forcing food crops onto an ever-decreasing stock of land available for swidden farming (rotating farm plots in and out of fallow to allow for the recovery of soil fertility). Fallow times quickly fell below the needed three to five years, and those engaged in food-crop production, especially women, found themselves increasingly dependent on inputs such as fertilizer to insure continuing harvests from the increasingly depleted land. Second, household incomes became ever more dependent on a shrinking number of crops, lowering the resilience of both the local agroecology and their livelihoods to agricultural shocks, such as the blight that struck coconut trees at the turn of the twenty-first century.

The surge in men's agricultural income was critical for women, as it allowed them to maintain their larger farms even as maize prices rose. Because men's incomes were rising about as quickly as women's, these changes did not upset household power relations. Further, there were relatively few sources of stress within these households, as they now had enough income to more than meet their material needs, even in the context of rising food prices. However, women's incomes became somewhat less diverse as many women, seeing a reduced profit from petty trading, began to use their agricultural profits for the purchase of seeds and fertilizers that further improved their farm productivity as fallow times decreased. Women's incomes may have risen steeply after the freeing of global agricultural markets, but some of this increase came at the cost of their economic resilience.

By 2020 nearly all the children in Dominase and Ponkrum could speak English, thanks to ever-improving standards in the public schools as well as to increased access to the nearby mission school facilitated by the new roads and improved incomes. The electrification of the villages allowed children to complete their nightly homework and so improved their overall performance in school. The first generation of children to benefit from these educational opportunities began to matriculate into secondary school, while others took wage-paying jobs in cities and towns across Ghana. The fertility rate in these villages began to fall noticeably as women focused more and more on agricultural labor, infant mortality declined, and the children families did have were more successful and, therefore, more able to care for their parents in old age.

These developments took place against a background of uncertainty. Without effective regulation, the Gulf of Guinea fishery collapsed in 2018, and the supplies of fish that had once provided much of the protein in the diets of Dominase and Ponkrum residents were severely curtailed and extraordinarily expensive. A development project in the Eguafo Traditional Area encouraged residents to raise livestock in an effort to address this protein deficit. However, villager participation in the project was largely limited to selecting between sheep, goats, or cattle. There was no real dialogue between project staff and the residents about previous experiences with livestock in these villages that had gone wrong. A few residents suggested the project would work better if it aimed at farming grasscutter, or even at a broad effort to repopulate the area with grasscutter, but they were ignored. Many project staff members were repulsed by the idea of eating a giant rodent and dismissed the idea out of hand. Without listening to the villagers' ideas, giving them no chance to explain the previous history of livestock in these villages, the project introduced sheep to most households at highly subsidized prices. This experiment came to a rapid end after one too many sheep broke into farm fields and did significant damage. The sheep were quickly sold off to buyers in Cape Coast and Elmina, which prevented the project from amounting to a total loss for the villagers.

Diets then shifted toward purchased chicken, which was expensive and therefore could not completely replace the lost protein from fish. Rising food prices began to cut into the rising household incomes in Dominase and Ponkrum, and the purchasing power of the residents began to fall. Men were most greatly affected by this trend, as their wage incomes did not keep pace with inflation. Women's incomes, heavily tied to agricultural production, largely kept pace with inflation, closing the gap between their incomes and those of their husbands. This resulted in increased stress between husbands and wives. *Kwashiorkor* returned to the villages, as children's diets overemphasized carbohydrates over proteins. Health issues prevented some children from attending school as often as they should have and hampered their academic progress and future job prospects.

By 2020 it was also clear that the minor rainy season could not support a full second harvest, as it had in the past. Without this second harvest, households had to spend even more of their incomes on food, and less of their food needs were supplied from their own farms. While women's incomes were most directly affected by this change, the well-being of nearly everyone in these villages became much more closely tied to national and ever more global markets for agricultural commodities. Initially, this was not a problem. However, as American production of staple crops such as maize and soy fell after 2025 due to climate change, the worldwide price for foods reliant on these crops began to rise. Women were able to hold even against this trend as international prices of maize and related foods rose. However, the prices of palm oil, citrus, and coconuts lagged behind the prices of staple foods, and the purchasing power of men's agricultural income began a rapid downward slide.

The shades of disaster that lurked behind the new prosperity in Dominase and Ponkrum came to the fore in 2028, when the price of gasoline skyrocketed as the government removed its subsidy under intense pressure from the World Trade Organization. This push was the consequence of an almost-total failure to understand the importance of this subsidy for the well-being of agricultural producers in Ghana. This failure to grasp the importance of the fuel subsidy was the result of a heavy reliance on per capita use as a measure of the dependence of the Ghanaian population on gasoline and, therefore, their ability to absorb a price shock when the subsidy was dropped. Those against these subsidies argued that per capita use of such products as gasoline were too low to have a significant impact on the everyday lives of most Ghanaians and, therefore, subsidies were an unnecessary market distortion.

This argument, however, misread the remarkable efficiency of the Ghanaian taxi and *tro-tro* system. As a result, when the end of the subsidy pushed these de facto providers of public transportation past the threshold of profitability, transportation became far too expensive for many Ghanaians, and their livelihoods were greatly affected. The price of the trip from Dominase and Ponkrum to Elmina tripled, dramatically cutting into market profits and wages. When coupled with rising food prices, these new transportation costs created a situation in which, for most households in these villages, men's incomes no longer dominated household incomes or even facilitated purchases needed to replenish the material needs of the households, such as farm tools. As in the past, men began to withdraw from local labor markets and fall back on their farms. Women's farms shrank to allow men to plant larger farms, and men began to replace tree crops such as palm with maize. Typically, these men sold their palm trees to an *akpeteshi*-maker, who knocked them over and harvested their sap. The loss of these trees was widespread around the villages.

Within a year or two the residents realized this agricultural fallback was no longer viable. The near-total loss of the minor rainy season coupled with increasingly unpredictable rainfall during the major rainy season made growing adequate food nearly impossible. Increasing farm sizes was not possible, as households were already farming as much land as they could manage by hand. Further, pressure on land resources began to rise as the adult children of various households returned to these villages with their families, seeking farmland in the wake of job-losses proceeding from the rapidly shrinking Ghanaian economy. Fallow cycles for fields fell to a year or less in some cases, resulting in the overutilization of the soils and most households' complete dependence on fertilizer. As household incomes and purchasing power contracted, fertilizers became more and more difficult to obtain. There were years in which farmers had to try to raise crops on depleted soils without fertilizers. Even when they could acquire fertilizers, the unstable rainfall led to problems.

Starting in 2040, intense land pressure, in the absence of needed inputs and stable rainfall, contributed to a trend of failing farms in areas around these villages. Nearly all the remaining trees in the area were cut and sold for firewood or lumber as residents tried to eke out a living from the land around the villages. As the decade wore on, the residents, unable to support themselves from the local environment, began to trickle out of Dominase and Ponkrum, much as they had in the late 1960s. By 2050 both villages were nearly completely abandoned as only the heads of land-controlling families remained with their households, awaiting the return of residents to take up the now-recovering but still moisture-parched lands.

Scenario 2. A Different Future: Escaping the Echo Chamber

In late 2009 the 15th Conference of the Parties (COP) to the United Nations Framework Convention on Climate Change met in Copenhagen. While this initial meeting failed to produce a durable agreement on a path forward for addressing global climate change, over the next two years an agreement that sought to limit overall global warming to three degrees Celsius by 2100 was hashed out. By 2012 it was ratified by every major country emitting greenhouse gases. For Ghana, this produced a mixed set of results. In 2011 the Ghanaian government experienced an unprecedented flow of revenue as its offshore oil reserves came online, though this flow was somewhat constrained by surprisingly level prices for petroleum as advanced economies moved rapidly toward clean-energy initiatives in their energy and transportation sectors. The constraints on this income, however, caused few problems in Ghana. Carrying relatively little national debt, the government quickly paid off existing debt and opened new lines of credit to pay for the rapid expansion of infrastructure, especially road networks and the country's electrical-generation capacity. By committing its new revenues to projects before they came online, the government was largely able to overcome the problem of absorptive capacity, where governments with greatly increased new revenues often lack the capacity to spend that money, leading to opportunities for theft and corruption. Dominase and Ponkrum benefited from this forward planning, first in the form of rural electrification in 2012 and, by 2013, in the form of paved roads in and around these villages.

The new transportation infrastructure greatly improved the efficiency of agricultural production in these villages. Farmers were able to move crops to market rapidly and cheaply, and the explosive growth of Ghana's economy created ready markets in towns such as Elmina and Cape Coast. The value of food crops rose dramatically as these cities demanded food for their populations, leading the residents of Dominase and Ponkrum to expand their farms between 2013 and 2016. This expansion only slowed when the amount of land under cultivation became so great that fallow times fell to less than two years, and agricultural production began to fall despite ever-larger farms.

In response to this falling production, which was well understood by farmers to be the consequence of overusing the land, households began to diversify their economies to maintain or increase their incomes while reducing the size of their farms. Most of the reduction in farmland under cultivation came as men's agricultural production shifted primarily to tree crops planted on much smaller farms than seen in previous years, and they began to take up wage employment in the booming economies of Cape Coast and Elmina. As these men began to earn substantial sums from wage employment, women were able to maintain larger farms, with higher farm incomes, without threatening the overall hierarchy of the household. They produced a great deal of food for market and used this income to pay for ever-scarcer fish as well as for chicken, and other meat for their households. Some women used their farm incomes to support petty trading activities, though these were somewhat less lucrative than in years past due to the ease of movement to and from markets. Other women used this income to purchase fertilizers to maintain the productivity of their fields, as the residents of the area transitioned back to a more-sustainable rotation of crops and fallow land.

Concurrently, the Copenhagen COP and the subsequent global climate accord marked the beginning of an explosion in global-emissions trading. As the United States adopted a cap-and-trade system for managing its emissions, the global-emissions trading market exploded to more than $300 billion per year. With so much available capital, efforts to expand carbon trading to existing carbon sinks along globalization's shoreline accelerated beyond existing efforts of the Reducing Emissions from Deforestation and Forest Degradation (REDD) and Clean Development Mechanism (CDM) projects to embrace a wide range of private-sector initiatives. Some of these early efforts were disastrous and resulted in fortress-conservation efforts that had serious impacts on the well-being of affected communities. However, nearly all these problematic initiatives failed quickly, costing the investors significant sums of money and driving the market away from fortress-conservation solutions. By 2018 the majority of these initiatives contained significant social-welfare components aimed at maintaining and improving the quality of life for affected communities, as the cost of such efforts was extremely small in relation to the profits generated by these projects.

In Dominase and Ponkrum the outcome of these climate-change initiatives was a revaluation of one long-standing product, acacia. Where farmers had once planted acacia to provide a steady source of charcoal for themselves and markets in nearby coastal towns, now this fast-growing tree was greatly valued for its ability to take up carbon. Throughout the Eguafo Traditional Area, land under acacia cultivation was incorporated into a single investment package negotiated by the paramount chief in consultation with village chiefs, government and academic advisers, and farmers' representatives. The annual revenues generated by these carbon credits were distributed to farmers according to the amount of acacia they cultivated, creating a financial incentive to allow these stands of trees to continue growing instead of cutting them to make charcoal. Heads of families prevented most new planting of these trees, arguing correctly that their growth precluded the growth of food crops in or around them. This created some friction in the community, but the income from the carbon credits was not very large, and levels of conflict over the growth of this tree remained low. However, one clearly uneven benefit of carbon trading in these villages was that those who already had stands of acacia (nearly all of them men) now had a secure source of income that required almost no agricultural labor, allowing them to take greater risks in finding wage employment outside the villages.

In 2017 the agricultural markets in advanced economies opened to largely unrestricted imports from globalization's shoreline, creating a surge in prices for select crops. An agricultural collective, organized by the paramount chief of the Eguafo Traditional Area, attracted a significant number of agricultural exporters, who paid locally competitive prices for farm produce. In Dominase and Ponkrum maize and citrus prices skyrocketed. This reversed the trend back toward smaller farms, as the huge (by local standards) profit margins on these crops enabled the purchase of fertilizers and seeds, which did away with the need for fallow time. Much of the land around these villages was planted with citrus crops that, once mature, required relatively little attention. As a result, household farm sizes grew dramatically, though much of this growth was in the cultivation of citrus. The growth of other food crops, such as maize, also increased. However, the expansion of these crops was constrained by the availability of household labor. Even under these new conditions of profitability, mechanization was not a viable option for agricultural production in these villages.

While the household incomes of Dominase and Ponkrum rose dramatically between 2010 and 2020, significant issues were underlying this otherwise-happy picture. First, the cost of food rose across this decade, especially as the 2018 collapse of the Gulf of Guinea fishery reduced local fish hauls. This decreasing availability of fish, coupled with increasing demand for food from the growing populations in coastal towns, drove the price of fish up steeply. Second, the overall trend toward less precipitation in the area, coupled with the lack of rainfall in the minor rainy season and the increasing unpredictability of the major season, resulted in lower levels of farm productivity in these villages. To counter this trend, households had to buy more of their food. Thus, while incomes rose, much of this increase was spent on food purchases.

However, this impact was largely ameliorated by a pilot project—initiated after the Gulf of Guinea fishery collapse—aimed at improving the protein content in coastal West African diets. Project staff engaged residents of Dominase and Ponkrum in wide-ranging discussions of how to meet their protein needs. Livestock husbandry was quickly taken off the table after villages recounted their history of troubles with such animals. Instead, staff members were impressed with the villagers' emphatic support for grasscutter farming, which required good fences for all local farms and a limited amount of training. The project also promoted the planting on local farms of beans that could be intercropped with the maize that already dominated most women's production. What the project staff overlooked in their analysis was the fact that a market-oriented activity such as raising grasscutters was likely to be dominated by men. In many households women found themselves caring for animals they did not own and could not sell to meet household needs. Therefore, while the end result of this project was a recovery of the local grasscutter population and, through the consumption of grasscutters and the beans planted on women's fields, an increase in the overall protein intake of the villagers that all but eliminated *kwashiorkor* within two years, the project did little to change the position of women in their households and may have added a new burden to their daily labors.

By 2025 any increases in household income were the result of heavy engagement with markets, either via wage labor or through the sale of agricultural products. As a result, these households were extremely exposed

to economic shocks. Understanding that the globalization of rural economies was creating in these areas new vulnerabilities that might compromise
their long-term political, social, and environmental situations, in 2018
the World Bank had turned away from a universal view of strategic food
reserves as being a market distortion. Instead, the World Bank began to
promote a case-by-case approach to these reserves. If they were properly
justified and organized, the World Bank would support them as insur-
ance that could preserve livelihoods, political stability, and environmental
health. This new view proceeded from evidence from globalization's shoreline that the negative outcomes of development and globalization—once
treated as outliers—were, in fact, much more common than previously
understood. The World Bank and other agencies were finally able to see
these challenges clearly because of substantial pressure from the carbon
markets, whose investments would be threatened by insecurity in food and
livelihood among people living near carbon sinks.

The Ghanaian government took advantage of this policy shift to justify
the creation of its own strategic reserve, using petroleum revenues to pay for
the subsidized fertilizers and seed it provided for rural farmers in order to
generate surpluses needed to create a reserve of maize. By 2020 Ghana held
a million metric tons of maize in reserve against fluctuations in global food
prices. Having seen the remarkable success of this program in generating an
agricultural surplus, the government also justified the creation of a transparent, publicly accountable emergency agricultural fund to be spent, in case of
a food emergency, on subsidized seeds and fertilizer for the population.

This move proved prescient across the 2020s, as global food prices rose
steadily while American grain production began to fall off due to unexpect-
edly rapid warming of agricultural areas in the Midwest. While this created
a tremendous demand for Ghanaian maize, it also drove the price of maize
so high that much of the Ghanaian population could not afford it at global
market prices. In 2024 the Ghanaian government began to release some of
the maize in its strategic reserve to hold prices down on its internal markets
and provide farmers a season or two to transition toward the growth of
other food crops to supplement maize and maintain food supplies under
these new market conditions. The government tapped its emergency agricultural fund to provide inputs for staple crops such as cassava, yams, and
millet, which were key sources of food in various parts of the country. This
facilitated the expansion of these crops and preventing global price shocks
from rippling into a national food-security crisis.

By 2026 Ghanaian agricultural production had rediversified, with maize exports now complemented by substantial production of local staple crops. In Dominase and Ponkrum inputs to support the growth of cassava and yam enabled women to plant large amounts of these staples alongside their maize crops. With this new emphasis, most households met a substantial portion of their own food needs and were able to sell a great deal of surplus to those living in nearby coastal towns. While the well-being of residents of Dominase and Ponkrum was still closely linked to both national and global agricultural markets, vagaries in this connection were partly mitigated by the efforts of the government, which prevented full-scale shocks to agriculture that might produce significant food insecurity.

The residents of Dominase and Ponkrum recognized their well-being was closely tied to government policy, and however proactive that policy seemed to be at the moment, they had little faith in its long-term benevolence. Having identified their principal challenges as unstable and declining rainfall and the rising cost of fertilizer when government subsidies were inadequate, residents connected to a growing global network of communities that exchanged experiences, ideas, and encouragement without relying on development agencies or professionals. The mobile phone was ubiquitous in nearly all parts of the world, and even the cheapest handset had Internet capabilities, however limited. The residents of Dominase and Ponkrum began to send queries to this network, looking for suggestions on how to shift their strategies, techniques, or crops to facilitate greater productivity under declining rainfall and fertilizer availability.

Responses came back from around the world. Some of the most productive came from small, self-contained farms in the United States that had long ago shifted from the industrial agricultural model to one of fostering complex local agricultural ecosystems that generate the food and fertilizers needed via the careful husbanding of plants, crops, and animals. Residents experimented with some of these techniques, developing several new strategies for locally sustainable farming. For example, one farmer, after several seasons of experimentation, developed a useful means of raising grasscutters on fallow land while harvesting their droppings for fertilizer on active fields. Other farmers dug and lined earthen cisterns on the tops of hills near their farms and created controlled drip-irrigation channels that had the effect of evening out the irregular rainfall of the major rainy season. These and other innovations allowed residents to maintain their productivity, even in the face of an unstable environment and declining access to fertilizers.

By 2030 Ghana was a carbon-*negative* country. By engaging fruitfully with global carbon markets and investing heavily in clean energy sources in its northern areas, the country was taking up more carbon than it generated each year. Ghana had defined a new path for development, away from high-carbon, material-intensive definitions of what it meant to be developed and toward low-carbon but high quality-of-life situations in most communities in the country. Dominase and Ponkrum were fully electrified, linked to a grid that provided cheap energy via solar and hydropower. Throughout Ghana the rolling blackouts of the late twentieth and early twenty-first centuries were a thing of the past. Carbon credits and healthy incomes from the export of maize crops enabled residents to earn incomes that were more than sufficient to meet their food and material needs without the constant toil that had marked life in the early twenty-first century. Villagers began to build houses of locally produced brick and roofed with fired ceramic tiles produced in Elmina and Cape Coast.

By 2050 Dominase had disappeared, the last residents having moved to Ponkrum for the sake of convenience. Ponkrum, now a town of some 500 residents, was best described as an agricultural suburb of Elmina. It had comfortable residential homes surrounded on all sides by stands of acacia and farms of maize and citrus for export, intermixed with cassava, beans, yam, and other food crops for local consumption. Most farmers worked plots significantly smaller than those at the turn of the twenty-first century, but they earned many times more income from those small plots. Because of the high levels of agricultural productivity and the prevalence of wage labor in towns such as Elmina, there was little pressure to expand these farms. Those who did work the land did not have to spend ten hours a day, five or six days a week. Instead they spent a few hours a day at most on their farms, and this was mainly between April and September. The rest of the time they were able to enjoy the fruits of their labors with friends and family. While the rising sea-level had inundated parts of coastal towns such as Elmina and Cape Coast, affected residents relocated to higher ground, and the need to rebuild kept local labor markets active. Global efforts to manage and restore large fisheries, including an effort in the Gulf of Guinea, met with some success, and fish catches began to rise again.

Two Stories, Two Implications

As these two scenarios illustrate, how we think about globalization and development will have a tremendous impact on how the economy, environment, and quality of life play out in particular places along globalization's shoreline. The second scenario shows it is possible to create a more sustainable, pleasant future without micromanaging every aspect of the economy, environment, and society, forcing them into particular alignments. Instead, by incorporating flexibility, and a real concern for actual events on globalization's shoreline, into our policy and project-design processes, we can build a sustainable future. In short, if we can get out of the way of those living on globalization's shoreline, we might be able to get to a desirable future. This future does not require a complete rethinking of the world economy or global geopolitics. If the international and bilateral development organizations can make the shift away from economic and development dogma and toward realism, then there is no need to do away with those organizations. Instead, they can become a powerful means by which policies align the interests of advanced economies with those of globalization's shoreline—to the benefit of all. If national governments, and their associated economic and development departments and ministries, come to see the plight of those living along globalization's shoreline as a problem that compromises their own national interests, we can create conversations between governments, between agencies, and between people in the advanced economies and those along globalization's shoreline that result in solutions amenable (or at least acceptable) to everyone.

In other words, the business-as-usual scenario, as played out in Dominase and Ponkrum, will play out in locally specific ways in thousands of places along globalization's shoreline. The outcomes of this scenario will vary from place to place. Some will see economic growth—perhaps, even environmentally sustainable economic growth. Most places will see significant trade-offs, such as economic growth at the expense of local environmental quality. Still others will be caught in a series of events that bring nothing but problems and challenges. How these various outcomes will weigh against one another is difficult to say. However, given our experiences up to this point, it seems safe to predict that the cases involving significant trade-offs and seriously negative outcomes will outweigh the overwhelmingly positive cases. It seems likely that these trade-offs and negative outcomes will aggregate in important ways—whether in terms of the overall function of global carbon sinks or in terms of shifts in the global food supply—that have reverberating effects impacting everyone on Earth. However, if we do not start trying to understand, measure, and address these challenges now, we will be caught in a reactive cycle, addressing each new challenge as it manifests itself. This is a classic case of treating the symptoms of the problem, not the cause, and over the next century will likely lock us into a losing battle against environmental change and economic stagnation.

If business-as-usual is likely to result in significant challenges to human well-being throughout the world, a world outside the echo chamber presents hope for a sustainable future. Here again, while the outcomes of this scenario are specific to the situation of Dominase and Ponkrum, they reflect broad trends toward improved standards of living via increased livelihoods security, the creation of local practices that result in the sustainable use of natural resources over the long term, and the creation of small yet stable markets for global goods across globalization's shoreline. In the Upper Guinea Forest, these trends might reflect a move toward smallholder sustainable forestry secured by subsidies based on carbon credits, thus fostering stable, secure livelihoods and the sustainable use of forest resources. At the edge of the Sahara, we might see efforts to foster communal property-ownership that allows for the continuous movement of livestock herds required to maintain environmental quality and livelihoods.

Not all these locally specific solutions will work. Some will fail at the local level and result in unsustainable outcomes in terms of livelihoods and environment, or both. Others will appear sustainable at the local level but will contribute to shifts in global processes, such as the carbon cycle, that in aggregate are ultimately unsustainable. If, however, we adjust our measurements of these outcomes, in terms of both what we measure and who does the measuring, we are likely to recognize such issues earlier, and more accurately, than we do today. This will allow for proactive efforts to avoid negative impacts downstream, rather than waiting for the negative outcome to materialize. Perhaps more important (and more numerous) than the negative cases will be the success stories. If success stories can be circulated rapidly and widely, other communities in similar economic and environmental situations might be able to draw on these cases for motivation and new ideas to create their own solutions. In this world, it seems to me, the balance will tip heavily toward success stories that drive down atmospheric concentrations of greenhouse gases, sustain the environment, protect the global food supply, and preserve human well-being around the world.

This will not be a perfect world. Massive income inequality will persist at the global scale, as there seems to be no politically feasible way of erasing that in 50 or 100 years. However, at the very least there is a chance to build a world that affords every person living in it the opportunity to enjoy leisure, comfort, and happiness in a way that is impossible under current conditions, and unlikely under business-as-usual in the future. This goal is not easily measured using such factors as income, life expectancy, or even infant mortality. Instead, it is highly qualitative and locally specific. However, it is achievable, and it is necessary, if anyone on Earth is to enjoy a comfortable, enjoyable quality of life in the future.

Chapter 14

Uncertainty Is Hope

This book, at its heart, is an effort to lay bare a colossal failure of imagination behind the creation of economic and environmental policy and development projects. If there is one thing the histories of so many of these policies and projects have in common, it is the urge to organize, control, and somehow influence a complex, unruly world to create new opportunities for people, wherever they might live. While these efforts have usually been undertaken with the best of intentions, they have resulted in a woefully inadequate, often incorrect understanding of life along globalization's shoreline. The urge to control and fix the events and processes in play in these areas is evident in existing policy initiatives, such as PRSPs. This urge pervades efforts to address the long-term failure of development and globalization in order to meaningfully change the situations of those living along this shoreline. The clearest example of this, but hardly the only, is the MVP, which is predicated on problems and solutions designed in advanced economies and implemented in villages along globalization's shoreline in a manner that marginalizes community participation.

The significance of this problem cannot be overstated. There are several billion people living along globalization's shoreline who are addressing economic and environmental change in their everyday lives. In aggregate, how they choose to manage the challenges life presents them, and leverage the opportunities that emerge in the context of these changes, will impact the global economy and environment with significant ramifications for everyone on the planet. Yet, we understand very little about what is actually happening along this shoreline, and we show relatively little interest in getting a firm handle on the size and scope of these aggregate impacts. As a result, the residents of globalization's shoreline have largely been pushed to one side, ignored except when their consent is necessary for a government or some other organization to leverage funds needed for a particular project or policy.

Our failure to understand what is really happening on globalization's shoreline continues to constrain even innovative efforts to move development forward. In recent years, some development thinkers have moved away from the idea of devising plans, policies, and projects that will directly and predictably ameliorate the challenges of life on globalization's shoreline. Writers such as economist William Easterly have, instead, begun to argue that, in the face of our long history of failure, a productive path forward for development is to create the conditions within which local populations can devise their own development paths. In principal, I think this is the most productive path left for development, and for our hopes of a sustainable future.

However, these emerging approaches to development, with those in advanced economies working to establish conditions in which local development pathways might emerge, are still greatly constrained by some common assumptions about development and globalization—most clearly that these processes will, in the long run, improve the quality of life for people everywhere and that they are still relatively new processes along most parts of the shoreline. These assumptions are reflected in the fact that even the more open-ended efforts to explain previous failures rely on *one* key issue to unlock the potential of development, a key issue that tends to be a focus of those in advanced economies, or at least those associated with institutions in the advanced economies.

For example, the economist Hernando de Soto argues that the absence of clear titles to common-law property holdings in the developing world, along with other institutional barriers to unlocking the capital in these property holdings, are the principal barriers to meaningful development in much of the world. Here, as in microcredit lending, the presumption is that access to capital will enable people to unlock their potential and develop themselves. This is not an overly constrained vision of development and how to get there. Instead, it is an argument for a catalyst that can start the development process in different parts of the world, even though that process might take different forms. The same might be said of Easterly's argument that inadequate, or inappropriate, governance is the critical barrier to development. He does not lay out a constrained set of problems that hinder development or interventions that might overcome these problems. Instead, he argues for improved forms of governance that can empower creative people to find their own paths to development. In both cases the authors may see development as an open-ended and locally specific process, but they see the means to this end as particular (and closely related) problems: governance and property rights.

However, it is not clear to me that those living along globalization's shoreline see governance and property rights as being the principal barriers to the improvement of their conditions of life. De Soto's argument overlooks significant problems attendant with assigning property rights to the poor, such as the impact on livelihoods and the local environment that comes with such privatization. In rural Ghana people's lives are largely organized around local structures of authority. This includes issues of land management. Heads of families live and work among the other farmers in the area and can see the economic and environmental results of various efforts and initiatives, which allows them to manage land resources sustainably.

In 2005, I ran an analysis of the land uses around these villages and realized the planting of acacia was taking up a substantial amount of land that had once lain fallow. I knew from the farmers that land planted with acacia could not be planted with crops, even if the acacia were cut down; therefore, it was clear the rapid expansion of acacia planting, if unchecked, was going to generate a shortage of arable land in the near future. I brought a few maps to Dominase and Ponkrum and sat with heads of families to discuss this issue. All but one were completely unsurprised by my findings, and three had already banned the further planting of acacia. A fourth told me, "I know it is bad for the land, but I won't stop." In short, these family heads had already identified a land-use problem and chosen to act as they saw fit because they lived on and worked that land, and because they had the capacity to enforce their decisions.

If landholding around these villages were privatized, this local check on land use would be removed, triggering first ecological collapse and then economic collapse. There is not enough land around these villages simply to grant every man a permanent plot large enough to enable the field-rotation system that currently preserves local soil fertility. The privatization of landholding would result in either smaller overall farm sizes as households tried to maintain some fallow fields in their landholdings, or the steady overfarming of their plots. In either case farm outputs and incomes would drop, likely challenging the ability of these households to support themselves through agriculture. To buy fertilizer, some households might take loans against their homes and land, and in good years they might raise enough crops to meet their needs and pay off the loans. However, under conditions of uncertain precipitation, there will be many years where inauspicious timing of rainfall, or insufficient amounts, offset gains from the use of fertilizers, leaving households unable to pay off their loans. When the loans come due, these households could find themselves landless. De Soto neither acknowledges this as a likely scenario (indeed, something similar played out in Southeast Asia under the green revolution) nor offers suggestions about how to avoid, or address, these sorts of challenges.

While Easterly has conducted substantial analytic exercises to demonstrate that the style and quality of governance in a particular country have greater influence on overall development outcomes than factors such as the geographic characteristics of the country, this is not the same as identifying the main cause of development failures. It is merely a relative argument, with governance as a better predictor than geography of development outcomes. Further, this argument is predicated on national-scale data and traditional metrics of development, such as GDP. As has been argued repeatedly in this book, these metrics often have little bearing on the actual situations in particular communities that, when aggregated, create national statistics.

Development and globalization do not directly cause anything to happen. They create opportunities and challenges that are then addressed or mobilized by particular people with reference to their situations in particular places. These processes defy singular catalysts that might unleash their development potential. Further, given the long emergency already in place along globalization's shoreline, it is doubtful there is much potential (at least as we think of it in conventional economics) to be unleashed through traditional means of economic growth. There are not enough resources to make this possible. Any changes in life along the shoreline of globalization will have to come via a rather different path than that once charted by the advanced economies. These people and countries cannot be seen as modern-day relics of the former circumstances of advanced economies, moving through the same stages of economic growth and social development. That path closed long ago by virtue of the emergence of those advanced economies and their economic and environmental clout.

Therefore, we face a world of uncertainty as we move forward with efforts to build a sustainable future. Some see such uncertainty as a challenge to be overcome, a problem to be banished through more policies, more data, and more analysis founded on prevalent understandings of globalization and development. While I appreciate that mentality, especially the can-do philosophy behind it, I believe it is doomed to fail. As the case of Dominase and Ponkrum has shown, many of the very problems we seek to address through globalization and development *were caused by* globalization and development. We cannot treat the problem with more of its cause.

It is clear that more of the same is ultimately unproductive, and that we do not know how to fix all the world's problems. We probably overlook significant problems every day, as our measurements fail to capture them, and we are likely mismeasuring many of those we can see. However, this is not failure; this is hope. If we acknowledge that these are, indeed, significant problems that must be addressed if we wish to build a sustainable future, then we can abandon the baggage of decades of failure. We can open ourselves up to innovation that might be unimaginable from within the echo chamber of contemporary globalization and development.

Once we start down the path of the unimaginable, the fantastic can occur. This is why the interface and database model of interaction with globalization's shoreline is so exciting. I am thrilled by the fact that I have no idea what sorts of information will emerge from such a massive, evolving database. Which development, globalization, and environmental issues and interventions will be confirmed by this database as important, and which will be cast aside as irrelevant, are unknown. Nobody knows because these questions have never been asked in a way that would allow for real, unconstrained answers.

This uncertainty, for me, is hope. There are more than 6.5 billion people on this planet. Surely at least several of them have innovative and exciting ideas about how to address the challenges facing their lives, ideas that might be applicable in other places or be philosophically innovative. We will not know unless we ask, unless we actively go looking for these ideas and empower those who have them to express them to the world.

Acknowledgments

This book draws on work I have been doing for more than 13 years. To adequately thank and acknowledge everyone who had something to do with all the different field seasons, writing projects, presentations, and thinking out loud that brought me to the place from which I wrote this book is impossible. That said, there are a large number of people who played such a significant role that I cannot, in good conscience, avoid acknowledging their contributions.

First and foremost, I owe a tremendous debt to the people of Dominase and Ponkrum. They took me in as a 24-year-old graduate student back in 1997, and their generosity never ceased. Whether teaching me about how to farm the land around the villages, testing my shaky Fante, or sitting around and chatting after a meal, the people of these villages opened their lives and livelihoods to me. Without them, there is no research, and certainly no book. I hope it does justice to their experiences, efforts, and abilities.

Among the people of these villages, a few require special mention. Francis Quayson has been my research assistant since my first day in Ponkrum in 1997. Over the time we have worked together, Francis has evolved from an interpreter and manual laborer into a research partner, suggesting questions during interviews and contributing to the overall research design of entire field seasons. The book is dedicated to his children (Jennifer and Edward) and mine (Cleary, RJ and Evie). I don't know if their lives will be as entwined as Francis's and my own have been, but as this book shows, they certainly will not live out their lives without an impact on one another. And if they cannot learn to work together in ways that previous generations have not, I have grave concerns for their children.

Samuel Mensah was one of the first people to welcome me to Ponkrum. He was on my field crew for every field season. Samuel taught me a great deal about farming around these villages, even as his farm drove me insane with its absurd variety of crops. He was an agricultural tinkerer, and so each inventory of his farm would yield at least one or two unique crops that he was just trying out. One of the hardest workers I ever met, Samuel plowed through all sorts of injuries and discomfort without a word of complaint, until I begged him to take a day or two off. Unfortunately, Samuel was not complaining to anyone in 2006 as he sickened, and he died of unknown causes a few months after the summer field season ended. I was devastated when Francis called with the news. When fieldwork resumes in Ponkrum (as it inevitably will), I will feel his loss again.

Joe Dadzie, Johnson Gyesi, and Ernest Mensah all worked for me during field seasons spanning archaeological excavation, household inventories, and farm-mapping exercises. I was fortunate to have a field team that was as good-humored as it was hard working. They made eighteen months of fieldwork go all too quickly. Kwame Ackon, Kwesi Awotwe, and Ekow Ackon welcomed me to Dominase, supported my project from the beginning, and taught me more than anyone should know about *akpeteshi*. Kwame passed away in late 2009, and my life will be a little less full in his absence. Nana Kofi Akuansanuah, the chief of Ponkrum, welcomed my presence in the village and facilitated much of my work. Finally, the support and friendship of Nana Kwamena Ansah IV, the Paramount Chief of the Eguafo Traditional Area to which Dominase and Ponkrum belong, was invaluable.

Many other Ghanaian colleagues participated in this project. Professor Kofi Awusabu-Asare and James Eshun, both of the Department of Geography and Tourism at the University of Cape Coast, partnered with me in 2006 in my study of changing livelihoods in these villages. From interpreting the surveys that structured our interviews to conceiving an appropriate community project at the end of the research project, they made a massive data-collection exercise run smoothly. They also ran a parallel study in January of 2007 to capture the effects of seasonality on these livelihoods, which we plan to publish shortly. Simon Mariwa, Foster Frempong, Ernest Kwame Asante and Gerald Atampugre, all graduate students in the Department of Geography and Tourism at the University of Cape Coast, were invaluable as field enumerators during the 2006 field season. Ben Kankpeyeng and Bossman Murey, both of the Department of Archaeology at the University of Ghana, participated in archaeological excavations at Dominase. Bossman spent a month with me in Dominase and Ponkrum in April 2000, and his ideas and presence set the stage for a very successful excavation. Ben provided amusement and bush-driving lessons that mostly seemed to involve me getting out and pushing. Raymond Agbo, of the Ghana Museums and Monuments Board, worked with me to train some of his staff in archaeological excavation and artifact storage, and was a friend and sounding board in every field season. Julius Fobil of the School of Public Health at the University of Ghana provided a place to crash, and constructive criticism and ideas (usually delivered over several beers) during my work in Ghana between 2004 and 2006.

Chris DeCorse was my dissertation advisor at Syracuse, and remains a friend and colleague today. He was nothing short of fantastic as an advisor, and remains the standard of scholarship to which I try to hold myself. Gerard Chouin brought me to Dominase and Ponkrum when I was looking for a dissertation site. Without him, I never would have heard of these villages, let alone visited them. During my first three field seasons in Ghana, Gerard and his family were amazingly generous hosts whenever I drifted back in after a week or two in Ponkrum and Dominase. Sam Spiers was a fantastic help in my archaeological efforts in Dominase, working on my preliminary excavations in 1998, teaching me that HP Sauce makes nearly anything palatable, and offering counsel through the 2000 field season as he excavated a few kilometers away in Eguafo. Greg Cook and Natalie Swanepoel provided companionship and moral support during various field seasons. Literally dozens of participants in a Syracuse University/Earthwatch field school helped dig in Dominase in 2000, and I thank all of them for their efforts. Doug Armstrong, Theresa Singleton, and Peter Castro kept me very honest at my dissertation defense, and their input resulted in the foundations of what became chapters five and six in this book.

Rich Schein was my dissertation advisor at Kentucky. He gave me a lot of rope, but knew how to keep me in line. I've drawn on my experiences with Rich as I advise my own graduate students. John Pickles, Sue Roberts, the late Tom Leinbach, and J.P. Jones III contributed to my development as a geographer, and to my dissertation. The geography graduate-student community at Kentucky also deserves mention. My work benefited immensely from being in the intellectual environment they created, and from the questions and ideas routinely kicked around in Miller Hall or Lynaugh's.

Since coming to South Carolina, I have been fortunate to call a collegial, supportive department home. Carl Dahlman, who was a cohort ahead of me at Kentucky, and two years ahead of me at South Carolina, was the person who first noticed that globalization seemed to come and go from Dominase and Ponkrum, and he urged me to write about it. Roger Coate and Gordon Smith, each in their capacity as Director of the Walker Institute for International and Area Studies at the University of South Carolina, supported my research in these villages. Without Walker Institute support, I would not have been able to go to Dominase and Ponkrum in 2004, right after the road was improved. Will Graf has been a steadying force as a mentor, and was of great help in preparing the proposal that resulted in National Geographic Society funding for the 2006 field season. Marcia Castro joined the project in 2006 to examine the health situation in these villages, bringing fresh eyes to a project that was for me nearly a decade old.

I wrote this book in a hurry, trying to keep up with the words that were coming out of my head. The first draft took about a month to write, fueled by a lot of coffee (thanks to the lovely people at Cool Beans and Immaculate Consumption) and a constant loop of music that involved Doves' absolutely brilliant album *Kingdom of Rust*, U2's *No Line on the Horizon*, and pretty much everything ever performed by Mogwai. Writing the first draft was the easy part. Editing took another six months, and involved the comments of friends, colleagues, students and family. Thanks go to Pamela Mullins-Baker, Ron Atkinson, Mike Finewood, Kathleen Carr, Chris Van Dyke, Bob Greeley, Paul Kingsbury, Mary Thompson, Laura Ware, and the inimitable and irrepressible Brent McCusker. Pat Coate did a wonderful job copy-editing the draft I submitted to publishers. Thanks also go to Nate Kettle, Andrew Hoskins, Monica Fisher, and Melanie Feakins for their comments and contributions to some of the articles that became the backbone of this book. Any shortcomings of the book probably relate to the things I did not take on board from these readers.

I did not realize how fortunate I was when Colleen Mohyde decided she wanted to represent this book. I'm not sure all authors are lucky enough to have an agent who "gets" what they are doing, but I do know that this luxury greatly facilitated my experience with the publication process. After my first phone call with Laurie Harting at Palgrave Macmillan, I knew that I had found an editor who shared my goal of making this book accessible to as broad an audience as possible. Working with Laurie and her extended production team—especially Heather Faulls and Tiffany Hufford—has been a wonderful experience.

An assorted crowd of friends keeps me going every day. Without them, this book would never have happened. Thanks to Paul Kingsbury, Jon Adams, Sean Patel, Sam Walker, Ben Yocum, Brent McCusker, Brian King, Jeff Bury, Amy Mills, John Kupfer, and Molly Brown for keeping me sane.

I am fortunate to have the family I do. My mother, Kathleen Carr, reads most of my work, even the discipline-specific journal articles, and makes a serious effort to stay abreast of what I do. She is a wonderful sounding board for all things career and life. My brothers Tom and Morgan are better than I deserve. I hope they are as proud of me as I am of them. My father, Robert E. Carr, died in December 2002. He was my hero, and I still feel the loss every day. More than 15 years ago, as I entered graduate school, he challenged my reasons for going into archaeology, insistently asking "but why?" It took me years to realize that he was not dismissing academic pursuits, but trying to force me to think about why I worked on the projects I worked on, and what I was going to do with the knowledge I gathered. While I have been trying to answer that question for the past 13 years, and I suspect I will still be trying for the rest of my life, I think this book is a pretty good first cut, and his question and influence worth a dedication.

The highest complement I can pay my wife, Therese, is that she makes me a better person. We have supported each other through the hardships and frustrations of fieldwork, from when she came to Ghana in 2000 for three months, to tolerating several six-week absences during the summer in subsequent years. We supported each other through deep personal losses, as she lost her father suddenly in 2001, 18 months before my father died. There are no words to convey what she means to me. A graduate student at South Carolina, upon hearing about my constant trips to Ghana for fieldwork, remarked "Your wife must be really cool." He has no idea. My children, Cleary Jo, RJ, and Evie, have been leveling and centering forces in my life since their arrival. They are probably adding years to my life with their presence, and my inability to avoid smiling around them is making those added years a lot of fun.

Notes

1 Taking It All Apart

1. This is not to suggest that the local inhabitants are the victims of inadequate education or a backward worldview, but instead to highlight the ways in which events from outside their experience are incorporated into that worldview, often with significant consequences for how people view themselves and their place in the world.
2. This figure includes funds freed by debt relief.
3. According to the World Bank, the 66 high-income economies are Andorra; Antigua and Barbuda; Aruba; Australia; Austria; Bahamas; Bahrain; Barbados; Belgium; Bermuda; Brunei Darussalam; Canada; Croatia; Cayman Islands; Channel Islands; Cyprus; Czech Republic; Denmark; Estonia; Equatorial Guinea; Faeroe Islands; Finland; France; French Polynesia; Germany; Greece; Greenland; Guam; Hong Kong, China; Hungary; Iceland; Ireland; Isle of Man; Israel; Italy; Japan; Republic of Korea; Kuwait; Liechtenstein; Luxembourg; Macao, China; Malta; Monaco; Netherlands; Netherlands Antilles; New Caledonia; New Zealand; Northern Mariana Islands; Norway; Oman; Portugal; Puerto Rico; Qatar; San Marino; Saudi Arabia; Singapore; Slovak Republic; Slovenia; Spain; Sweden; Switzerland; Trinidad and Tobago; United Arab Emirates; United Kingdom; United States; and the Virgin Islands (U.S.).
4. http://www.un.org/millenniumgoals/2008highlevel/pdf/newsroom/ MDG_Report_2008_Progress_Chart_en_r8.pdf.
5. A detailed survey of health conditions in these villages nine years later confirmed that the overall health of the population is surprisingly good.
6. Perhaps the clearest writer in this category is the geographer Richard Peet, whose book *Unholy Trinity: The IMF, World Bank and WTO* links a sound analysis of these institutions to the author's particular political stance on their workings and existence.
7. For those familiar with the literature, this claim obviously echoes upon the work of many schools of development critique, from dependency theorists such as Andre Günder Frank to more recent post-structurally inspired efforts of authors such as Arturo Escobar. However, I do not make this claim out of any particular theoretical allegiance. As will be illustrated in the next several chapters, events on the ground in coastal Ghana bear out many of the dependency theorists' claims, while at the same time they call for more nuanced interpretation.

8. Here my argument drifts more toward the post-structural end of the spectrum as I focus my argument and analysis at the community level, instead of the macroeconomic level. I am searching for and thinking about the agency of individuals on globalization's shoreline as a central part of how globalization and development actually work.

2 Getting to the "Beach"

1. Brashares, Justin S.; Arcese, Peter; Sam, Moses K.; Coppolillo, Peter B.; Sinclair, A. R. E.; Balmford, Andrew "Bushmeat Hunting, Wildlife Declines, and Fish Supply in West Africa," *Science* 306 (5699). 1180–1183.

3 A Day at the Beach

1. Wednesdays and Sundays are exceptions to this. Generally speaking, nobody goes to the farm on Wednesdays as it is treated as a compulsory day of rest from farming. On Sundays many in these villages attend one of the two churches in Ponkrum (one is Catholic, the other Apostolic, an evangelical sect) in the morning before paying a short visit to their farms.

4 Living with Uncertainty

1. Owusu, K., & Waylen, P. (2009). Trends in spatio-temporal variability in annual rainfall in Ghana (1951–2000). *Weather* 64(5), 115–120, Owusu, K., Waylen, P., & Qiu, Y. (2008). Changing rainfall inputs in the Volta basin: implications for water sharing in Ghana. *Geojournal* 71(4), 201–210.
2. Ghana will be bringing its reserves of oil online in 2011. While this will create a new, large flow of revenue for the country, it will do nothing to diversify the economy away from primary commodities, and the problems they pose for development.
3. This can become a self-fulfilling prophecy, however, for when large traders start buying a particular currency, they can create a shortage of that currency on global markets that will drive the price of that currency (and their investments) up. Thus, large investors with billions of dollars can more or less manipulate currency markets through their own investments, ensuring their own profits.
4. For an outstanding discussion of this issue, see J. Scott, *Seeing Like a State: How Certain Schemes to Improve the Human Condition Have Failed* (New Haven, Conn.: Yale University Press, 1998); and T. Mitchell, *Rule of Experts: Egypt, Techno-Politics, Modernity* (Berkeley: University of California Press, 2002).

5 Nothing Has Always Been Like This

1. I must, however, confess to an interesting anomaly. In the last week of my final excavations in 2000, we uncovered two small patches of Late Stone Age ceramics that stylistically date at latest to the seventeenth century (Chris

DeCorse, Personal Communication, December 18, 2009). These artifacts suggest there was some form of settlement where modern Dominase
stands before the nineteenth century. However, there is no archaeological
evidence suggesting continuous occupation of this settlement across this
entire time span.

2. Anyane, S. L. 1963: *Ghana Agriculture: Its Economic Development from
   Early Times to the Middle of the Twentieth Century.* Accra: Oxford University
   Press., p.6.
3. DeCorse, C. R., 2001: *An Archaeology of Elmina: Africans and Europeans
   on the Gold Coast, 1400–1900.* Washington, DC: Smithsonian Institution
   Press. p.32.
4. Britton, K. O., Orr, D., and Sun, J. "Kudzu" in R.Van Driesche et al.,
   2002, *Biological Control of Invasive Plants in the Eastern United States,*
   USDA Forest Service Publication FHTET-2002–04, Washington, D.C.:
   United States Department of Agriculture. 325–30.
5. Anyane 1963, 31.
6. Hopkins, A. G., 1973: *An Economic History of West Africa.* New York:
   Columbia University Press, 133; McPhee, A., 1971: *The Economic
   Revolution in British West Africa,* 2nd Edition. London: Frank Cass
   and Company; McCann, J. C., 1999: *Green Land, Brown Land, Black
   Land: An Environmental History of Africa, 1800–1990.* Portsmouth, NH:
   Heinemann; Anyane 1963, 31.
7. Hopkins 1973, 176–77.
8. Hopkins 1973, 126; Lynn, M., 1997: *Commerce and Economic Change in
   West Africa: The Palm Oil Trade in the Nineteenth Century.* Cambridge:
   Cambridge University Press.
9. Hopkins 1973, 177; McPhee 1971, 41
10. Hopkins 1973, 177; Hill, P., 1970: *Rural Capitalism in West Africa.*
    Cambridge: Cambridge University Press. Hopkins 1973, 22; McPhee
    1971, 41; McCann (1999, 129) cites Fairhead and Leach (Fairhead, J and
    M. Leach 1998, *Reframing Deforestation: global analyses and local reali-
    ties – studies in West Africa.* , London: Routledge) for a slightly different
    set of statistics: 500 tons in 1900; 22,631 tons in 1910; and 200,000 tons
    in 1930.
11. Hopkins 1973, 177.
12. See DeCorse, C. R., 1992: Culture Contact, continuity and change in
    the Gold Coast, AD 1400–1900. *The African Archaeological Review*
    10 pp.163–196 for discussion of burial practices along this part of the
    coast.
13. McFee 1971, 117; McCann 1999, 130.
14. Robertson, C. C., 1984: *Sharing the Same Bowl: A Socioeconomic History of
    Women and Class in Accra, Ghana.* Bloomington, IN: Indiana University
    Press, 33.
15. McFee 1971, 120.
16. Hopkins 1973, 197; Robertson 1984, 33.
17. McFee 1971, 120; Hopkins 1973, 196.
18. McFee 1971, 117.
19. McFee 1971, 118; Hopkins 1973, 196.

20. Owusu, J. H., 1998: Current Convenience, Desperate Deforestation: Ghana's Adjustment Program and the Forestry Sector." *Professional Geographer* 50(4) pp. 418–436, 424.
21. Owusu 1998, 425.
22. Eguafo Abrem Management Committee 1955 "Application for Funds to Improve Feeder Roads." Letter to the Chairman, The National Food Board, Accra. Dated 29th June. Ref. No. 37/54/12.
23. This situation was not unusual in sub-Saharan Africa at this time. The economic outlook for much of the region was extremely positive across the 1960s.

6 The Tide Goes Out

1. There is a great deal of evidence from authors such as Polly Hill that rural livelihoods throughout Ghana were doing well at this time.
2. Huq, M. M. 1989: *The Economy of Ghana: The First 25 Years Since Independence.* St. Martin's Press, New York., 106; Owusu 1998, 424.
3. Owusu 1998, 424.
4. Eguafo-Abrem Management Committee 1955.
5. Annan, G. 1955. Letter dated 9th October to the Government Agent in Cape Coast.
6. Eguafo-Abrem Local Council 1957 "Feeder Roads" Letter to the Chairman, District Development Committee, Government Agent's Office, Cape Coast. Dated 24th September. Ref. No. 37/5/12.
7. Tabatabai, H. 1988: Agricultural Decline and Access to Food in Ghana. *International Labour Review.* 127(6) pp.703–34, 706.
8. Timber was not the only export in Ghana to run into significant problems at this time. The history of cocoa exports there charts a similarly complex decline that links national political-economic issues with a shifting global market for cocoa. The collapse of cocoa revenues had a much greater effect on the trajectory of Ghanaian history through the 1970s and early 1980s than did the decline of the timber sector. However, in Dominase and Ponkrum only a few residents were raising cocoa. These cocoa growers were focused on limited production, as part of a larger farm. Nobody was working cocoa fields full time, as in other parts of Ghana, and nobody relied on cocoa for their entire livelihood. Therefore, it is likely that, from the perspective of those living in these villages, the impact of this round of cocoa price instability was limited. For a discussion of the rise and fall of cocoa in Ghana, see Tabatabai 1988; Herbst, J., 1993: *The Politics of Reform in Ghana, 1982–1991.* Berkeley: University of California Press.; Austin, G., 1996: National poverty and the "vampire state" in Ghana: a review article. *Journal of International Development* 8(4): 553–573; Austin, G., 2003: African rural capitalism, cocoa farming and economic growth in colonial Ghana. In Falola, T. (ed.) *Ghana and Africa in the World: Essays in Honor of Adu Boahen,* pp. 437–453. Africa World Press, Trenton, NJ.
9. Eguafo-Abrem Management Committee 1955.
10. Dand, R. 1999: The International Cocoa Trade. Boca Raton, FL: CRC Press. 25.

11. Gyesi, E.; Agyepong, G. T.; Ardayfio-Schandorf, E.; Enu-Kwesi, L.; Nabila, J. S.; and Owusu Bennoah, E.; 1995. "Production pressure and environmental change in the forest-savannah zone of Southern Ghana" Global Environmental Change 5(4). 361.
12. Gyesi, et al. 1995, 362.
13. I know the name of the last chief, but I choose not to use it here in a speculative and potentially derogatory context.
14. Ghana underwent structural adjustment beginning in 1983. This program and future economic reforms were aimed at such goals as removing subsidies and price controls, the removal of subsidies in health and education, and the selling off of state-owned enterprises. The implementation of this program initially created significant urban unemployment and economic dislocation, while at the same time it raised the cost of such services as education and health care.

7 The Tide Comes Back In

1. Hill, P., 1956: The Gold Coast Cocoa Farmer: A Preliminary Survey. Oxford University Press: London; Hill, P., 1963: The Migrant Cocoa-Farmers of Southern Ghana: A Study in Rural Capitalism. Cambridge: Cambridge University Press; Hill, P.,1970: Rural Capitalism in West Africa. Cambridge: Cambridge University Press.

8 Scaling Up: Why the Lessons of Dominase and Ponkrum Matter to the World

1. Lewis, Simon L.; Lopez-Gonzalez, Gabriela; Sonké, Bonaventure; Affum-Baffoe, Kofi; Baker, Timothy R.; Ojo, Lucas O.; Phillips, Oliver L.; Reitsma, Jan M.; White, Lee; Comiskey, James A.; Djuikouo K., Marie-Noël; Ewango, Corneille E. N.; R. Feldpausch, Ted; Hamilton, Alan C.; Gloor, Manuel; Hart, Terese; Hladik, Annette; Lloyd, Jon; Lovett, Jon C.; Makana, Jean-Remy; Malhi, Yadvinder; Mbago, Frank M.; Ndangalasi, Henry J.; Peacock, Julie; Peh, Kelvin S.-H.; Sheil, Douglas; Sunderland, Terry; Swaine, Michael D.; Taplin, James; Taylor, David; Thomas, Sean C.; Votere, Raymond; and Wöll, Hannsjörg; "Increasing Carbon Storage in Intact African Tropical Forests," Nature 457 (February 19, 2009): 1003–6.
2. See http://www.nature.org/initiatives/climatechange/features/art29432.html?src=news.
3. Schlenker, Wolfram (Columbia University) and Roberts, Michael (North Carolina State University), "Nonlinear Temperature Effects Indicate Severe Damages to U.S. Crop Yields under Climate Change," August 24, 2009, in the online version of Proceedings of the National Academy of Sciences.
4. Most of these projects take a highly paternalistic attitude toward affected communities, a significant barrier to project success I will address in chapter 12.
5. Organization for Economic Cooperation and Development, Agricultural Policies in OECD Countries at a Glance (Paris: OECD, 2008), 93, http://

titania.sourceoecd.org/vl=2718222/cl=13/nw=1/rpsv/cgibin/fulltextew.
pl?prpsv=/ij/oecdthemes/99980002/v2008n10/s1/p11.idx.

6. Anderson, Kym; Martin, Will; and Van Der Mensbrugghe, Dominique;
"Would Multilateral Trade Reforms Benefit Sub-Saharan Africa?" World
Bank Policy Research Working Paper 3616, June 2005 (revised October 2005),
http://www-wds.worldbank.org/external/default/WDSContentServer/
IW3P/IB/2005/06/21/000112742_2005062115823/Rendered/PDF/
wps3616.pdf.

7. Of course, foreign aid budgets are not only about helping poorer countries but also about exerting political influence over the policies of other
countries. As a result, we are not likely to see a dramatic contraction of the
foreign aid budgets of advanced economies, no matter how successful such
agricultural restructuring might be.

9   Losing the Signal in the Noise

1. Unless noted otherwise, all figures regarding GDP in this chapter are taken
from the World Bank's official figures.

2. Ratha, Dilip; and Xu, Zhimei; "Migration and Remittances in Senegal,"
in *Migration and Remittances Factbook,* Migration and Remittances Team,
Development Prospects Group, World Bank, Washington, DC: The World
Bank. 170.

3. Van Vlaenderen, Hilde; Mansour Tall, Serigne; and Gaye, Gora; "Senegal,"
in *Till to Tiller: Linkages between International Remittances and Access to
Land in West Africa,* eds. Cotula, Lorenzo; and Toulmin, Camilla; with
van Vlaenderen, Hilde; Mansour Tall, Serigne; Gaye, Gora; Saunders,
Jacqueline; Ahiadeke, Clement; and Anarfi, John K. London: International
Institute for Environment and Development (IIED), July 2004).

4. Equatorial Guinea would likely be an outstanding example of this phenomenon, but the data required to calculate the GINI coefficient for the
country have not been gathered or made available by the government.

5. CIA World Factbook. (https://www.cia.gov/library/publications/the-
world-factbook/ accessed 18 December 2009).

6. For discussion, see A. Deaton, *The Analysis of Household Surveys: A
Microeconometric Approach to Development Policy* (Baltimore: World Bank
and Johns Hopkins University Press, 1997); and E. Aryeetey, "Household
Asset Choice among the Rural Poor," paper presented at ISSER – University
of Ghana—Cornell University International Conference on "Ghana at the
Half Century," Accra 2004 http://www.isser.org/publications/older/
Poor%20Household%20Asset%20Choice%20in%20Ghana%201.pdf on 17
December 2009).

7. Several factors lead me to this conclusion, not least of which is the fact
that nearly every individual reported expenditures much larger than their
incomes, sometimes more than twice as large. Having lived in these villages for more than a year and a half, I have come to have a good sense of
the level of consumption taking place in most households. The expenses
reported by residents roughly align with the consumption I have seen.
Therefore, I conclude that they are greatly underreporting their incomes.

8. This example draws loosely on a study of PEIndicators of which I was coauthor: Edward R. Carr, Nathan P. Kettle, and Andrew Hoskins, "Evaluating Poverty-Environment Dynamics," *International Journal of Sustainable Development & World Ecology*16(2) (2009): 87–93.

9. A. Osuntogun, *Applied Poverty-Environment Indicators: The Case of Nigeria* (Washington, D.C.: Environment Department, World Bank, 2002).

10 The Long Emergency on the Shoreline of Globalization: It Is Not Their Problem

1. While these economies continue to grow, some will do so at rates that drop below population growth rates, which means reductions in per capita economic productivity and therefore reductions in per person wages.

2. Kolbert, Elizabeth. "Running on Fumes," *New Yorker*, November 5, 2007.

3. This figure is meant more for illustration that as a rigorous statement of wage levels in the United States, as wages vary dramatically across regions and economic sectors. I arrived at this figure by using data from the U.S. Bureau of Labor Statistics, *National Compensation Survey: Occupational Wages in the United States, June 2006*. Taking the average national figure of $19.29 per hour and multiplying it by 7.5 hours results in a total of $144.68.

11 Understanding the World Anew

1. http://www.nytimes.com/2008/07/20/business/worldbusiness/20ping.html.

12 Truly Participatory Development

1. Robert Chambers's extensive body of work on issues of data collection in development is essential reading for anyone interested in this topic.

2. All quotes and information about the MVP are taken directly from various project Web sites, including that of the Millennium Village Project at http://www.earthinstitute.columbia.edu/mvp/about/index; and Millennium Promise at http:/www.millennium promise.org/site/PageServer?pagename=mv_building.

3. Sachs, J. D. and J. W. McArthur, "The Millennium Project: A Plan for Meeting the Millennium Development Goals," *The Lancet* 365 (2005): 347

4. Klugman, J. 2002, *A Sourcebook for Poverty Reduction Strategies* Vol 1. World Bank: Washington, DC.

5. Klugman, J. "Overview," in 2002, *A Sourcebook for Poverty Reduction Strategies* Vol 1. World Bank: Washington, DC.

6. For details of the Zambia example, see B. P. Mpepo and V. Seshamani, "Zambia's PRSP Process: From Exclusion to Inclusion, Confrontation to Cooperation," *Participatory Learning and Action* 51 (2002): 59–63.

For Further Reading

While this book does not contain extensive references, the ideas it expresses are influenced by, and drawn from, the work of many people in many fields. These readings (many of which are drawn from the syllabi of my graduate and undergraduate courses, and my own published work) are not meant to be an exhaustive bibliography, but a means of facilitating further exploration for readers who take an interest in a particular topic in this book. Therefore, they represent a range of perspectives on each topic, from various points in time, that will facilitate the interested reader's understanding of the development and scope of each topic.

Contemporary writing on globalization and development that promote, to a greater or lesser extent, the misunderstandings of both globalization and development that drove the writing of this book:

Collier, P., 2008: *The Bottom Billion: Why the Poorest Countries are Failing and What Can Be Done About It*. Oxford: Oxford University Press.

De Soto, H., 2003: *The Mystery of Capital: Why Capitalism Triumphs in the West and Fails Everywhere Else*. New York: Basic Books.

Easterly, W., 2002: *The Elusive Quest for Growth: Economists' Adventures and Misadventures in the Tropics*. Boston: MIT Press.

———, 2007: *The White Man's Burden: Why the West's Efforts to Aid the Rest Have Done So Much Ill and So Little Good*. New York: Penguin.

Fisman, R.; and Miguel, E.; 2008: *Economic Gangsters: Corruption, Violence, and the Poverty of Nations*. Princeton, NJ: Princeton University Press.

Kaplan, R. D., 1997: *The Ends of the Earth: From Togo to Turkmenistan, from Iran to Cambodia, a Journey to the Frontiers of Anarchy*. New York: Vintage.

———, 2001: *The Coming Anarchy: Shattering the Dreams of the Post Cold War*. New York: Vintage.

Perkins, J., 2005: *Confessions of an Economic Hit Man*. New York: Plume.

———, 2008: *The Secret History of the American Empire: The Truth About Economic Hit Men, Jackals, and How to Change the World*. New York: Plume.

Sachs, J. D., 2005: *The End of Poverty: Economic Possibilities for Our Time*. New York: Penguin Press.

———, 2009: *Common Wealth: Economics for a Crowded Planet*. New York: Penguin.

Readers interested in dependency theory should probably consult Gunder Frank's "Development of Underdevelopment" article first. Those interested in World Systems Theory should begin with Wallerstein's "Rise and Future Demise of World Capitalist System—Concepts for Comparative Analysis" article, or his book *World-Systems Analysis: An Introduction*:

Ahiakpor, J. C. W., 1985: The success and failure of Dependency Theory—the experience of Ghana. *International Organization 39*(3): 535–552.

Amin, S., 1976: *Unequal Development*. New York: Monthly Review Press.

Amsden, A. H., 2003: Comment: Good-bye dependency theory, hello dependency theory. *Studies in Comparative International Development 38*(1): 32–38.

Arrighi, G.; Silver, B. J.; and Brewer, B. D.; 2003: Comment: Good-bye dependency theory, hello dependency theory—response. *Studies in Comparative International Development 38*(1): 39–42.

Baran, P., 1957: On the roots of backwardness. In *The Political Economy of Growth*, 134–162. New York: Monthly Review Press.

Caporaso, J. A., 1978: Dependence, dependency, and power in global system—structural and behavioral-analysis. *International Organization 32*(1): 13–43.

Dietz, J. L., 1980: Dependency Theory—a review article. *Journal of Economic Issues 14*(3): 751–758.

Dos Santos, T., 1970: The structure of dependence. *American Economic Review 60*: 231–236.

Gunder Frank, A., 1966: The development of underdevelopment. *The Monthly Review 18*(4): 17–31.

———, 1967: *Capitalism and Underdevelopment in Latin America*. New York: Monthly Review Press.

———, 1978: *Dependent Accumulation and Underdevelopment*. New York: Monthly Review Press.

Prebisch, R., 1981: The Latin American periphery in the global system of capitalism. *CEPAL Review 13*: 143–150.

Schwartz, H., 2007: Dependency or institutions? Economic geography, causal mechanisms, and logic in the understanding of development. *Studies in Comparative International Development 42*(1–2): 115–135.

Smith, T., 1979: Underdevelopment of development literature—case of Dependency Theory. *World Politics 31*(2): 247–288.

Wallerstein, I., 1974: Rise and future demise of world capitalist system—concepts for comparative analysis. *Comparative Studies in Society and History 16*(4): 387–415.

———, 1974: *The Modern World-System*. Vol. 1: *Capitalist Agriculture and the Origins of the European World-Economy in the Sixteenth Century*. New York: Academic Press.

———, 1980: *The Modern World-System*. Vol. 2: *Mercantilism and the Consolidation of the European World-Economy, 1600–1750*. New York: Academic Press.

———, 1989: *The Modern World-System*. Vol. 3: *The Second Great Expansion of the Capitalist World-Economy, 1730–1840's*. San Diego: Academic Press.

———, 2004: *World-Systems Analysis: An Introduction*. Durham, NC: Duke University Press.

Wibbels, E., 2009: Cores, peripheries, and contemporary political economy. *Studies in Comparative International Development 44*(4): 441–449.

Readers interested in "post-development" and "anti-development" critiques of contemporary development theory and practice, as well as critiques of these schools of thought, should probably begin with Escobar's *Encountering Development* and Ferguson's *The Anti-Politics Machine* before branching into the rest of the readings.

Agrawal, A., 1996: Poststructuralist approaches to development: Some critical reflections. *Peace and Change 21*(4): 464–477.

Blakie, P., 2000: Development, post-, anti- and populist: A critical review. *Environment and Planning A 32*(6): 1033–1050.

Corbridge, S., 1998: Beneath the pavement only soil: The poverty of post-development. *Journal of Development Studies 34*(6): 138–148.

Curry, G. N., 2003: Moving beyond postdevelopment: Facilitating indigenous alternatives for "development." *Economic Geography 79*(4): 405–423.

Crush, J., ed., 1995: *Power of Development*. London: Routledge.

Escobar, A., 1995: *Encountering Development*. Princeton: Princeton University Press.

———, 1997: The making and unmaking of the Third World through development. In *The Post-Development Reader*, ed. Rahnema, M., and Bawtree, V., 85–93. London: Zed Books.

———, 2001: Culture sits in places: Reflections on globalism and subaltern strategies of localization. *Political Geography 20*: 139–174.

Ferguson, J., 1994: *The Anti-Politics Machine: Development, Depoliticization, and Bureaucratic Power in Lesotho*. Minneapolis: University of Minnesota Press.

Grischow, J.; and McKnight, G.; 2003: Rhyming development: Practising post-development in colonial Ghana and Uganda. *Journal of Historical Sociology 16*(4): 517–549.

Kapoor, I., 2004: Hyper-self-reflexive development? Spivak on representing the Third World "Other." *Third World Quarterly 25*(4): 627–647.

Lehmann, D., 1997: An opportunity lost: Escobar's deconstruction of development. *The Journal of Development Studies 33*(4): 568–578.

Little, P.; and Painter, M.; 1992: Discourse, politics, and the development process: Reflections on Escobar's "Anthropology and the Development Encounter." *American Ethnologist 22*(3): 602–616.

Matthews, S., 2004: Post-development theory and the question of alternatives: A view from Africa. *Third World Quarterly 25*(2): 373–384.

———, 2008: The role of the privileged in responding to poverty: Perspectives emerging from the post-development debate. *Third World Quarterly 29*(6): 1035–1049.

McKinnon, K., 2008: Taking post-development theory to the field: Issues in development research, Northern Thailand. *Asia Pacific Viewpoint 49*(3): 281–293.

Nederveen Pieterse, J., 1998: My paradigm or yours? Alternative development, post-development, and reflexive development. *Development and Change 29*: 343–373.

———, 2000: After post-development. *Third World Quarterly 21*(2): 175–191.

Pickles, J., 2001: Development "deferred": Poststructuralism, postdevelopment, and the defense of critical modernism. *Economic Geography 77*(4): 383–388.

Rahnema, M., ed., 1997: *The Post-Development Reader*. London: Zed Books.

Sidaway, J. D., 2007: Spaces of post development. *Progress in Human Geography 31*(3): 345–361.

Simon, D., 2006: Separated by common ground? Bringing (post)development and (post)colonialism together. *Geographical Journal 172*: 10–21.

———, 2007: Beyond antidevelopment: Discourses, convergences, practices. *Singapore Journal of Tropical Geography 28*(2): 205–218.

Sreerekha, M. S., 2008: Feminist post-development thought: Rethinking modernity, post-colonialism and representation. *Indian Journal of Gender Studies 15*(2): 409–413.

Yan, T.; and Qian, W. Y.; 2004: Environment migration and sustainable development in the upper reaches of the Yangtze River. *Population and Environment 25*(6): 613–636.

For more on rural life in Ghana:

Awusabo-Asare, K., 1990. Matriliny and the new intestate succession law of Ghana. *Canadian Journal of African Studies* 24, 1–16.

Carr, E. R., 2005: Development and the household: Missing the point? *Geojournal* 62(1): 71–83.

———, 2008: Men's crops and women's crops: The importance of gender to the understanding of agricultural and development outcomes in Ghana's Central Region. *World Development 36*(5): 900–915.

Quisumbing, A. R.; Otsuka, K.; Suyanto, S.; Aidoo, J. B.; and Payongayong, E.; 2001. Land, Trees and women: Evolution of land tenure institutions in Western Ghana and Sumatra Research Report 121. Washington, DC: International Food Policy Research Institute.

Quisumbing, A. R.; Payongayong, E.; Aidoo, J. B.; and Otsuka, K.; 1999. Women's land rights in the transition to individualized ownership: Implications for the management of tree resources in Western Ghana. *Food Consumption and Nutrition Division Discussion Paper No 58*. Washington, DC: International Food Policy Research Institute.

While they are set in Nigeria, I find T. M. Aluko's *One Man, One Matchet* and Chinua Achebe's *Things Fall Apart* and *Arrow of God* wonderful fictional representations of life in rural West Africa, and a valuable resource for gaining a feel for village life.

For more on adaptation to economic and environmental change:

Batterbury, S.; and Forsyth, T.; 1997: Fighting back: Human adaptations in marginal environments. *Environment 41*(6) 6–11, 25–30.

Carr, E. R., 2008: Between structure and agency: Livelihoods and adaptation in Ghana's Central Region. *Global Environmental Change 18*(4): 689–699.

Denton, F., 2002: Climate change vulnerability, impacts, and adaptation: Why does gender matter? *Gender and Development 10*: 10–20.

Grothmann, T.; and Patt, A.; 2005: Adaptive capacity and human cognition: The process of individual adaptation to climate change. *Global Environmental Change 15*: 199–213.

McCarthy, J. J.; Canziani, O. F.; Leary, N. A.; Dokken, D. J.; and White, K. S.; 2001: *Climate Change 2001: Impacts, Adaptation and Vulnerability*. Cambridge: Cambridge University Press.

Pelling, M.; and High, C.; 2005: Understanding adaptation: What can social capital offer assessments of adaptive capacity? *Global Environmental Change 15*: 308–319.

Risby, J.; Kandlikar, M.; Dowlatabadi, H.; and Graetz, D.; 1999: Scale, context and decision making in agricultural adaptation to climate variability and change. *Mitigation and Adaptation Strategies for Global Change 4*: 137–165.

Smit, B.; Burton, I.; Klein, R.; and Wandel, J.; 2000. An anatomy of adaptation to climate change and variability. *Climatic Change* 45, 223–251.

Smit, B.; and Wandel, J.; 2006. Adaptation, adaptive capacity and vulnerability. *Global Environmental Change* 16, 282–292.

How development thinks about livelihoods. This list serves as an introduction to how development thinks about livelihoods is heavily, but not exclusively, focused on African livelihoods. Interested readers should begin with Ellis' *Rural Livelihoods and Diversity in Developing Countries*; Chambers' and Conway's *Sustainable Rural Livelihoods: Practical Concepts for the 21st Century;* Scoones' "Sustainable Rural Livelihoods: A Framework for Analysis"; and Carney's *Sustainable Rural Livelihoods: What Contribution Can We Make?*

Ahmed, N.; Allison, E. H.; and Muir, J. F.; 2008: Using the sustainable liveli-hoods framework to identify constraints and opportunities to the development of freshwater prawn farming in southwest Bangladesh. *Journal of the World Aquaculture Society 39*(5): 598–611.

Allison, E. H.; and Horemans, B.; 2006: Putting the principles of the Sustainable Livelihoods Approach into fisheries development policy and practice. *Marine Policy 30*(6): 757–766.

Attfield, R.; Hattingh, J.; and Matshabaphala, M.; 2004: Sustainable develop-ment, sustainable livelihoods and land reform in South Africa: a conceptual and ethical inquiry. *Third World Quarterly 25*(2): 405–421.

Barrett, C. B.; Reardon, T.; and Webb, P.; 2001: Nonfarm income diversification and household livelihood strategies in rural Africa: Concepts, dynamics and policy implications. *Food Policy 26*(4): 315–331.

Batterbury, S., 2001: Landscapes of diversity: A local political ecology of livelihood diversification in south-western Niger. *Ecumene 8*(4): 437–464.

Bebbington, A., 2000: Reencountering development: Livelihood transitions and place transformations in the Andes. *Annals of the Association of American Geographers 90*(3): 495–520.

———, 2004: Livelihood transitions, place transformations: Grounding glo-balization and modernity. In *Latin America Transformed. Globalization and Modernity.* 2nd ed., ed. Gwynne R., and Kay, C. 173–192. : London: Arnold.

Bebbington, A.; Bebbington, D. H.; Bury, J.; Lingan, J.; Munoz, J. P.; and Scurrah, M.; 2008: Mining and social movements: Struggles over livelihood and rural territorial development in the Andes. *World Development 36*(12): 2888–2905.

Binns, T., 2009: Making development work in Africa (part 1): uplifting liveli-hoods. *Geography 94*: 28–37.

Breusers, M., 2001: Searching for livelihood security: Land and mobility in Burkina Faso. *The Journal of Development Studies 37*(4): 49–80.

Bryceson, D. F., 2002: The scramble in Africa: Reorienting rural livelihoods. *World Development 30*(5): 725–739.

Buchy, M., 2005: In search of sustainable livelihoods systems: Managing resources and change. *Development and Change 36*(2): 414–415.

Buchy, M., 2007: Managing natural resources for sustainable livelihoods: Uniting science and participation. *Development and Change* 38(2): 356–358.

Carney, D. ed., 1998: *Sustainable Rural Livelihoods: What Contribution Can We Make?* London: Department for International Development.

Carr, E. R., 2008: Between structure and agency: Livelihoods and adaptation in Ghana's Central Region. *Global Environmental Change* 18(4): 689–699.

Carr, E. R.; and McCusker, B.; 2009: The co-production of land use and livelihoods change: Implications for development interventions. *Geoforum* 40(4): 568–579.

Chambers, R.; and Conway, G.; 1992: *Sustainable Rural Livelihoods: Practical Concepts for the 21st Century.* Sussex: Institute of Development Studies.

Cleaver, F., 1998: Choice, complexity, and change: Gendered livelihoods and the management of water. *Agriculture and Human Values* 15(4): 293–299.

De Sherbinin, A.; VanWey, L. K.; McSweeney, K.; Aggarwal, R.; Barbieri, A.; Henry, S.; Hunter, L. M.; Twine, W.; and Walker, R.; 2008: Rural household demographics, livelihoods and the environment. *Global Environmental Change-Human and Policy Dimensions* 18(1): 38–53.

Ellis, F., 1998: Household strategies in rural livelihood diversification. *The Journal of Development Studies* 35(1): 1–38.

———, 2000: *Rural Livelihoods and Diversity in Developing Countries.* Oxford: Oxford University Press.

Ellis, F.; and Kutenguke, M.; 2003: Livelihoods and rural poverty reduction in Malawi. *World Development* 31(9): 1495–1510.

Francis, E., 2000: *Making a Living: Changing Livelihoods in Rural Africa.* New York: Routledge.

Gilling, J.; Jones, S.; and Duncan, A.; 2001: Sector approaches, sustainable livelihoods and rural poverty reduction. *Development Policy Review* 19(3): 303–319.

Gladwin, C. H.; Thomson, A. M.; Peterson, J. S.; and Anderson, A. S.; 2001: Addressing food security in Africa via multiple livelihood strategies of women farmers. *Food Policy* 26: 177–207.

Glavovic, B. C., 2003: Neighbors, worlds apart: Livelihood prospects in Malawi and Mozambique. In *Contesting Development: Pathways to Better Practice, Proceedings of the Third Biennial Conference of the International Development Studies Network of Aotearoa, New Zealand,* ed. Storey, D., Overton, J., and Nowak, B. New Zealand: Massey University.

Gliessman, S., 2009: Building sustainable livelihoods while conserving biodiversity. *Journal of Sustainable Agriculture* 33(4): 359–360.

Hanson, K. T., 2005: Landscapes of survival and escape: Social networking and urban livelihoods in Ghana. *Environment and Planning A* 37(7): 1291–1310.

Hussein, K., 2002: Food security: Rights, livelihoods, and the World Food Summit—five years later. *Social Policy and Administration* 36(6): 626–647.

Malley, Z. J. U.; Mzimbiri, M. K.; and Mwakasendo, J. A.; 2009: Integrating local knowledge with science and technology in management of soil, water and nutrients: implications for management of natural capital for sustainable rural livelihoods. *International Journal of Sustainable Development and World Ecology* 16(3): 151–163.

McCusker, B.; and Carr, E. R.; 2006: The co-production of livelihoods and land use change: Case studies from South Africa and Ghana. *Geoforum 37*(5): 790–804.

Mohamed, N.; and Dodson, B.; 1998: Sustainable rural livelihoods? Evaluating the potential of small-scale aquaculture in the Western Cape. *Development Southern Africa 15*(1): 103–121.

Mudimu, G. D., 1996: Urban agricultural activities and women's strategies in sustaining family livelihoods in Harare, Zimbabwe. *Singapore Journal of Tropical Geography 17*(2): 179–194.

Orr, A.; and Mwale, B.; 2001: Adapting to adjustment: Smallholder livelihood strategies in Southern Malawi. *World Development 29*(8): 1325–1343.

Osbahr, H.; Twyman, C.; Adger, W. N.; and Thomas, D. S. G.; 2008: Effective livelihood adaptation to climate change disturbance: Scale dimensions of practice in Mozambique. *Geoforum 39*(6): 1951–1964.

Scoones, I., 1998: Sustainable rural livelihoods: A framework for analysis. *IDS Working Paper 72*. Sussex: Institute for Development Studies.

Shackleton, C.; Shackleton, S.; and Cousins, B.; 2001: The Role of land-based strategies in rural livelihoods: The contribution of arable production, animal husbandry, and natural resource harvesting in communal areas in South Africa. *Development Southern Africa 18*(5): 582–604.

Small, L. A., 2007: The Sustainable Rural Livelihoods Approach: A Critical Review. *Canadian Journal of Development Studies-Revue Canadienne D Etudes Du Developpement 28*(1): 27–38.

Sneddon, C. S., 2000: "Sustainability" in Ecological Economics, Ecology and Livelihoods: A Review. *Progress in Human Geography 24*(4): 521–549.

Sutherland, A. J.; Irungu, J. W.; Kang'ara, J.; Muthamia, J.; and Ouma, J.; 1998: Household food security in semi-arid Africa—the contribution of participatory adaptive research and development to rural livelihoods in Eastern Kenya. *Food Policy 24*(4): 363–390.

Syampungani, S.; Chirwa, P. W.; Akinnifesi, F. K.; Sileshi, G.; and Ajayi, O. C.; 2009: The Miombo woodlands at the cross roads: Potential threats, sustainable livelihoods, policy gaps and challenges. *Natural Resources Forum 33*(2): 150–159.

Thomas-Slayter, B.; and Bhatt, N.; 1994: Land, livestock, and livelihoods—changing dynamics of gender, caste, and ethnicity in a Nepalese village. *Human Ecology 22*(4): 467–494.

Verrest, H.; and Post, J.; 2007: Home-based economic activities/livelihoods and space in Paramaribo, Suriname. *International Development Planning Review 29*(2): 161–184.

For more on gender, livelihoods and rural development (again, mostly in Africa), see:

Bassett, T., 2002: Women's cotton and the spaces of gender politics in northern Côte d'Ivoire. *Gender, Place and Culture 9*(4): 351–370.

Boserup, E., 1970: *Women's Role in Economic Development*. London: George Allen and Unwin.

Carney, J. A., 1996: Converting the wetlands, engendering the environment: The intersection of gender with agrarian change in The Gambia. In *Liberation*

Ecologies: Environment, Development, Social Movements, ed. Peet, R.; and Watts, M. London: Routledge.

Carney, J. A.; Watts, M.; 1990: Manufacturing dissent: Work, gender and the politics of meaning in a peasant society. *Africa 60*(2): 207–241.

———; 1991: Disciplining women? Rice, mechanization and the evolution of Mandinka gender relations in Senegambia. *Signs: Journal of Women in Culture and Society 16*(4): 651–681.

Carr, E. R., 2005: Development and the household: Missing the point? *Geojournal 62*(1): 71–83.

Carr, E. R., 2008: Men's crops and women's crops: The importance of gender to the understanding of agricultural and development outcomes in Ghana's Central Region. *World Development 36*(5): 900–915.

Chant, S., 2005: Household decisions, gender and development: A synthesis of recent research. *American Anthropologist 107*(4): 738–739.

Grigsby, W. J., 2004: The gendered nature of subsistence and its effect on customary land tenure. *Society and Natural Resources 17*: 207–222.

Jackson, C., 1993: Women/nature or gender/history? A critique of ecofeminist "development." *The Journal of Peasant Studies 20*(3): 389–419.

———, 1997: Post poverty, gender and development. *Ids Bulletin-Institute of Development Studies 28*(3): 145–155.

———, 1998: Rescuing gender from the poverty trap. In *Feminist Visions of Development: Gender Analysis and Policy*, ed. Jackson, C.; and Pearson, R.; 39–64. London: Routledge.

Kandioti, D., 1998: Gender, power and contestation: "Rethinking bargaining with patriarchy." In *Feminist Visions of Development: Gender Analysis and Policy*, ed. Jackson, C; and Pearson, R.; 135–151. London: Routledge.

Leach, M., 1992: Gender and the environment: Traps and opportunities. *Development in Practice 2*: 12–22.

MacKenzie, F., 1990: Gender and land rights in Murang'a District, Kenya. *Journal of Peasant Studies 17*(4): 609–643.

———, 1995: "A Farm is Like a Child Who Cannot be Left Unguarded": Gender, land and labour in Central Province, Kenya. *IDS Bulletin 26*(1): 17–23.

———, 1999: Betterment and the gendered politics of maize production, Murang'a District, Central Province, Kenya. *Canadian Journal of African Studies 33*(1): 64–97.

Mama, A., 2005: Demythologising gender in development: Feminist studies in African contexts. *IDS Bulletin 35*(4): 121–124.

Meinzen-Dick, R. S.; Brown, L. R.; Feldstein, H. S.; and Quisumbing, A. R.; 1997: Gender, property rights, and natural resources. *World Development 25*(8): 1303–1315.

O'Reilly, K., 2006: "Traditional" women, "modern" water: Linking gender and commodification in Rajasthan, India. *Geoforum 37*(6): 958–972.

———, 2007: "'Where the knots of narrative are tied and untied': The dialogic production of gendered development spaces in north India." *Annals of the Association of American Geographers 97*(3): 613–634.

Parpart, J., 1995: Post-Modernism, gender and development. In *Power of Development*, ed. Crush, J., 253–265. London: Routledge.

Pearson, R.; and Jackson, C.; 1998: "Introduction: Interrogating Development: Feminism, Gender and Policy." In *Feminist Visions of Development: Gender Analysis and Policy*, ed. Jackson, C.; and Pearson, R.; London: Routledge.

Peters, P. E., 1995: Uses and abuses of the concept of "Female-headed Households" in research on agrarian transformation and policy. In *Women Wielding the Hoe: Lessons from Rural Africa for Feminist Theory and Development Practice*, ed. Bryceson, D. F., 93–108. Oxford: Berg Publishers.

Rathgeber, E., 2005: Gender and development as a fugitive concept. *Canadian Journal of Development Studies-Revue Canadienne D Etudes Du Developpement* 26: 579–591.

Rocheleau, D.; Thomas-Slayter, B.; and Wangari, E.; 1996: Gender and environment: A feminist political ecology perspective. In *Feminist Political Ecology: Global Issues and Local Experiences*, ed. Rocheleau, D.; Thomas-Slayter, B.; and Wangari, E.; 3–23. New York: Routledge.

Shiva, V., 1989: "Development, Ecology and Women." *Staying Alive*. London: Zed Books.

Valdivia, C.; and Gilles, J.; 2001: Gender and resource management: Households and groups, strategies and transitions. *Agriculture and Human Values* 18: 5–9.

The history of Ghana is represented by a huge number of works of which the following comprise a only a very small sample. This history (especially economic history) has been highly politicized, and therefore its interpretation has changed over time. However, everything that I have listed here served, in some manner or other, as source material for my work in Ghana:

Anyane, S. L., 1963: *Ghana Agriculture: Its Economic Development From Early Times to the Middle of the Twentieth Century*. Accra: Oxford University Press.

Austin, G., 1996: National poverty and the "vampire state" in Ghana: A review article. *Journal of International Development* 8(4): 553–573.

———, 2003: African rural capitalism, cocoa farming and economic growth in colonial Ghana. In *Ghana and Africa in the World: Essays in Honor of Adu Boahen*, ed. Falola, T., 437–453. Trenton, NJ: Africa World Press.

———, 2005: *Labour, Land and Capital in Ghana: From Slavery to Free Labour in Asante, 1807–1956*. Rochester, NY: University of Rochester Press.

Berg, E. J., 1971: Structural transformation versus gradualism: Recent economic development in Ghana and the Ivory Coast. In *Ghana and the Ivory Coast: Perspectives on Modernization*, ed. Foster, P.; and Zolberg, A. R. Chicago: University of Chicago Press.

Berry, S., 1997: Tomatoes, land and hearsay: Property and history in Asante in the time of structural adjustment. *World Development* 25(8): 1225–1241.

Bowdich, T. E., 1966 (1819): *Mission from Cape Coast to Ashantee*. London: Frank Cass and Co., Ltd.

Brydon, L., 1987: Women and the family: Cultural change in Avatime, Ghana, 1900–80. *Development and Change* 18: 251–269.

Buliř, A., 1998: *The Price Incentive to Smuggle and the Cocoa Supply in Ghana, 1950–96*. IMF Working Paper no. WP/98/88. Washington, DC: International Monetary Fund.

Chouin, G., 1998: *Eguafo: Un Royaume Africain "Au Coeur Francois" (1637–1688): Mutations Socio-Economiques et Politique Europeenne d'un Etat de la Cote de L'Or (Ghana) Au XVIIE Siecle*. Paris: AFERA.

Cruickshank, B., 1966 (1853): *Eighteen Years on the Gold Coast of Africa*. Vols. 1 and 2. New York: Barnes and Noble, Inc.

DeCorse, C. R., 1992: Culture contact, continuity and change in the Gold Coast, AD 1400–1900. *The African Archaeological Review 10*: 163–196.

———, 2001: *An Archaeology of Elmina: Africans and Europeans on the Gold Coast, 1400–1900*. Washington, DC: Smithsonian Institution Press.

Esseks, J. D., 1971: Political independence and economic decolonization: The case of Ghana under Nkrumah. In *Ghana and the Ivory Coast: Perspectives on Modernization*, ed. Foster, P.; and Zolberg, A. R. Chicago: University of Chicago Press.

Fairhead, J.; and Leach, M.; 1998. *Reframing Deforestation: Global analyses and local realities—studies in West Africa*. London: Routledge.

Grier, B., 1992: Pawns, porters, and petty traders—women in the transition to cash crop agriculture in colonial Ghana. *Signs: Journal of Women in Culture and Society 17*(2): 304–328.

Hart, K., 1973: Informal income opportunities and urban employment in Ghana. *Journal of Modern African Studies 11*(1): 61–90.

Hayford, J. E. C., 1970 (1903): *Gold Coast Native Institutions*. London: Frank Cass and Co., Ltd.

Herbst, J., 1993: *The Politics of Reform in Ghana, 1982–1991*. Berkeley: University of California Press.

Hill, P., 1956: *The Gold Coast Cocoa Farmer: A Preliminary Survey*. London: Oxford University Press.

———, 1963: *The Migrant Cocoa-Farmers of Southern Ghana: A Study in Rural Capitalism*. Cambridge: Cambridge University Press.

———, 1970: *Rural Capitalism in West Africa*. Cambridge: Cambridge University Press.

Hopkins, A. G., 1973: *An Economic History of West Africa*. New York: Columbia University Press.

Huq, M. M., 1989: *The Economy of Ghana: The First 25 Years Since Independence*. New York: St. Martin's Press.

Kapur, I.; Hadjimichael, M. T.; Hilbers, P.; Schiff, J.; and Szymczak, P.; 1991: *Ghana: Adjustment and Growth, 1983–1991*. Washington, DC: International Monetary Fund

Killick, T., 1978: *Development Economics in Action: A Study of Economic Policies in Ghana*. New York: St. Martin's Press.

Krassowski, A., 1974: *Development and the Debt Trap: Economic Planning and External Borrowing in Ghana*. London: Croom Helm.

Kraus, J., 1971: Political change, conflict and development in Ghana. In *Ghana and the Ivory Coast: Perspectives on Modernization*, ed. Foster, P.; and Zolberg, A. R. Chicago: University of Chicago Press.

Lynn, M., 1997: *Commerce and Economic Change in West Africa: The Palm Oil Trade in the Nineteenth Century*. Cambridge: Cambridge University Press.

McCann, J. C., 1999: *Green Land, Brown Land, Black Land: An Environmental History of Africa, 1800–1990*. Portsmouth, NH: Heinemann.

McPhee, A., 1971: *The Economic Revolution in British West Africa*, 2nd ed. London: Frank Cass and Co., Ltd.

Morgan, W. B., 1963: Food imports of West Africa. *Economic Geography 39*: 351–362.

Owusu, J. H., 1998: Current convenience, desperate deforestation: Ghana's adjustment program and the forestry sector. *Professional Geographer 50*(4): 418–436.

Panford, K., 1997: Ghana: A decade of IMF/World Bank's policies of adjustment (1985–1995). *Scandinavian Journal of Development Alternatives and Area Studies 16*(2): 81–105.

Rattray, R. S., 1923: *Ashanti*. Oxford: Clarendon Press.

Robertson, C. C., 1984: *Sharing the Same Bowl: A Socioeconomic History of Women and Class in Accra, Ghana*. Bloomington, IN: Indiana University Press.

Tabatabai, H., 1988: Agricultural decline and access to food in Ghana. *International Labour Review 127*(6): 703–34.

Chapter 6 is heavily drawn from an article I wrote on environmental migration (see reference below). For more on the role of the environment, versus other factors such as a changing economy, in the movement of populations, see:

Bates, D. C., 2002: Environmental refugees? Classifying human migrations caused by environmental change. *Population and Environment 23*(5): 465–477.

Carr, E. R., 2005: Placing the environment in migration: Economy, environment, and power in Ghana's Central Region. *Environment and Planning A 37*(5): 925–946.

Dow, K.; Carr, E. R.; with Douma, A.; Han, G.; and Hallding, K.; 2005: Linking water scarcity to population movements: From global models to local experiences. *SEI Poverty and Vulnerability Programme Report*. Stockholm.: Stockholm Environment Institute.

Gidwani, V.; and Sivaramakrishnan, K.; 2003: Circular migration and the spaces of cultural assertion. *Annals of the Association of American Geographers 93*(1) 186–213.

Hugo, G., 1996: Environmental concerns and international migration. *International Migration Review 30*(1): 105–131.

Kibreab, G., 1997: Environmental causes and impact of refugee movements: A critique of the current debate. *Disasters 21*(1): 20–38.

Lawson, V. A., 1998: Hierarchical households and gendered migration in Latin America: Feminist extensions to migration research. *Progress in Human Geography 22*(1): 39–53.

———, 2000: Arguments within geographies of movement: The theoretical potential of migrants' stories. *Progress in Human Geography 24*(2): 173–189.

Lonergan, S., 1998: The role of environmental degradation in population displacement. *Global Environmental Change and Human Security Project Research Report I*. Victoria, BC: University of Victoria.

McGregor, J., 1993: Refugees and the environment, In *Geography and Refugees: Patterns and Processes of Change*, ed. Black, R.; and Robinson, V.; 157–170. London: Belhaven.

———, 1994: Climate-change and involuntary migration—implications for food security. *Food Policy 19*(2): 120–132.

McHugh, K. E., 2000: Inside, outside, upside down, backward, forward, round and round: A case for ethnographic studies in migration. *Progress in Human Geography 24*(1): 71–89.

Myers, N., 2002: Environmental refugees: A growing phenomenon of the 21st century. *Philosophical Transactions: Biological Sciences 357*(1420): 609–613.

Myers, N.; Kent, J.; 1995: *Environmental exodus: An emerging crisis in the global arena*. Washington, DC: Climate Institute.

Nash, A. E., 1999: Environmental refugees: Consequences and policies from a western perspective. *Discrete Dynamics in Nature and Society 3*(2–3): 227–238.

O'Lear, S., 1997: Migration and the environment: A review of recent literature. *Social Science Quarterly 78:* 608–618.

Ramlogan, R., 1996: Environmental refugees: A review. *Environmental Conservation 23*(1): 81–88.

Silvey, R.; and Lawson, V.; 1999: Placing the migrant. *Annals of the Association of American Geographers 89*(1): 121–132

Suhrke, A., 1994: Environmental degradation and population flows. *Journal of International Affairs 47*(2): 473–496

Swain, A., 1996: Environmental migration and conflict dynamics: Focus on developing regions. *Third World Quarterly 17*(5): 959–973.

Yan, T.; and Qian, W. Y.; 2004: Environment migration and sustainable development in the upper reaches of the Yangtze River. *Population and Environment 25*(6): 613–636.

Additional readings on sustainable development:

Banerjee, S. B., 2003: Who sustains whose development? Sustainable development and the reinvention of nature. *Organizational Studies 24*(1): 143–180.

Carr, E. R., 2008: Sustainable development. In the *Encyclopedia of Environmental Ethics and Philosophy*. Vol. 2. eds. Callicott, J. B.; and Frodeman, R.; 295–298. Detroit:Macmillan Reference USA.

Carr, E. R.; and Finewood, M.; 2010: Sustainable development. In *Handbook of Global Environmental Issues*, eds. Burns, W. C. G.; and Heinen, J. Mountain View, CA: World Scientific.

Clark, W. C.; and Dickson, N. M.; 2003: Sustainability science: The emerging research program. *Proceedings of the National Academy of Sciences 100*(14): 8059–8061.

Klauer, B., 1999: Defining and achieving sustainable development. *International Journal of Sustainable Development and World Ecology 6*: 114–121.

Martino, D.; Zommers, Z.; Bowman, K.; Brown, D.; Comim, F.; Kouwenhoven, P.; Manders, T.; Milimo, P.; Mohamed-Katerere, J.; De Oliviera, T.; 2007: Chapter 1: "Environment for Development." In *Fourth Global Environment Outlook*, 3–36. Valetta, Malta: Progress Press, Ltd.

Millennium Ecosystem Assessment Conceptual Framework Working Group, 2003: *Ecosystems and Human Well-Being: A Framework for Assessment*. Washington, DC: Island Press.

Scoones, I., 2007: Sustainability. *Development in Practice 17*(4–5): 589–596.

World Commission on Environment and Development, 1987: *Our Common Future*. Oxford: Oxford University Press.

Additional readings on development and conservation, and the negative effects of "fortress conservation" on both local populations and the natural resources:

Amend, S.; and Amend, T.; 1995: Balance sheet: Inhabitants in national parks—an unsolvable contradiction? In *National Parks without people? The South American experience,* ed. Amend, S.; and Amend, T.; 449–460. Gland, Switzerland: World Conservation Union.

Bedunah, D. J.; and Schmidt, S. M.; 2004: Pastoralism and protected area management in Mongolia's Gobi Gurvansaikhan National Park. *Development and Change 35:* 167–191.

Brandon, Redford, and Sanderson. 1998: *Parks in Peril: People, Politics, and Protected Areas.* Washington, DC: The Island Press.

Brockington, D.; and Igoe, J.; 2006: Eviction for conservation: A global overview. *Conservation and Society 4*(3): 424–470.

Brockington, D.; Igoe, J.; and Schmidt-Soltau, K.; 2006: Conservation, human rights, and poverty reduction. *Conservation Biology 20*(1): 250–252.

Cernea, M. M.; and Schmidt-Soltau, K.; 2003: The end of forcible displacements? Conservation must not impoverish people. *Policy Matters 12:* 42–51.

Neumann, R. P., 1997: Primitive ideas: Protected area buffer zones and the politics of land in Africa. *Development and Change 28:* 559–582.

Redford, K. H.; and Sanderson, S. E.; 2000: Extracting humans from nature. *Conservation Biology 14*(5): 1362–1364.

Wilkie, D. S.; Morelli, G. A.; Demmer, J.; Starkey, M.; Telfer, P.; and Steil, M.; 2006: Parks and people: Assessing the human welfare effects of establishing protected areas for biodiversity conservation. *Conservation Biology 20*(1): 247–249.

Additional readings on poverty-environment indicators:

Carr, E. R.; Kettle, N. P.; and Hoskins, A.; 2009: Evaluating poverty-environment dynamics. *International Journal of Sustainable Development and World Ecology 16*(2): 87–93.

Henninger, N.; and Hammond, A.; 2002: Environmental indictors relevant to poverty reduction. Washington, DC: World Bank.

Niemeijer, D., 2002: Developing indicators for environmental policy: Data-driven and theory-driven approaches examined by example. *Environmental Science & Policy 5:* 91–103.

Nunan, F.; Grant, U.; Bahiigwa, G.; Muramira, T.; Bajracharya, P.; Pritchard, D.; et al.; 2002: Poverty and the environment: measuring the links: A study of poverty-environment indicators with case studies from Nepal, Nicaragua and Uganda. *Issue paper No 2.* London: United Kingdom Department for International Development, Environment Policy Department.

Osuntogun, A., 2002: Applied poverty-environment indicators: The case of Nigeria. The World Bank: Washington, DC: .

Parris, T. M.; and Kates, R. W.; 2003: Characterizing and measuring sustainable development. *Annual review of environment resources 28:* 559–589.

Prennushi, G.; Rubio, G.; and Subbarao, K.; 2001: A sourcebook for poverty reduction strategies. In *Monitoring and Evaluation,* 105–130. Washington, DC: World Bank.

Reed, D.; and Tharakan, P.; 2004: Developing and applying poverty environment indicators. Washington, DC: WWF Macroeconomics Program Office.

Segnestam, L., 2002: Indicators of environment and sustainable development. *Theories and Practical Experience*. Washington, DC: World Bank.

Shyamsundar, P., 2002: Poverty-environment indicators. Paper no. 84, Environmental Economics Series. Washington, DC: World Bank.

Smeets, E.; and Weterings, R.; 1999: Environmental indicators: typology and overview. Copenhagen: European Environment Agency.

United Nations Commission on Sustainable Development 2001: Indicators of sustainable development: guidelines and methodologies. New York: United Nations.

For more on the Poverty Reduction Strategy, and Poverty Reduction Strategy Papers (PRSPs), see:

Arias, M., et al., 2004: From "donorship" to ownership? Moving towards PRSP round two. *Oxfam Briefing Paper 51*. Available at http://www.oxfam.org.uk/what_we_do/issues/democracy_rights/downloads/bp51_prsp.pdf

Gould, J., ed., 2005: *The New Conditionality: The Politics of Poverty Reduction Strategies.* : London: Zed Books.

International Monetary Fund and the International Development Association, 1999: Heavily Indebted Poor Countries (HIPC) Initiative—strengthening the link between debt relief and poverty reduction. Available at http://www.imf.org/external/np/hipc/0899/link.pdf

International Monetary Fund and the World Bank, 1999: Poverty Reduction Strategy Papers—operational issues. Available at http://www.imf.org/external/np/pdr/prsp/poverty1.htm

International Monetary Fund and the World Bank, 2000: Poverty Reduction Strategy Papers—progress in implementation. Available at http://www.imf.org/external/np/prsp/2000/prsp.htm

International Monetary Fund and the International Development Association, 2002: Review of the Poverty Reduction Strategy Papers (PRSP) approach: Main findings. Available at http://www.imf.org/external/np/prspgen/review/2002/031502a.pdf

Goldsbrough, D., et al., 2004: Evaluation of the IMF's role in Poverty Reduction Strategy Papers and the Poverty Reduction and Growth Facility. Washington, DC: Independent Evaluation Office, International Monetary Fund.

Klugman, J. (ed) 2002: *A Sourcebook for Poverty Reduction Strategies.* Washington, DC: World Bank. Available at http://go.worldbank.org/3I8LYLXO80/.

2003: Poverty Reduction Strategy Papers (PRSP): A rough guide. London: Bretton Woods Project. Available at http://www.brettonwoodsproject.org/topic/adjustment/PRSP%20rough%20guide/PRSP%20rough%20guide.pdf

United Nations Conference on Trade and Development, 2002: *Economic Development in Africa: From Adjustment to Poverty Reduction: What is New?* New York: United Nations. Available at http://www.unctad.org/en/docs/pogdsafricad2.en.pdf

Zuckerman, E., 2002: Poverty Reduction Strategy Papers and gender. *Conference on Sustainable Poverty Reduction and PRSP—Challenges for Developing Countries and Development Cooperation, Berlin, 2002*. Available at http://www.genderaction.org/images/PRSPs&Gender-GTZ.pdf

For more on the so-called Long Emergency, see:

Duncan, R. C., 1993: The life-expectancy of industrial civilization: The decline to global equilibrium. *Population and Environment 14*(4), 325–357.

Hirsch, R. L.; Bezdek, R.; and Wendling, R.; 2005: *Peaking of World Oil Production: Impacts, Mitigation and Risk Management.* Department of Energy, National Energy Technology Laboratory. Available at http://www.netl.doe.gov/publications/others/pdf/Oil_Peaking_NETL.pdf

Kunstler, J. H., 2005: *The Long Emergency: Surviving the Converging Catastrophes of the Twenty-first Century.* New York: Atlantic Monthly Press.

Kunstler, J. H., 2008: *World Made by Hand.* New York: Atlantic Monthly Press.

Meadows, D. H.; Meadows, D. L.; and Randers. J.; 1992: *Beyond the Limits: Confronting Global Collapse, Envisioning a Sustainable Future.* Post Mills, VT: Chelsea Green.

Meadows, D. H.; Meadows, D. L.; and Randers. J.; 2004: *Limits to Growth: The 30-year Update.* White River Junction, VT: Chelsea Green.

The critiques of data collection for development are many, but are perhaps best articulated in the work of Robert Chambers:

Chambers, R., 1995: *Rural Development: Putting the Last First.* Harlow, UK: Addison-Wesley Publishing Co.

———, 1997: *Whose Reality Counts?: Putting the First Last.* London: Intermediate Technology.

———, 2005: *Ideas for Development.* London: Earthscape Publications, Ltd.

———, 2008: *Revolutions in Development Inquiry.* London: Earthscan.

For more on the Millennium Village Project, see their websites (http://www.millenniumvillages.org/ and http://www.millenniumpromise.org/) and:

Sachs, J. D., 2005: *The End of Poverty: Economic Possibilities for Our Time.* New York: Penguin Press.

Broad, R.; and Cavanaugh, J.; 2006: The hijacking of the development debate: How Friedman and Sachs got it wrong. *World Policy Journal (Summer)*: 21–30.

Cabral, L.; Farrington, J.; and Ludi, E.; 2006: The Millennium Villages Project—a new approach to ending poverty in Africa? *Natural Resource Perspectives 101.* London: Overseas Development Institute.

Carr, E. R., 2008: The Millennium Village Project and African development: problems and potentials. *Progress in Development Studies 8*: 333–344.

Easterly, W., 2005: Reliving the '50s: The big push, poverty traps, and takeoffs in economic development. *Working Paper Number 65.* New York: Center for Global Development.

For more on the place of participation in development, see the previous references to the work of Robert Chambers under data collection, and:

Briggs, J.; and Sharp, J.; 2004: Indigenous knowledges and development: A post-colonial caution. *Third World Quarterly 254*: 661–676.

Cameron, J.; and Gibson, K.; 2005: Participatory action research in a poststructuralist vein. *Geoforum 36*: 315–331.

Chhotray, V., 2004: The negation of politics in participatory development projects, Kurnool, Andhra Pradesh. *Development and Change 35*: 327–352.

McKinnon, K., 2006: An orthodoxy of "the local": Post-colonialism, participation and professionalism in northern Thailand. *The Geographical Journal 172*: 22–34.

———, 2007: Postdevelopment, professionalism, and the politics of participation. *Annals of the Association of American Geographers 97*(4): 772–785.

Nightingale, A. J., 2005: "The experts taught us all we know": Professionalisation and knowledge in Nepalese community forestry. *Antipode 37*: 581–604.

O'Reilly, K., 2004: Developing contradictions: Women's participation as a site of struggle within an Indian NGO. *The Professional Geographer 56*(2): 174–184.

Parfitt, T., 2004: The ambiguity of participation: A qualified defence of participatory development. *Third World Quarterly 253*: 537–556.

Other scenarios of economic and environmental change include:

Carpenter, S. R.; Pingali, P. L.; Bennett, E. M.; and Zurek, M. B. ed., 2006: *Ecosystems and Human Well-Being: Scenarios,* Vol. 2. Washington, DC: Island Press.

Rothman, D. S.; Agard, J.; Alcamo, J.; et al.; 2007: The future today. In *Global Environment Outlook GEO-4: Environment for Development,* 395–454. Valetta, Malta: Progress Press Ltd.

Nakicenovic, N., et al., 2000: Special Report on Emissions Scenarios. *Working Group III of the Intergovernmental Panel on Climate Change.* Cambridge: Cambridge University Press.

Schwartz, P.; and Randall, D.; 2003: An abrupt climate change scenario and its implications for U.S. national security. Washington, DC: *United States Department of Defense.* Available at http://www.greenpeace.org/raw/content/international/press/reports/an-abrupt-climate-change-scena.pdf

Shell International, Ltd., 2005: The Shell global scenarios to 2025: The future business environment: trends, trade-offs and choices. Available at http://www-static.shell.com/static/aboutshell/downloads/our_strategy/shell_global_scenarios/exsum_23052005.pdf

Index